W9-DAS-798

INUYASHA

VOL. 49

Shonen Sunday Edition

STORY AND ART BY

RUMIKO TAKAHASHI

CONTENTS

THE STORY THUS FAR

Long ago, in the "Warring States" era of Japan's Muromachi period, dog-like half demon Inuyasha attempted to steal the Shikon Jewel—or "Jewel of Four Souls"—from a village. The village priestess, Kikyo, put a stop to his thievery with an enchanted arrow. Pinned to a tree, Inuyasha fell into a deep sleep, while mortally wounded Kikyo took the jewel with her into her funeral pyre. Years passed...

In the present day, Kagome, a Japanese high school girl, is pulled down into a well and transported into the past. There she discovers trapped Inuyasha—and frees him.

When the Shikon Jewel mysteriously reappears, demons attack. In the ensuing battle, the jewel *shatters*!

Now Inuyasha is bound to Kagome with a powerful spell, and the grudging companions must battle to reclaim the shattered shards of the Shikon Jewel to keep them out of evil hands...

LAST VOLUME Sesshomaru, Kohaku and Rin are trapped in the underworld. Kohaku is kept alive by the Shikon shard inside him, but Rin dies! Sesshomaru's grief turns out to be the key to the gateway to the living. His mother then resurrects Rin with the Meido Stone. Elsewhere, Inuyasha and the others battle a demon called the Flower Prince, who feeds on psychic pain. Then Kanna, following Naraku's orders, opens her magic mirror to release a crystalline warrior that mimics its opponent's weapons and attacks. It becomes clear that Naraku hopes that Kanna and Inuyasha will take each other out!

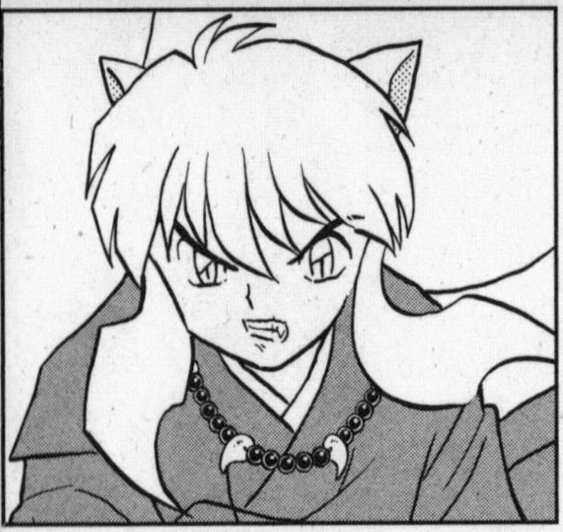

INUYASHA
Half-demon hybrid, son of a human mother and demon father. His necklace is enchanted, allowing Kagome to control him with a word.

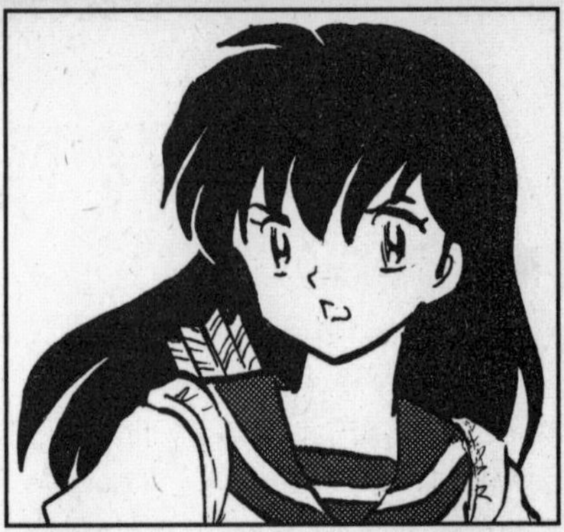

KAGOME
Modern-day Japanese schoolgirl who can travel back and forth between the past and present through an enchanted well.

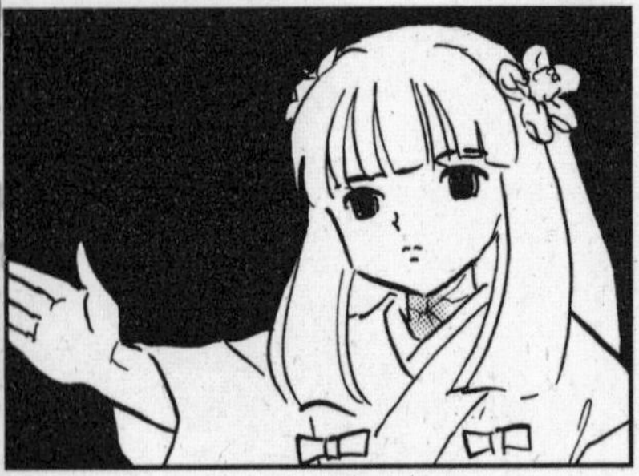

KANNA
Kanna is Naraku's first double. Her demonic mirror steals souls. Her loyalty to Naraku seems to be wavering.

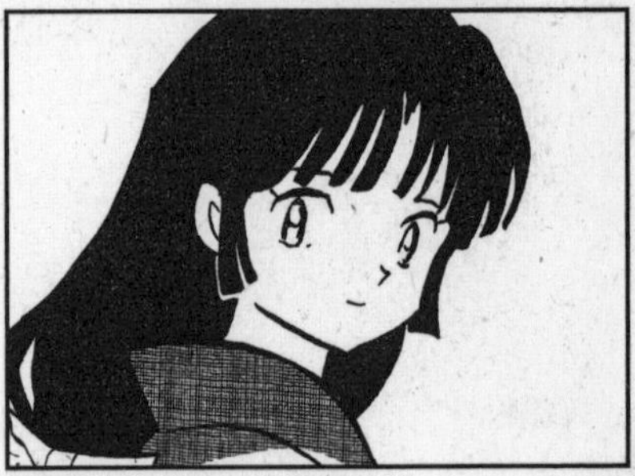

SANGO
A demon slayer from the village where the Shikon Jewel originated.

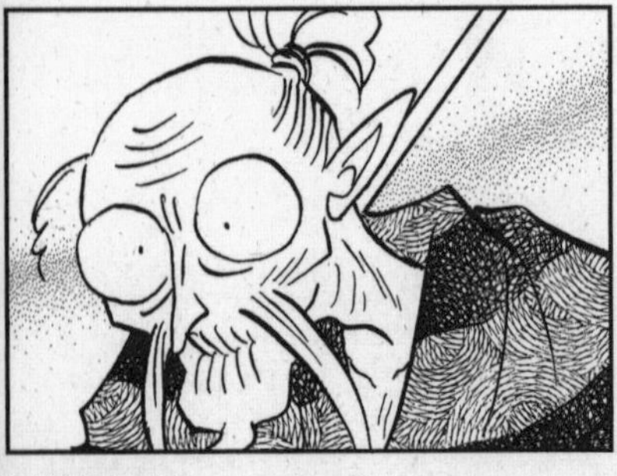

TOTOSAI
The fire-breathing old blacksmith who forged Inuyasha's blade Tetsusaiga and Sesshomaru's blade Tenseiga.

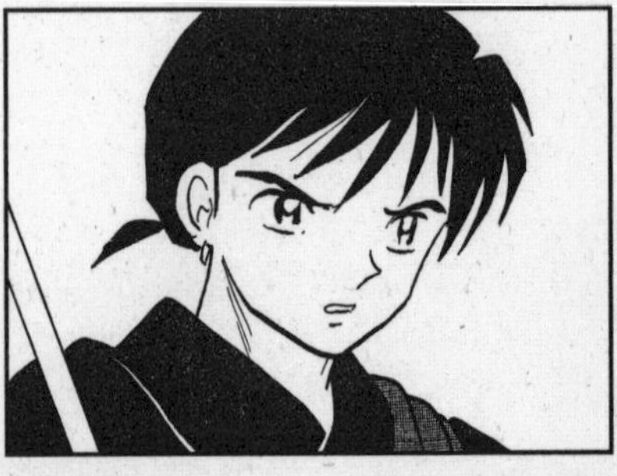

MIROKU
Lecherous Buddhist priest cursed with a mystical "hellhole" in his hand that is slowly killing him.

SCROLL 1

NULL

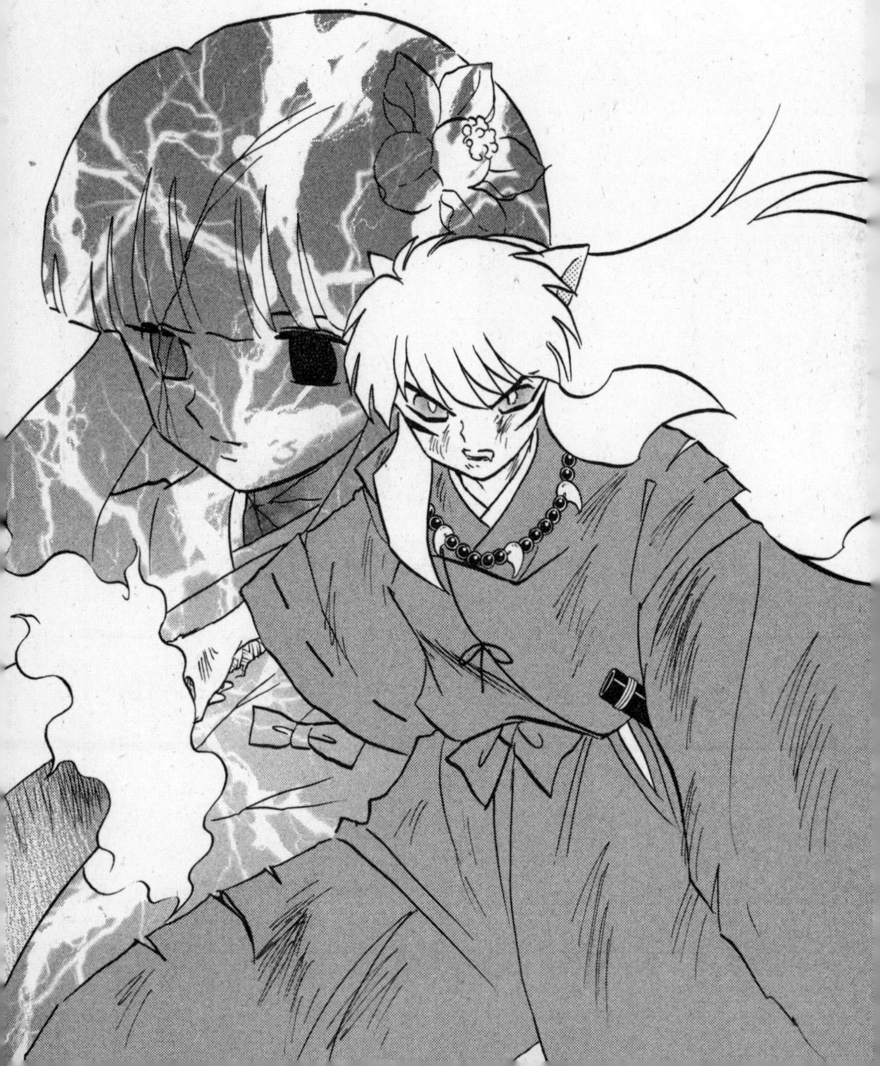

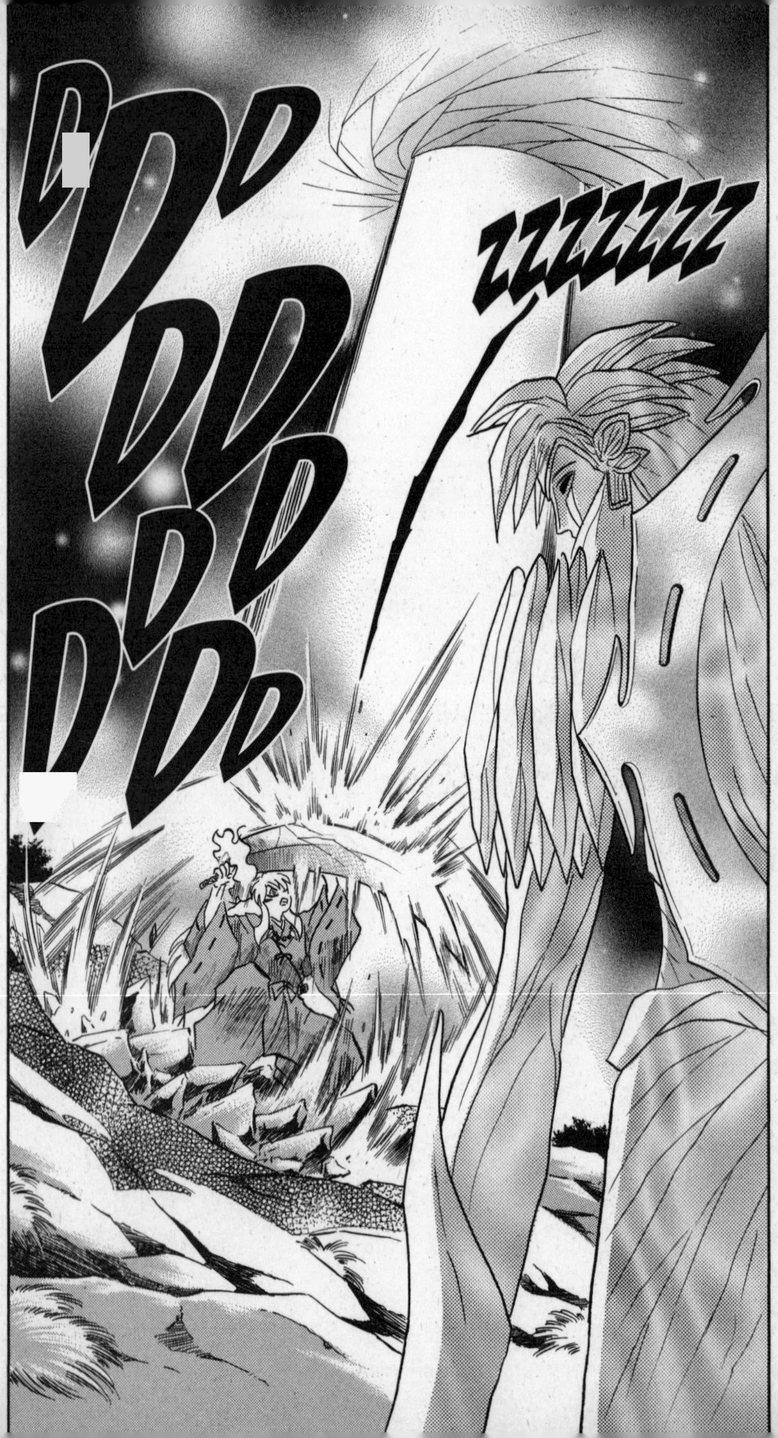
DDDDDDDDDDD
ZZZZZZZ

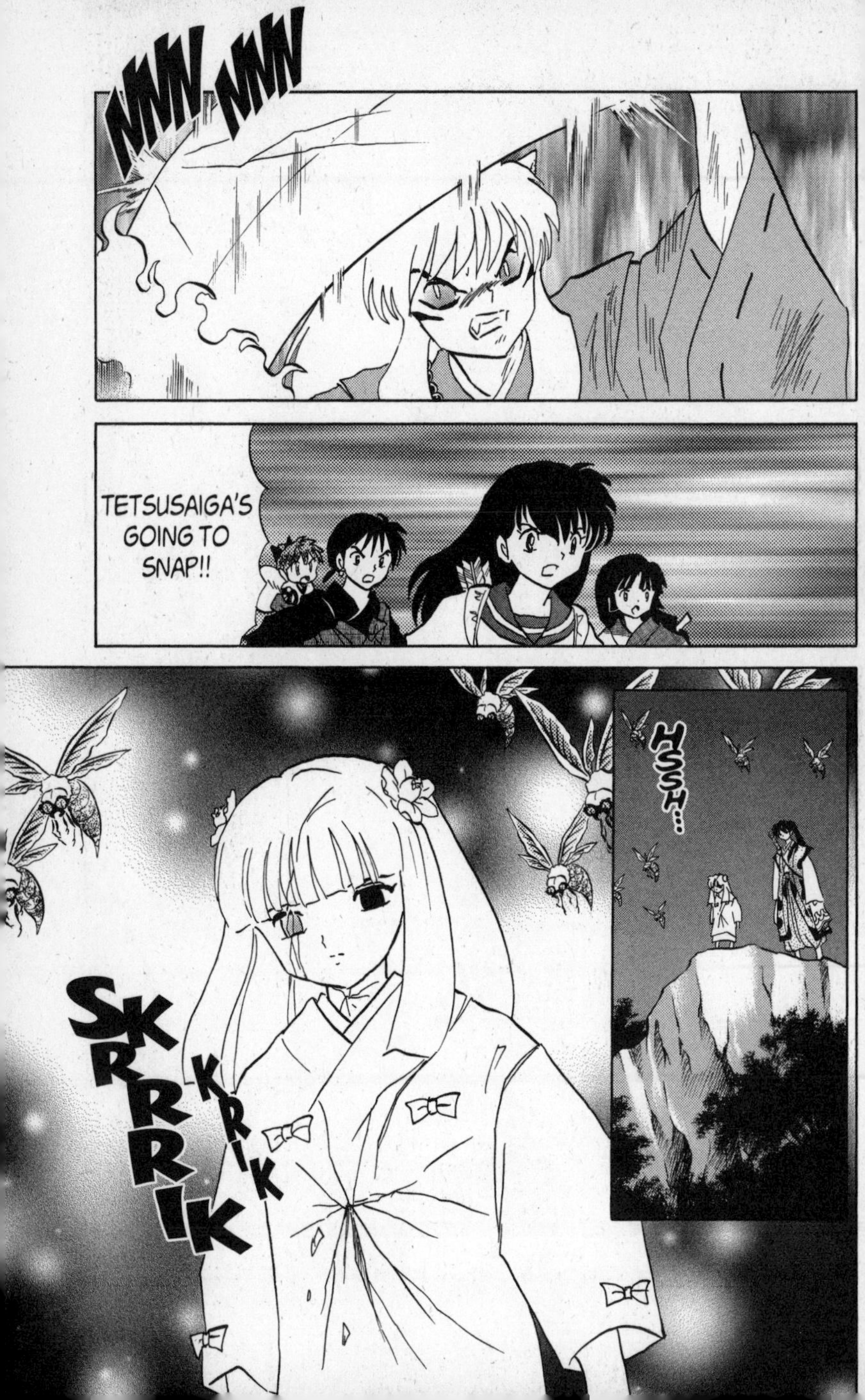
NNNN NNNN
TETSUSAIGA'S GOING TO SNAP!!
HSSH...
SKRRRIK
KRRIK

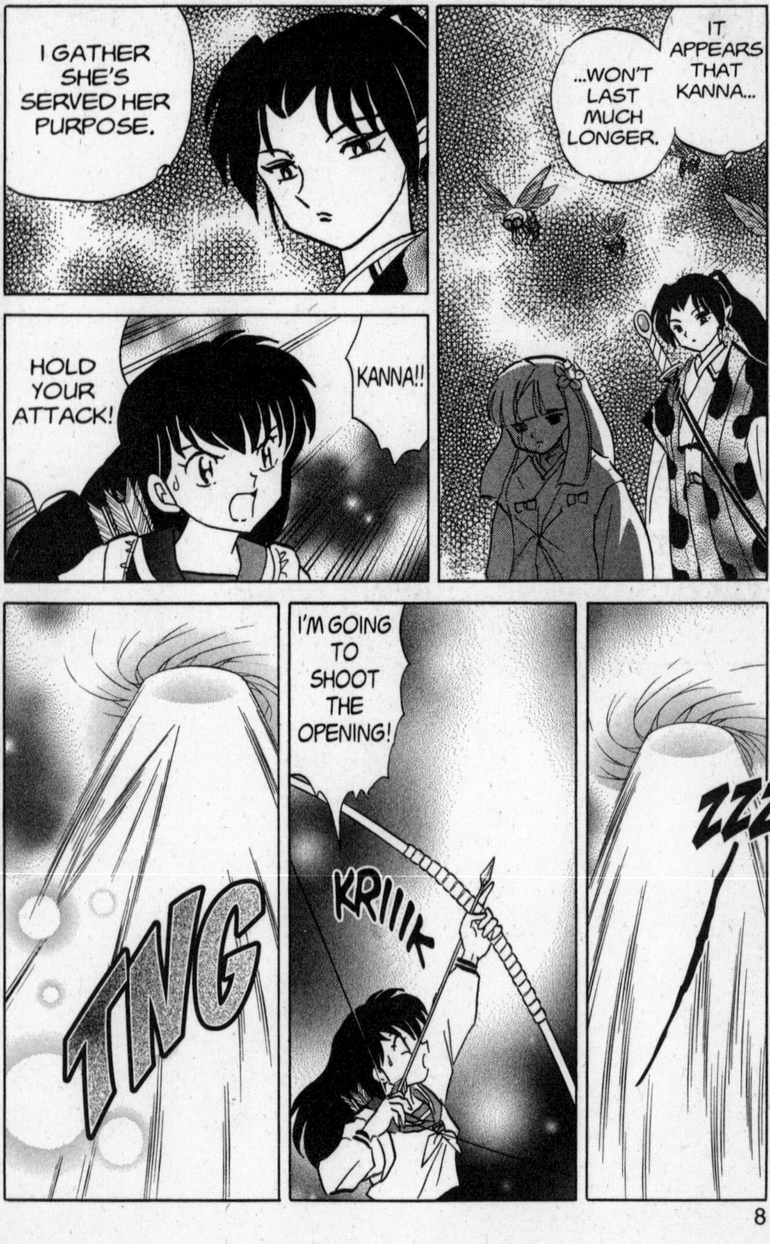
IT APPEARS THAT KANNA...
...WON'T LAST MUCH LONGER.
I GATHER SHE'S SERVED HER PURPOSE.
KANNA!!
HOLD YOUR ATTACK!
ZZZZ
I'M GOING TO SHOOT THE OPENING!
KRIIIK
TNG

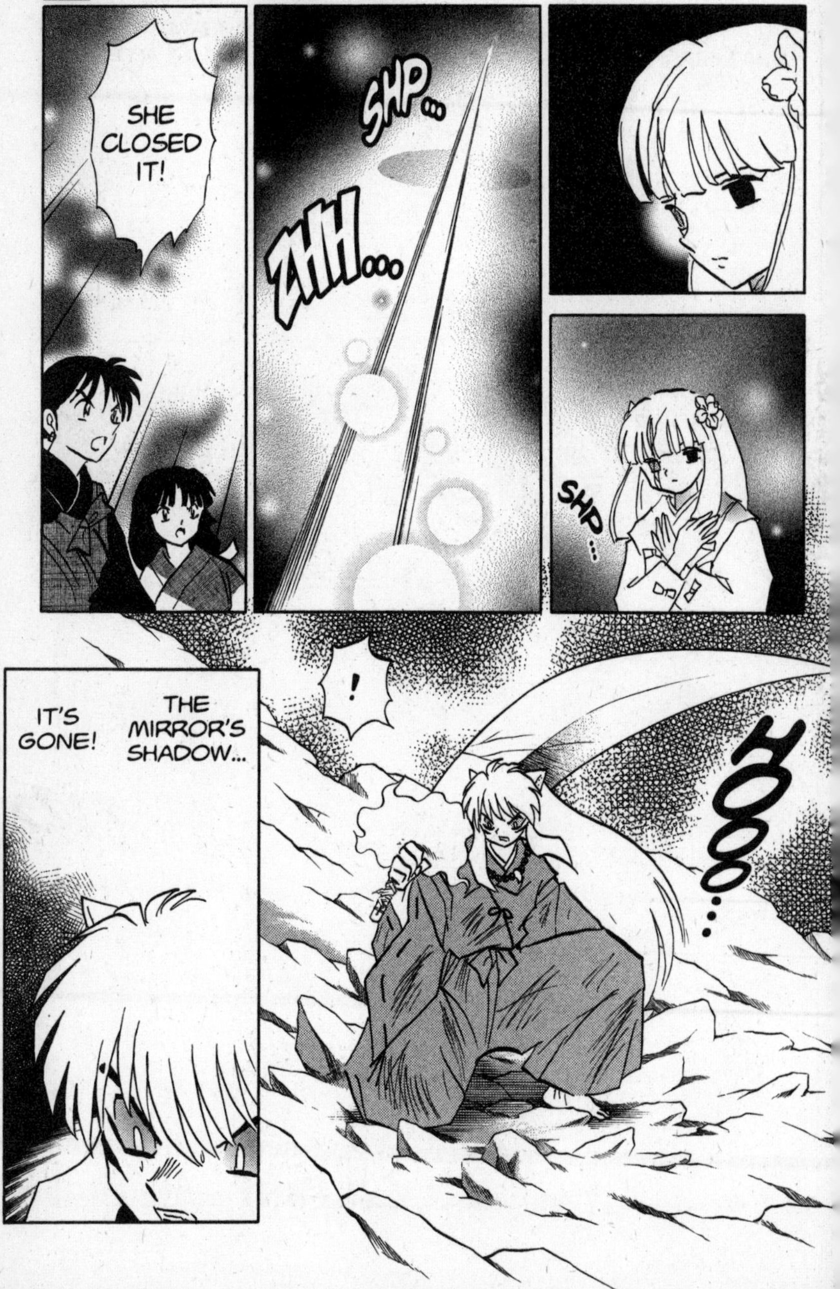
SHP...
SHP...
ZHH...
SHE CLOSED IT!
!
HOOO...
THE MIRROR'S SHADOW...
IT'S GONE!

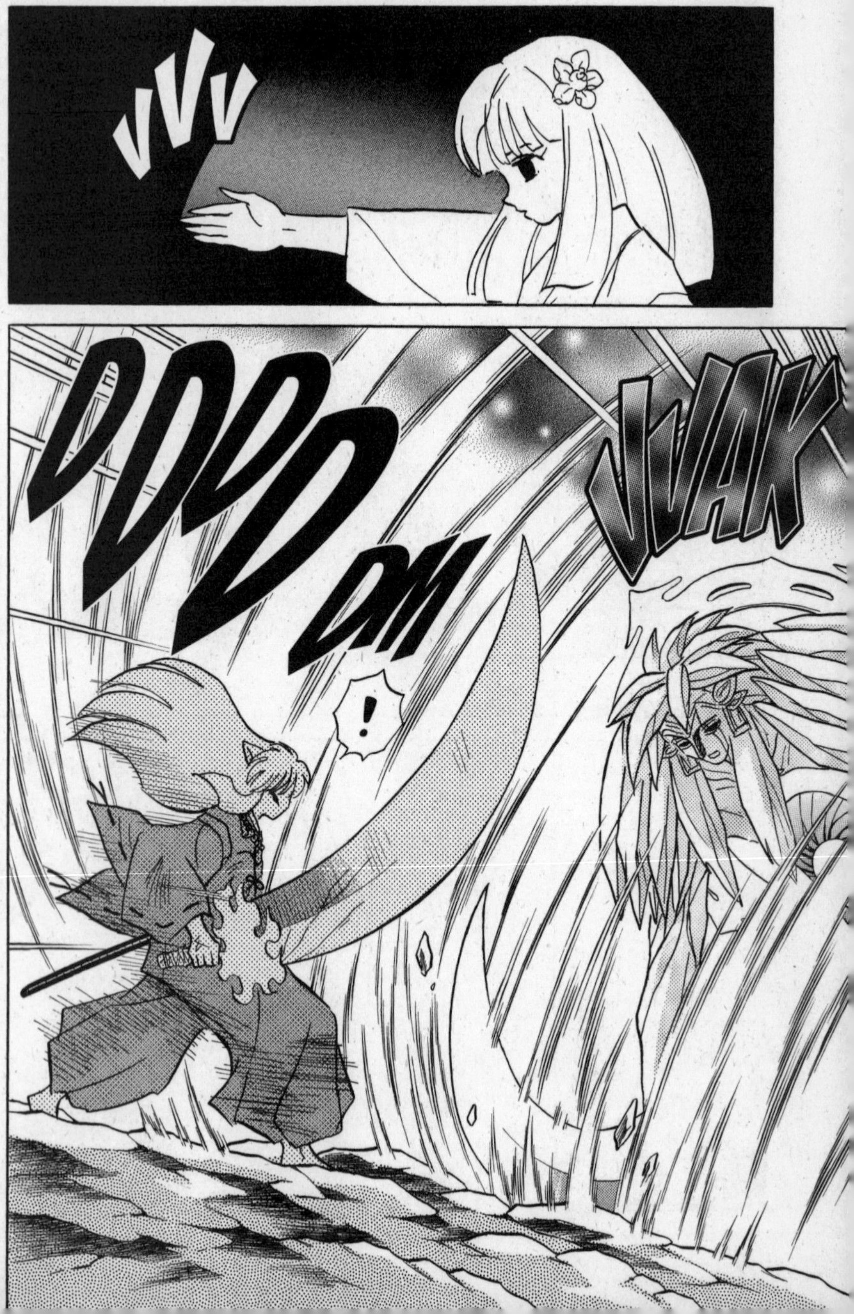
VVVV
JWAK
DDDDOM
!

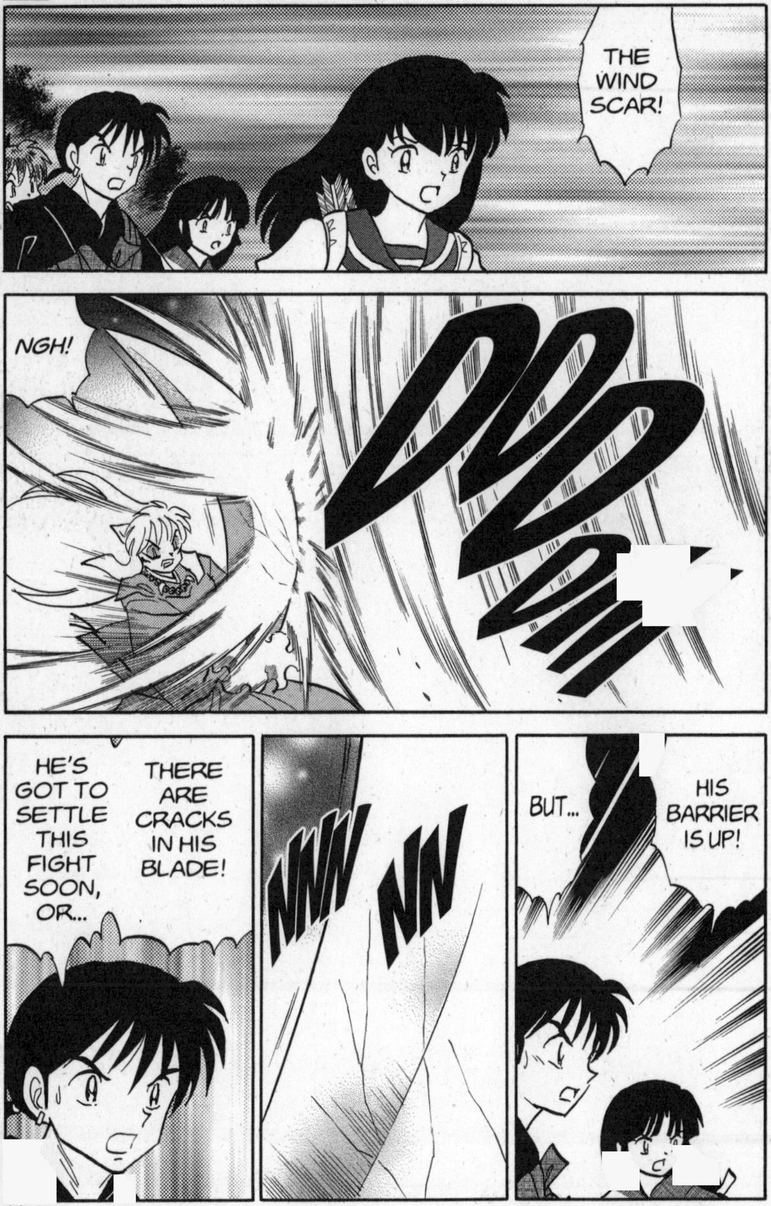
THE WIND SCAR!
NGH!
HIS BARRIER IS UP!
BUT...
THERE ARE CRACKS IN HIS BLADE!
HE'S GOT TO SETTLE THIS FIGHT SOON, OR...

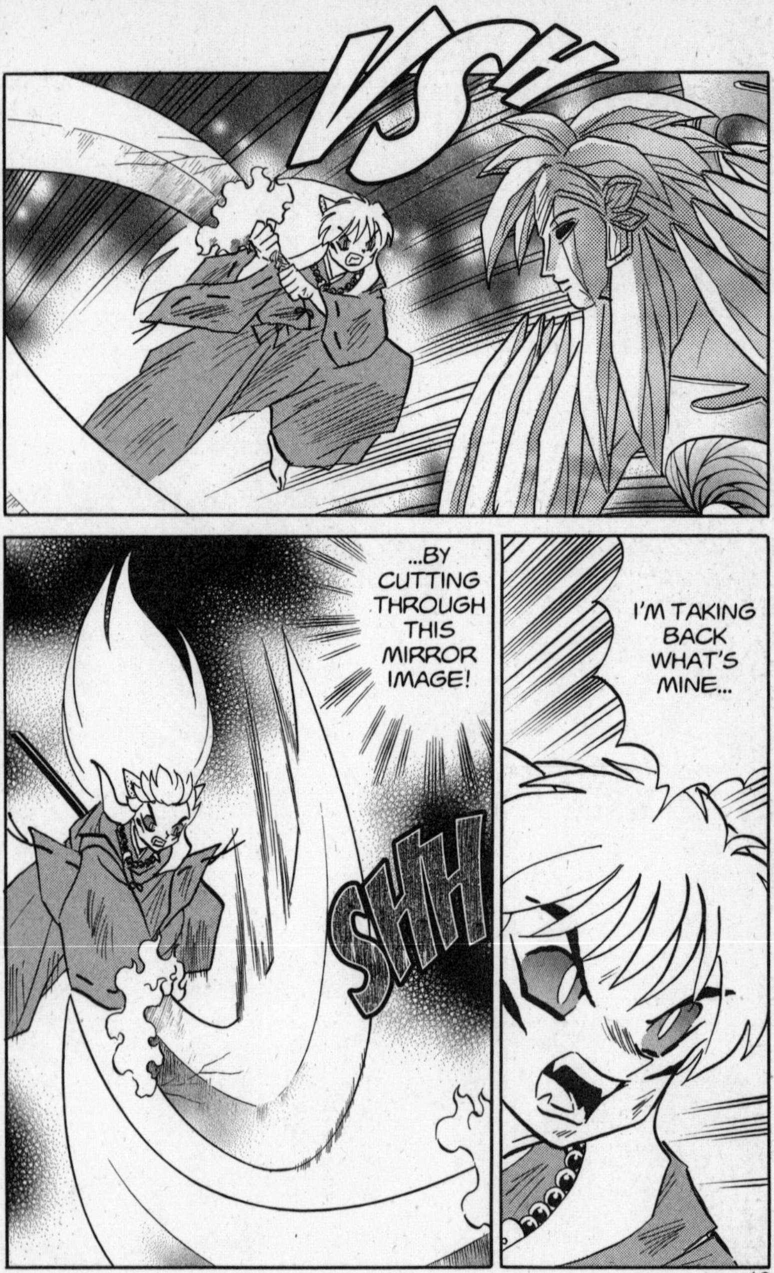
VSH
I'M TAKING BACK WHAT'S MINE...
...BY CUTTING THROUGH THIS MIRROR IMAGE!
SHH

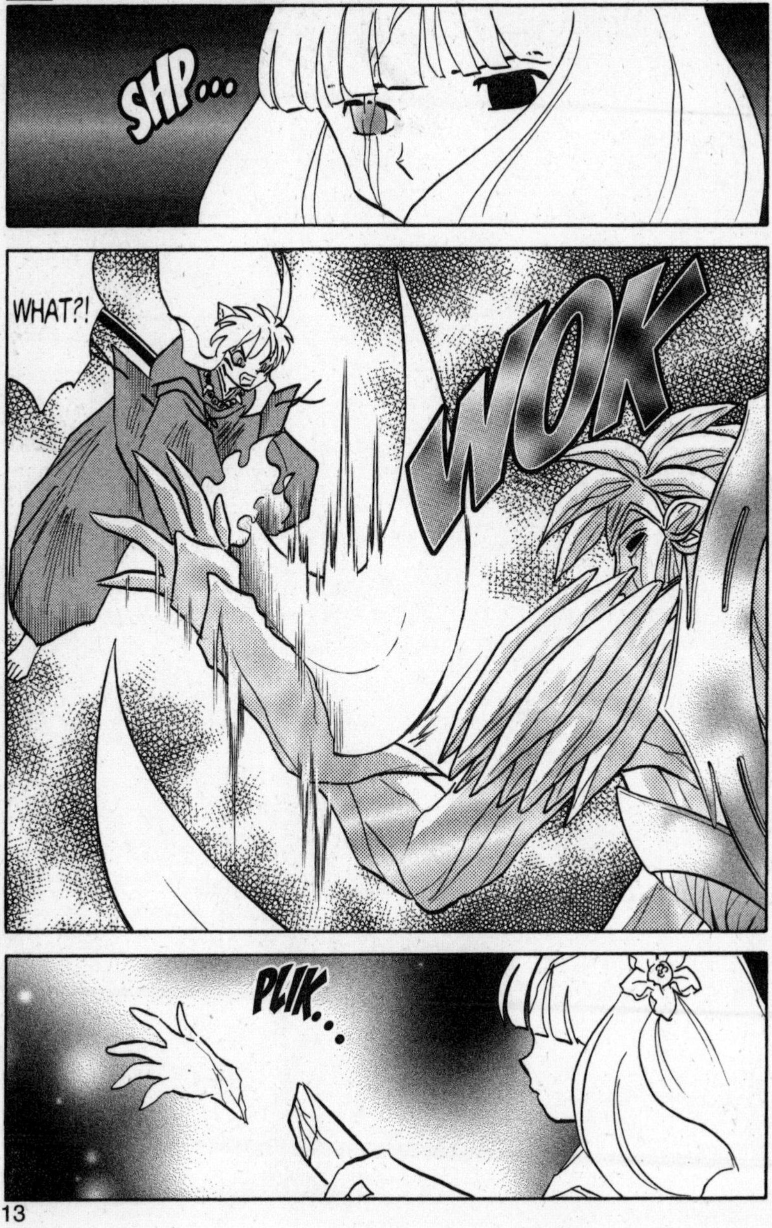
SHP...
WOK
WHAT?!
PLIK...

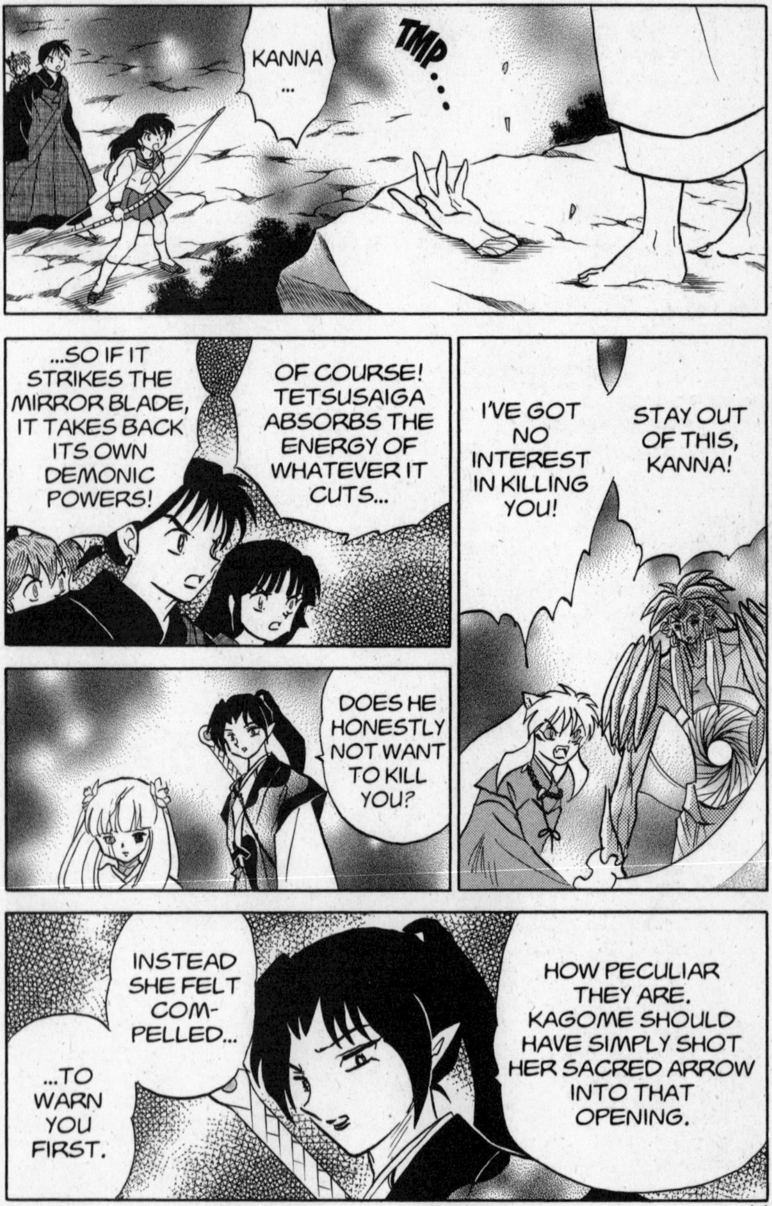
KANNA ...
TMP...
STAY OUT OF THIS, KANNA!
I'VE GOT NO INTEREST IN KILLING YOU!
OF COURSE! TETSUSAIGA ABSORBS THE ENERGY OF WHATEVER IT CUTS...
...SO IF IT STRIKES THE MIRROR BLADE, IT TAKES BACK ITS OWN DEMONIC POWERS!
DOES HE HONESTLY NOT WANT TO KILL YOU?
HOW PECULIAR THEY ARE. KAGOME SHOULD HAVE SIMPLY SHOT HER SACRED ARROW INTO THAT OPENING.
INSTEAD SHE FELT COM-PELLED...
...TO WARN YOU FIRST.

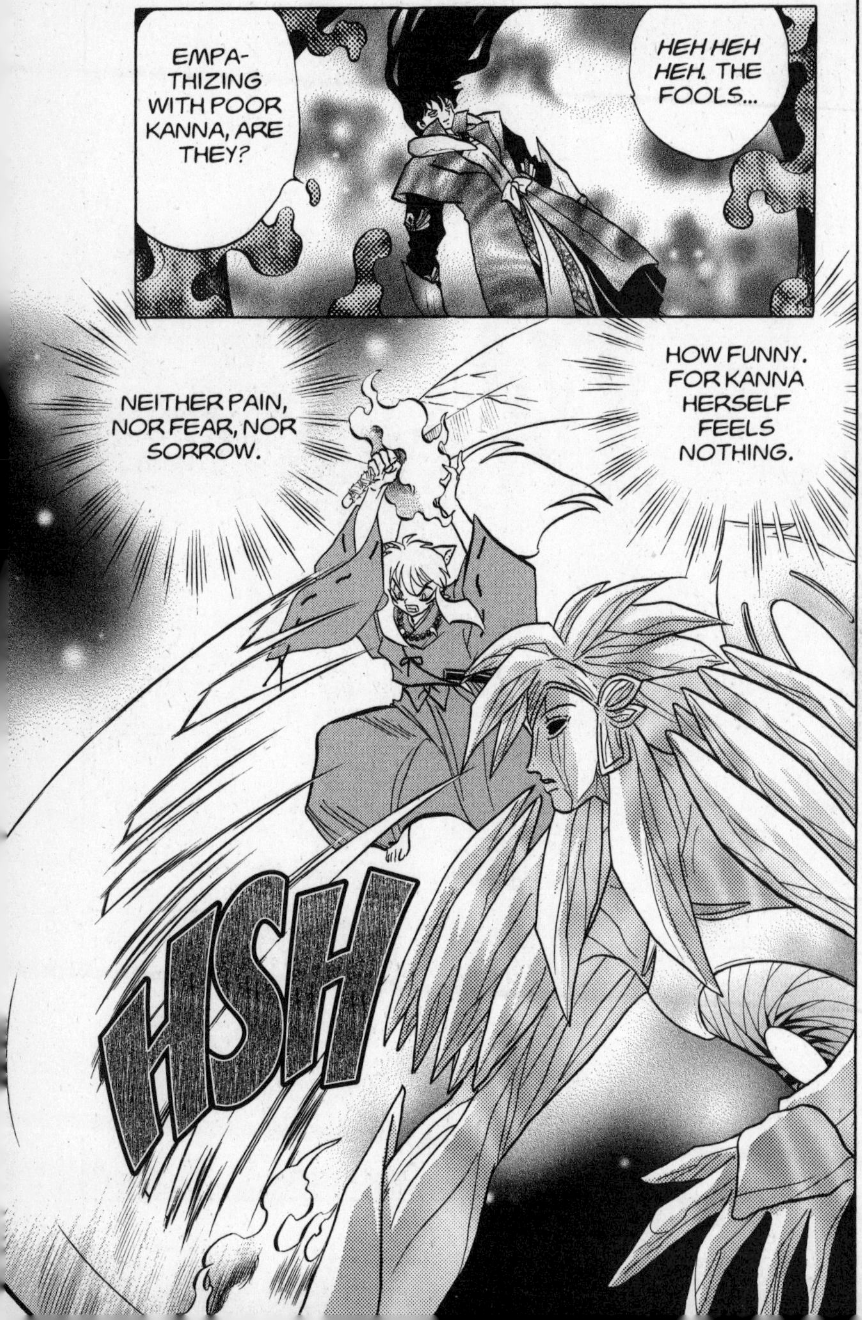
HEH HEH HEH. THE FOOLS...
EMPA-THIZING WITH POOR KANNA, ARE THEY?
HOW FUNNY. FOR KANNA HERSELF FEELS NOTHING.
NEITHER PAIN, NOR FEAR, NOR SORROW.
HSH

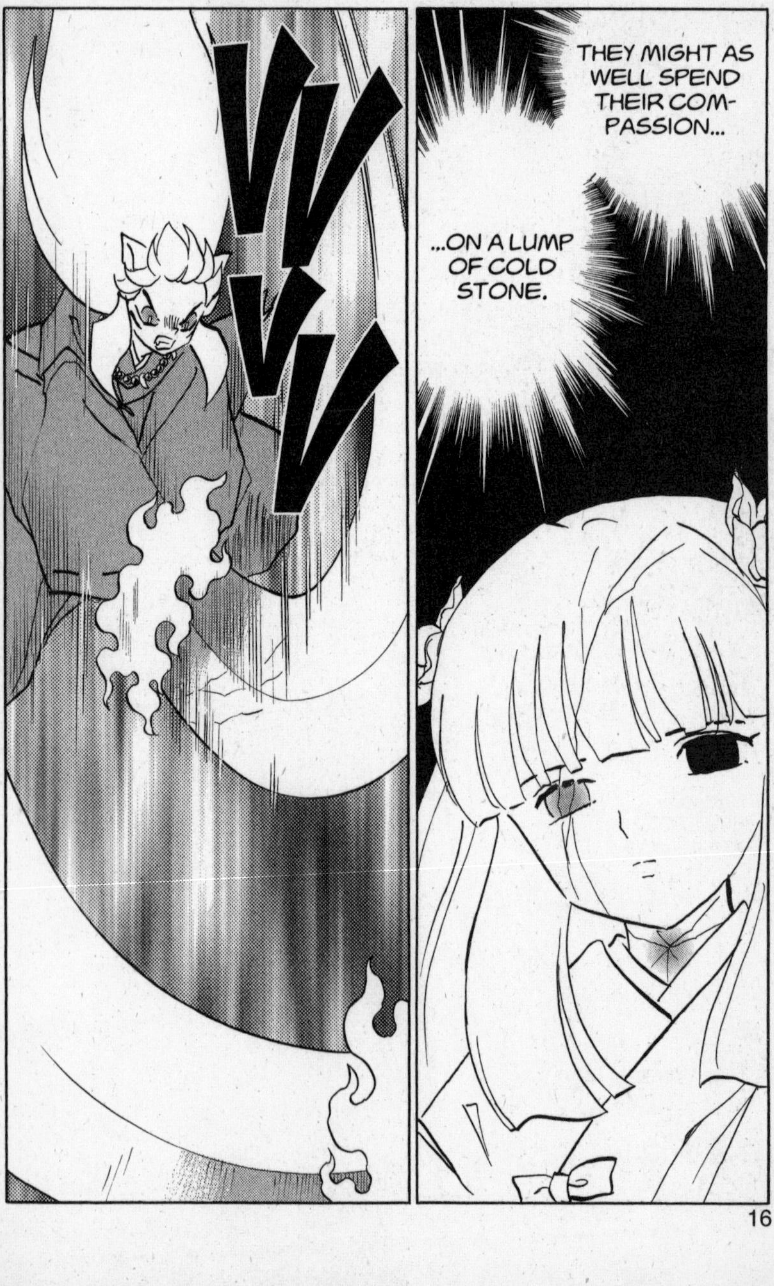
THEY MIGHT AS WELL SPEND THEIR COM-PASSION...
...ON A LUMP OF COLD STONE.

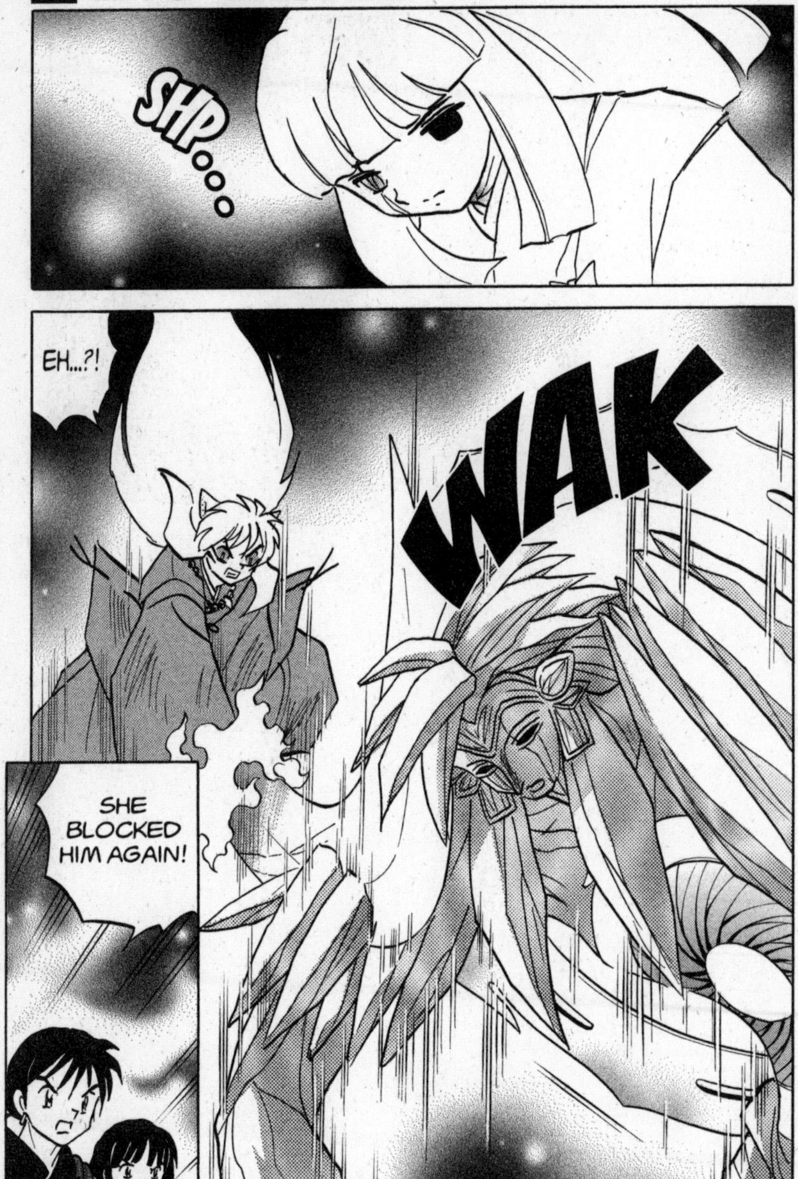
SHP...
WAK
EH...?!
SHE BLOCKED HIM AGAIN!

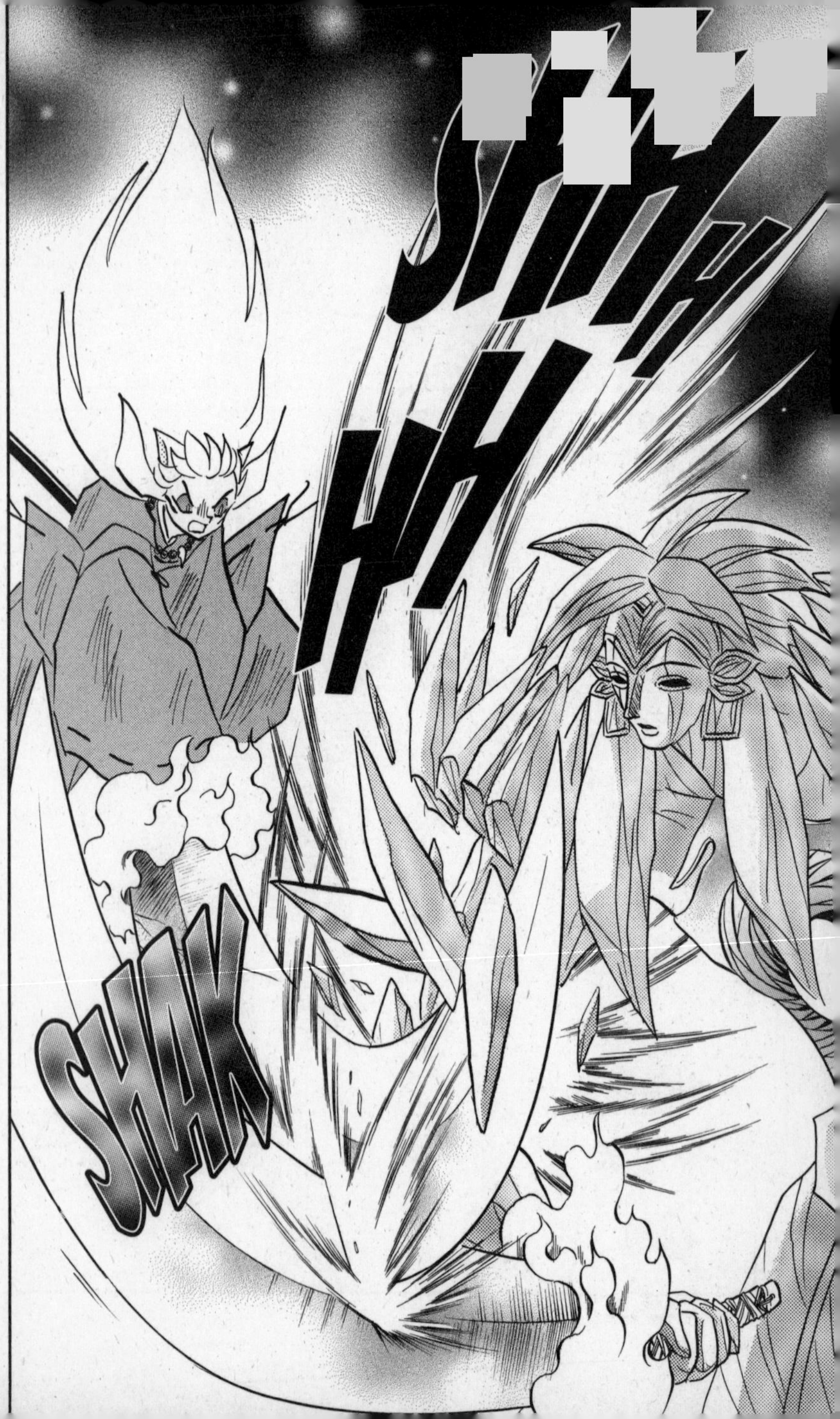
SHAK

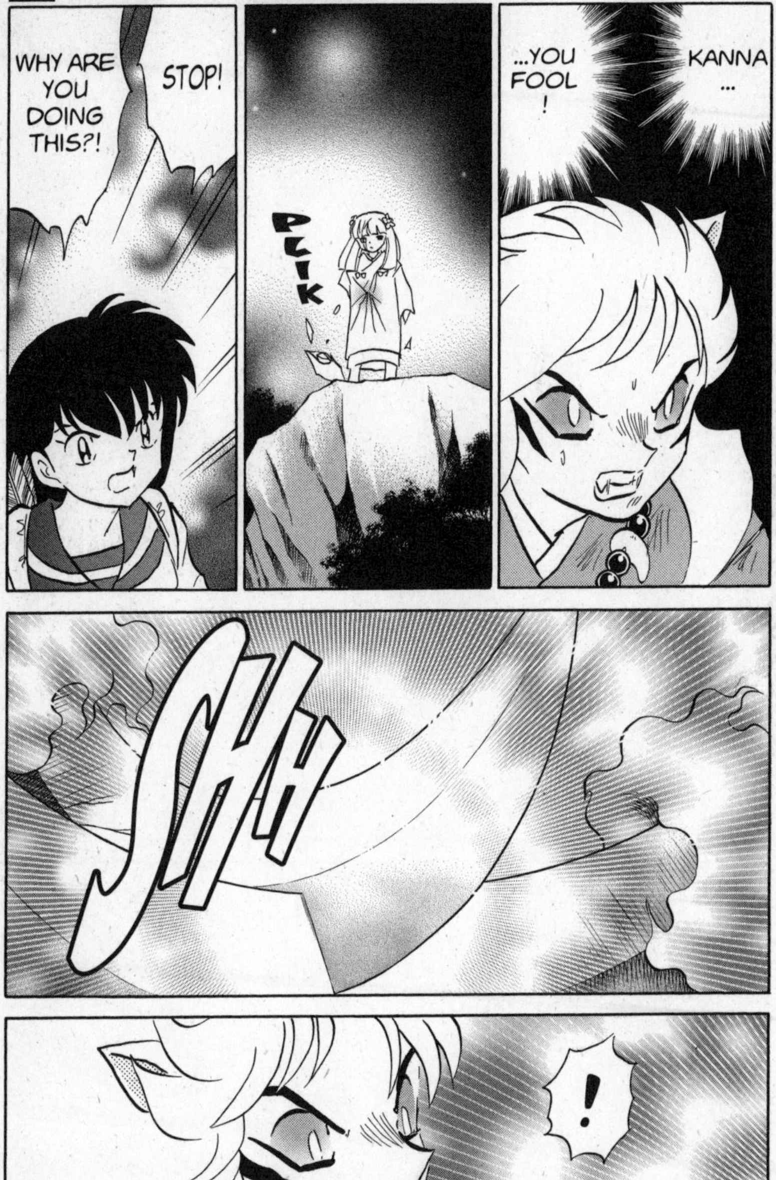
KANNA...
...YOU FOOL!
PLIK
STOP!
WHY ARE YOU DOING THIS?!
SHH
!

HOOOO

WOOM

KRK KRK KRK KRK

INU-YASHA!

DOOOM

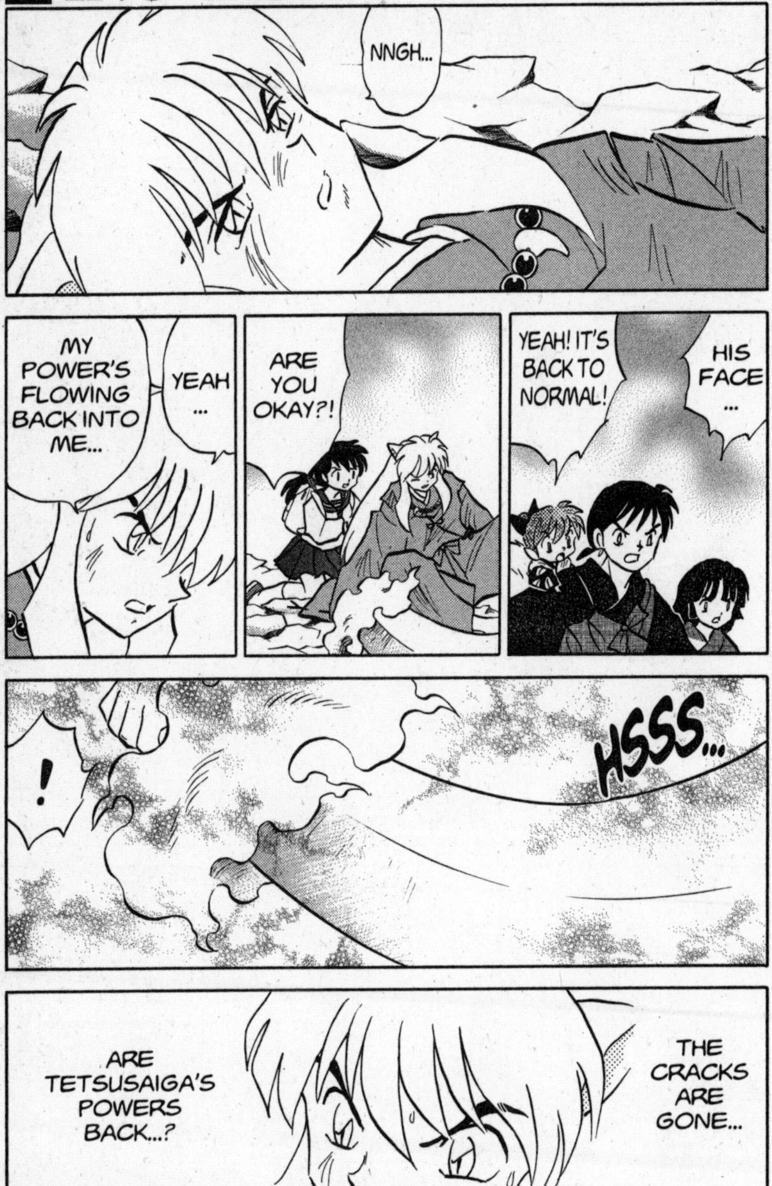
NNGH...
HIS FACE ...
YEAH! IT'S BACK TO NORMAL!
ARE YOU OKAY?!
YEAH ...
MY POWER'S FLOWING BACK INTO ME...
HSSS...
!
THE CRACKS ARE GONE...
ARE TETSUSAIGA'S POWERS BACK...?

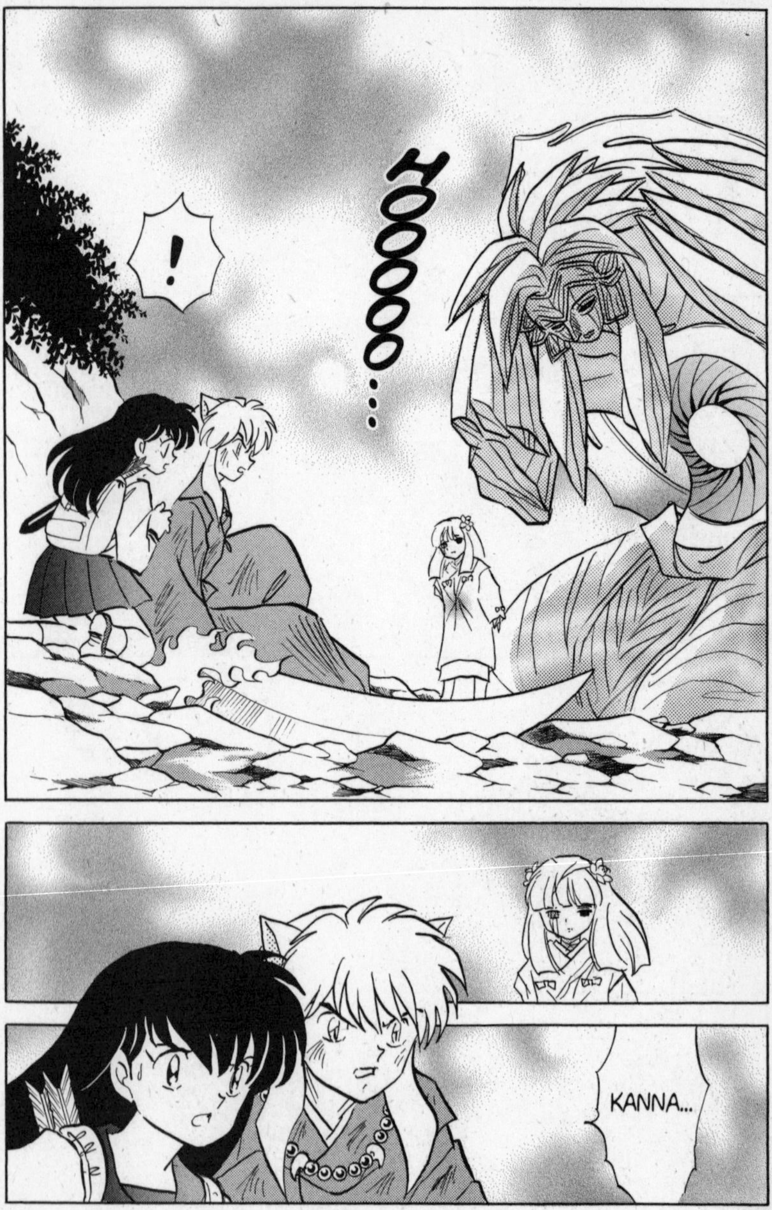
HOOOOO...
!
KANNA...

SCROLL 2
LAST WORDS

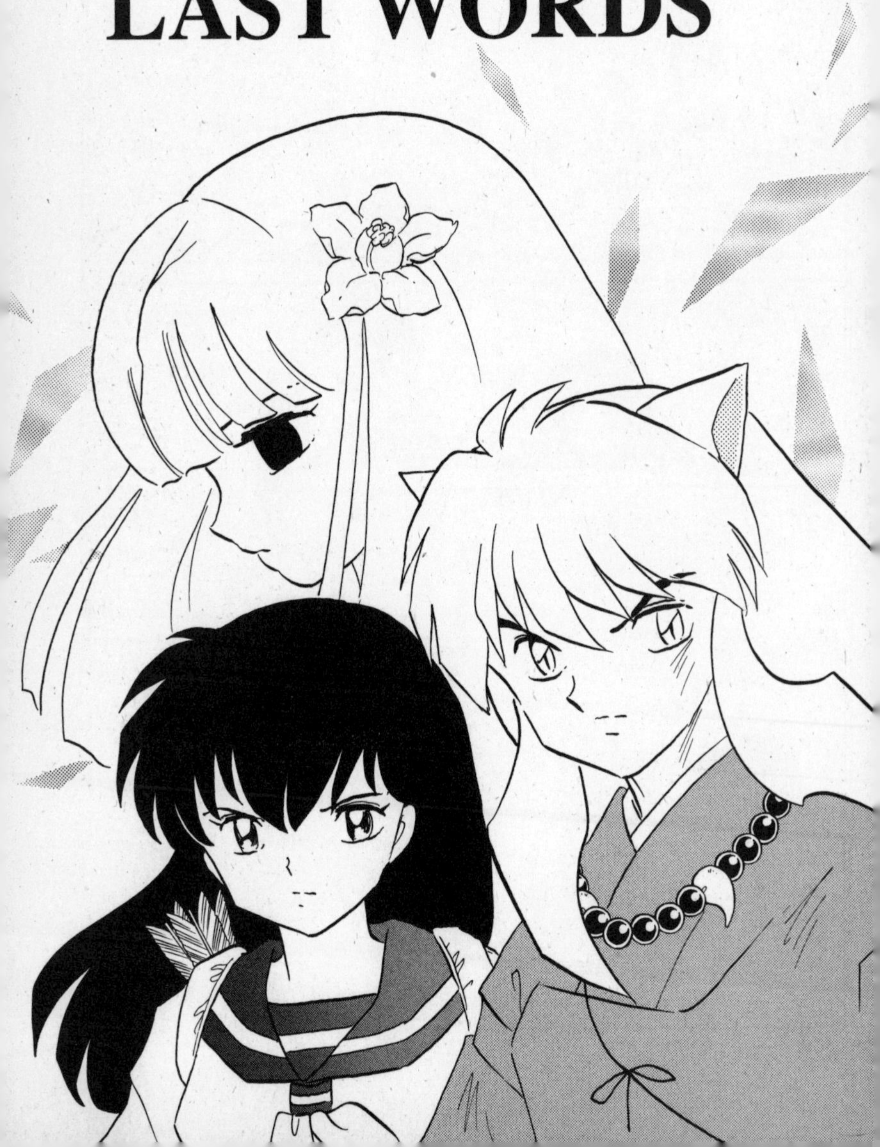

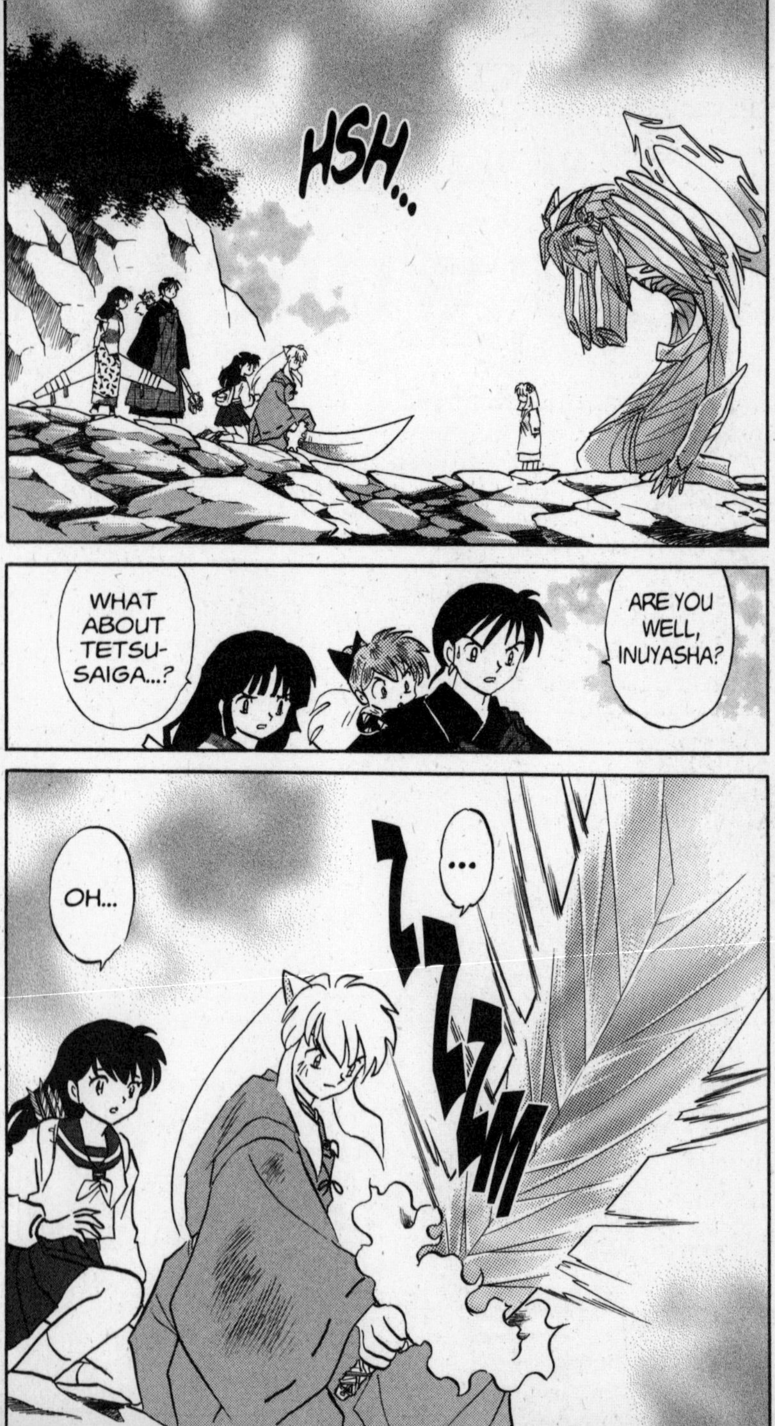
HSH...
ARE YOU WELL, INUYASHA?
WHAT ABOUT TETSU-SAIGA...?
...
ZZZM
OH...

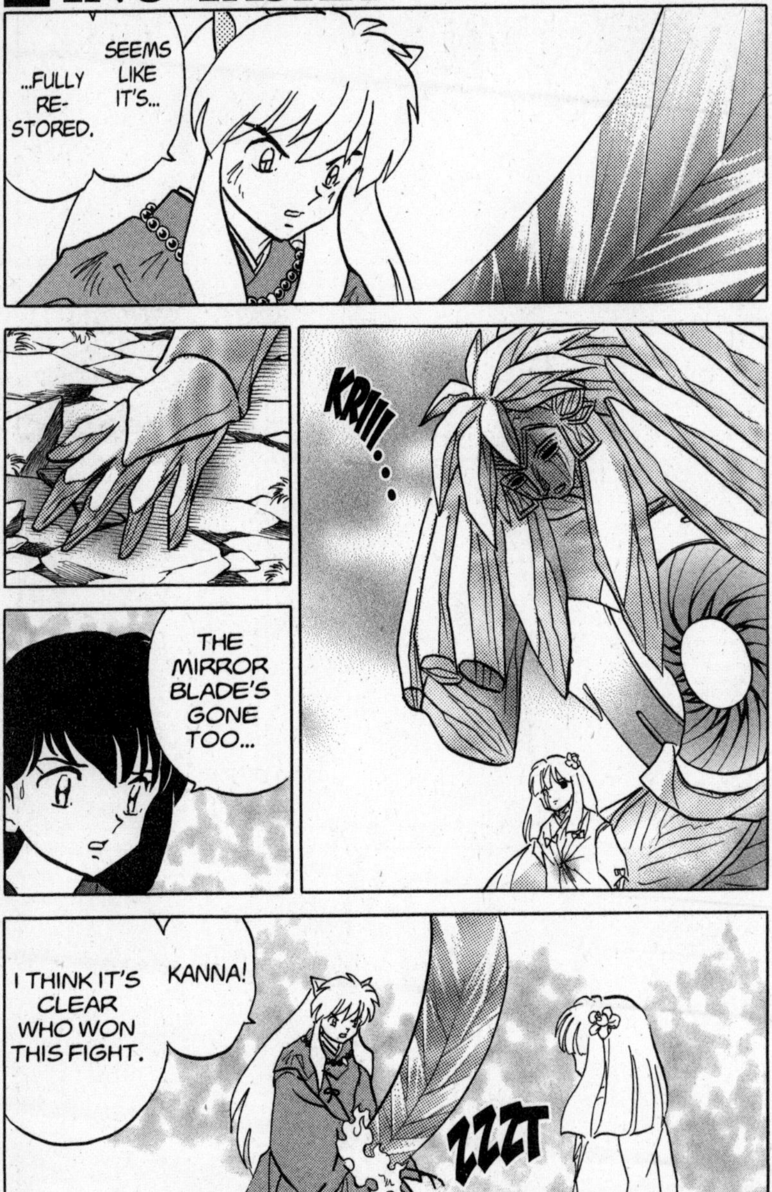
SEEMS LIKE IT'S...
...FULLY RE-STORED.
KRIII...
THE MIRROR BLADE'S GONE TOO...
KANNA!
I THINK IT'S CLEAR WHO WON THIS FIGHT.
ZZZT

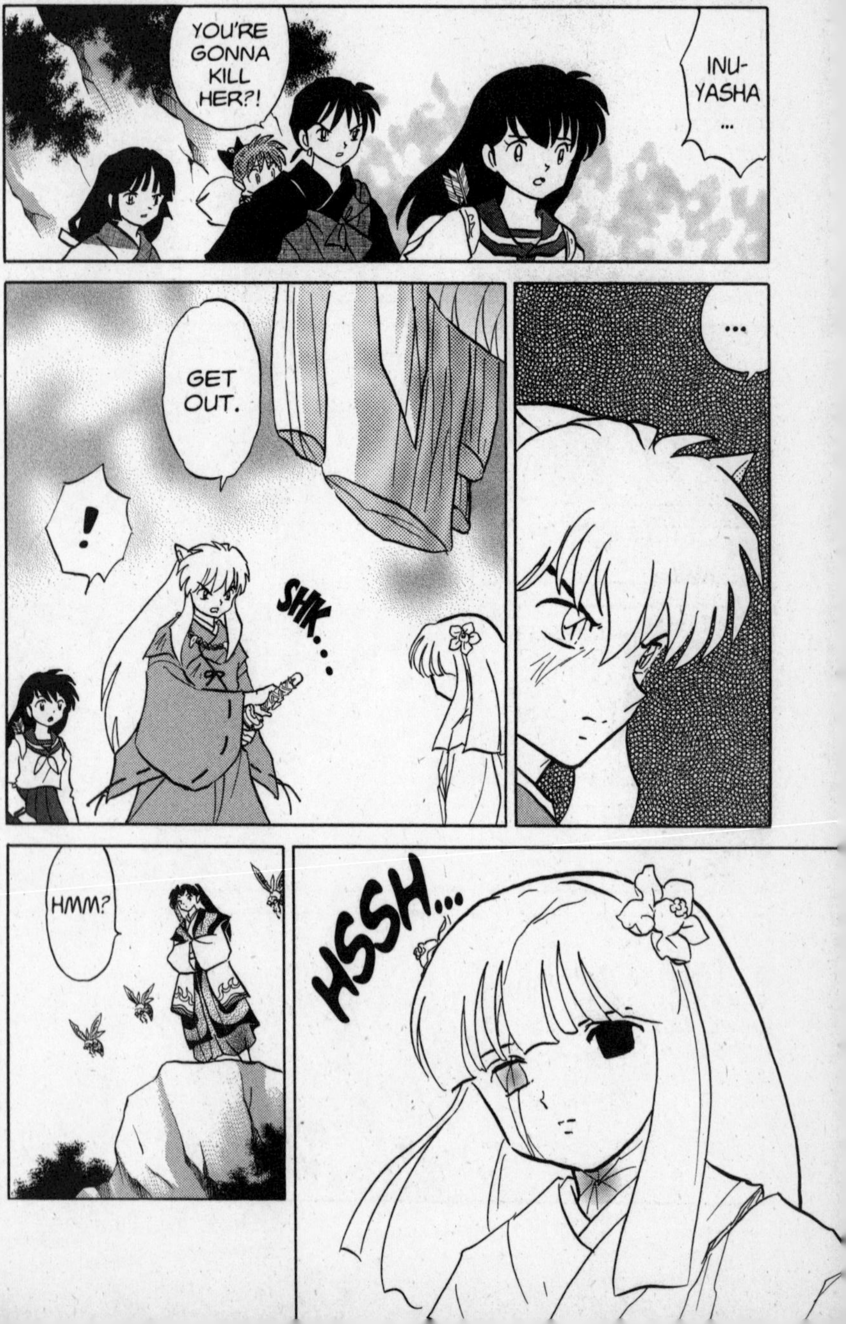
INU-YASHA ...
YOU'RE GONNA KILL HER?!
...
GET OUT.
!
SHK...
HSSH...
HMM?

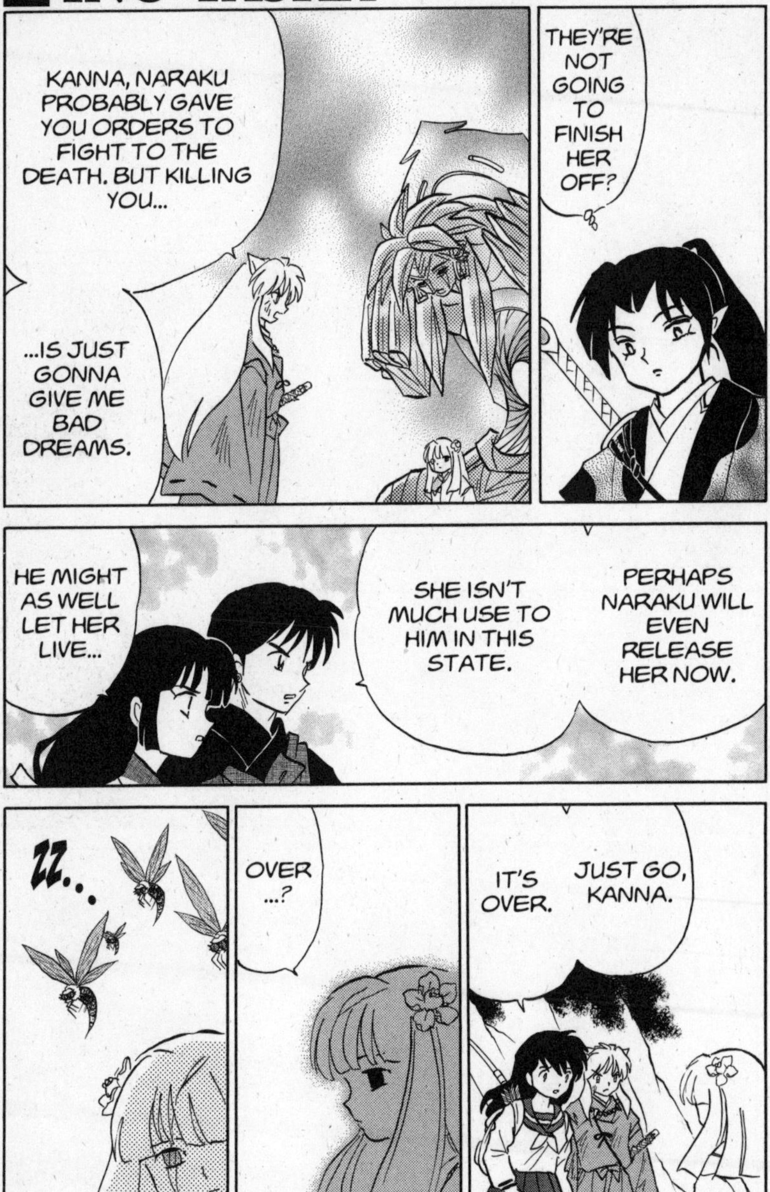
THEY'RE NOT GOING TO FINISH HER OFF?
KANNA, NARAKU PROBABLY GAVE YOU ORDERS TO FIGHT TO THE DEATH. BUT KILLING YOU...
...IS JUST GONNA GIVE ME BAD DREAMS.
PERHAPS NARAKU WILL EVEN RELEASE HER NOW.
SHE ISN'T MUCH USE TO HIM IN THIS STATE.
HE MIGHT AS WELL LET HER LIVE...
JUST GO, KANNA.
IT'S OVER.
OVER ...?
ZZ...

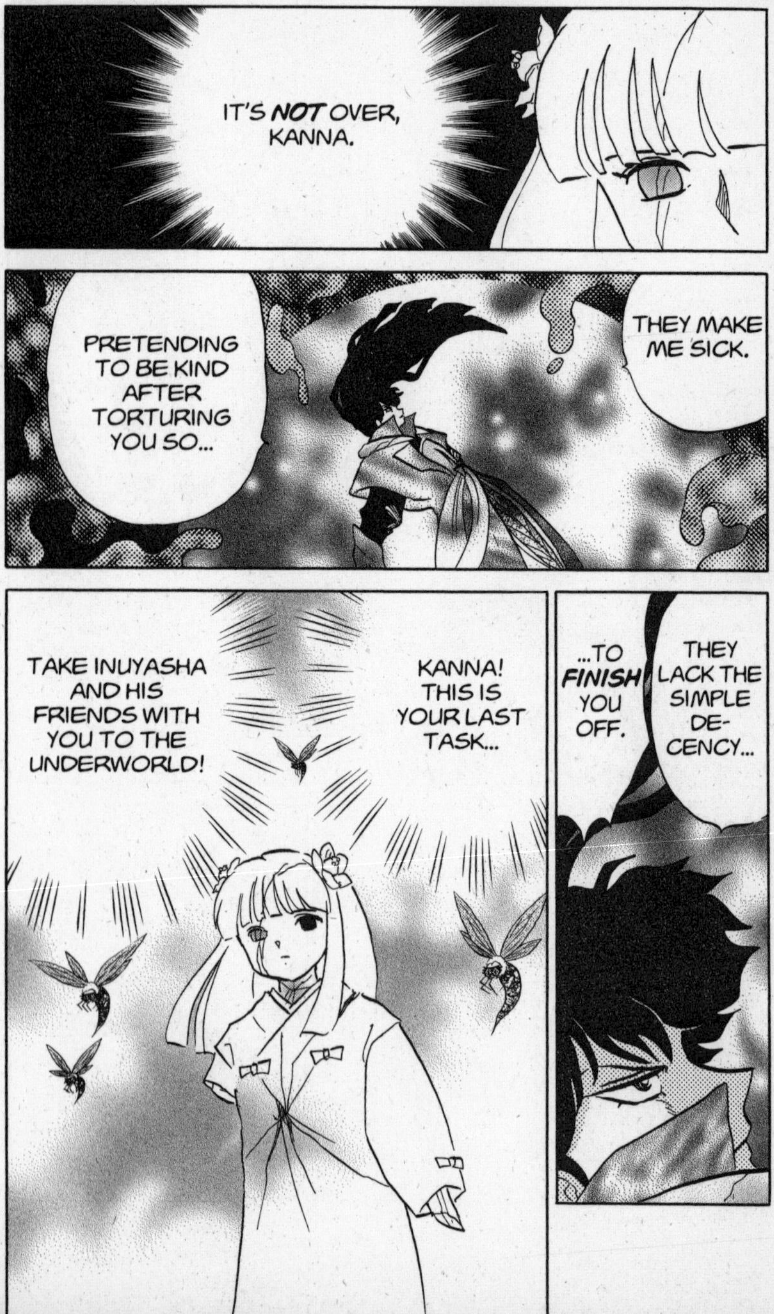
IT'S NOT OVER, KANNA.
THEY MAKE ME SICK.
PRETENDING TO BE KIND AFTER TORTURING YOU SO...
THEY LACK THE SIMPLE DE-CENCY...
...TO FINISH YOU OFF.
KANNA! THIS IS YOUR LAST TASK...
TAKE INUYASHA AND HIS FRIENDS WITH YOU TO THE UNDERWORLD!

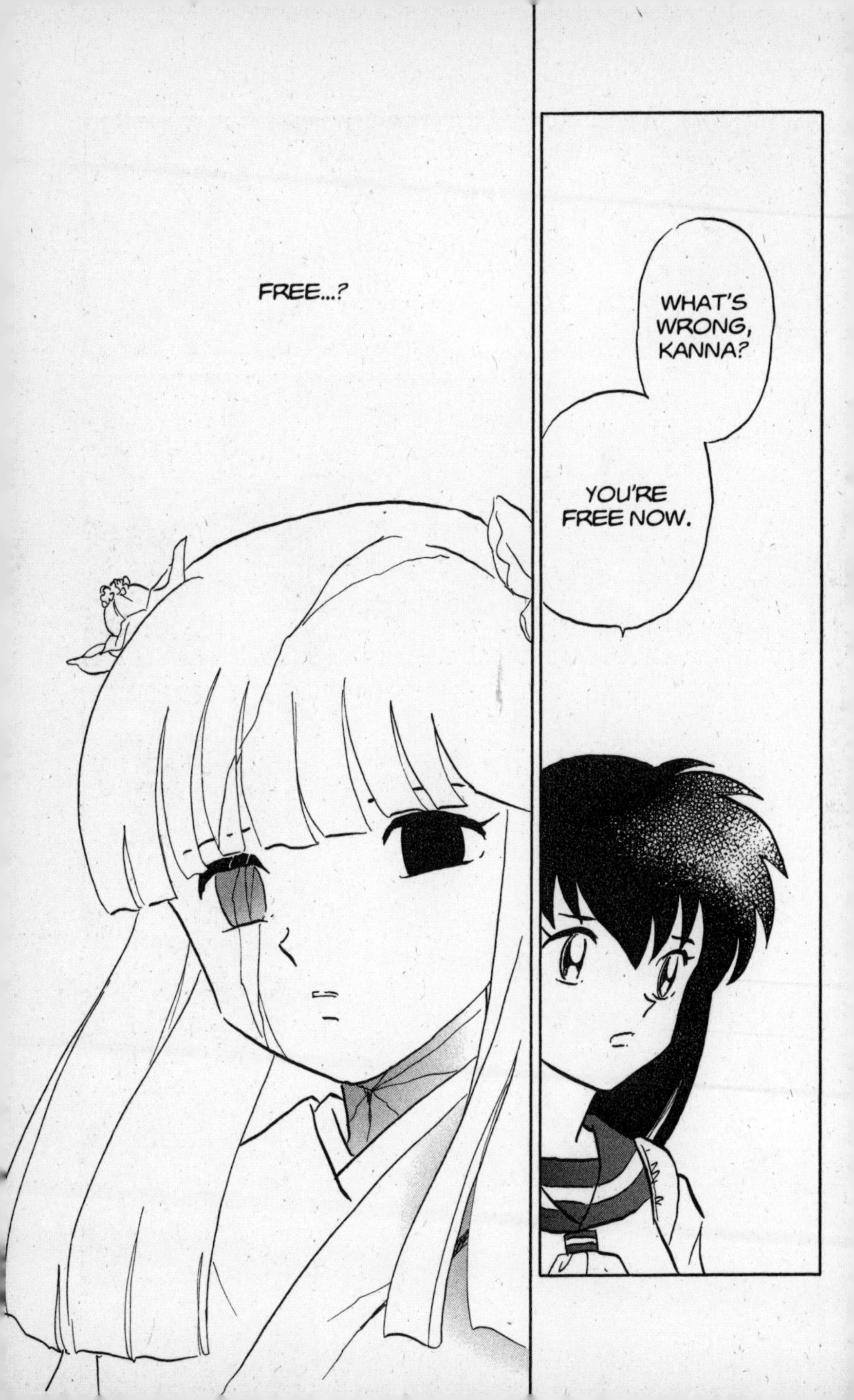
WHAT'S WRONG, KANNA?
YOU'RE FREE NOW.
FREE...?

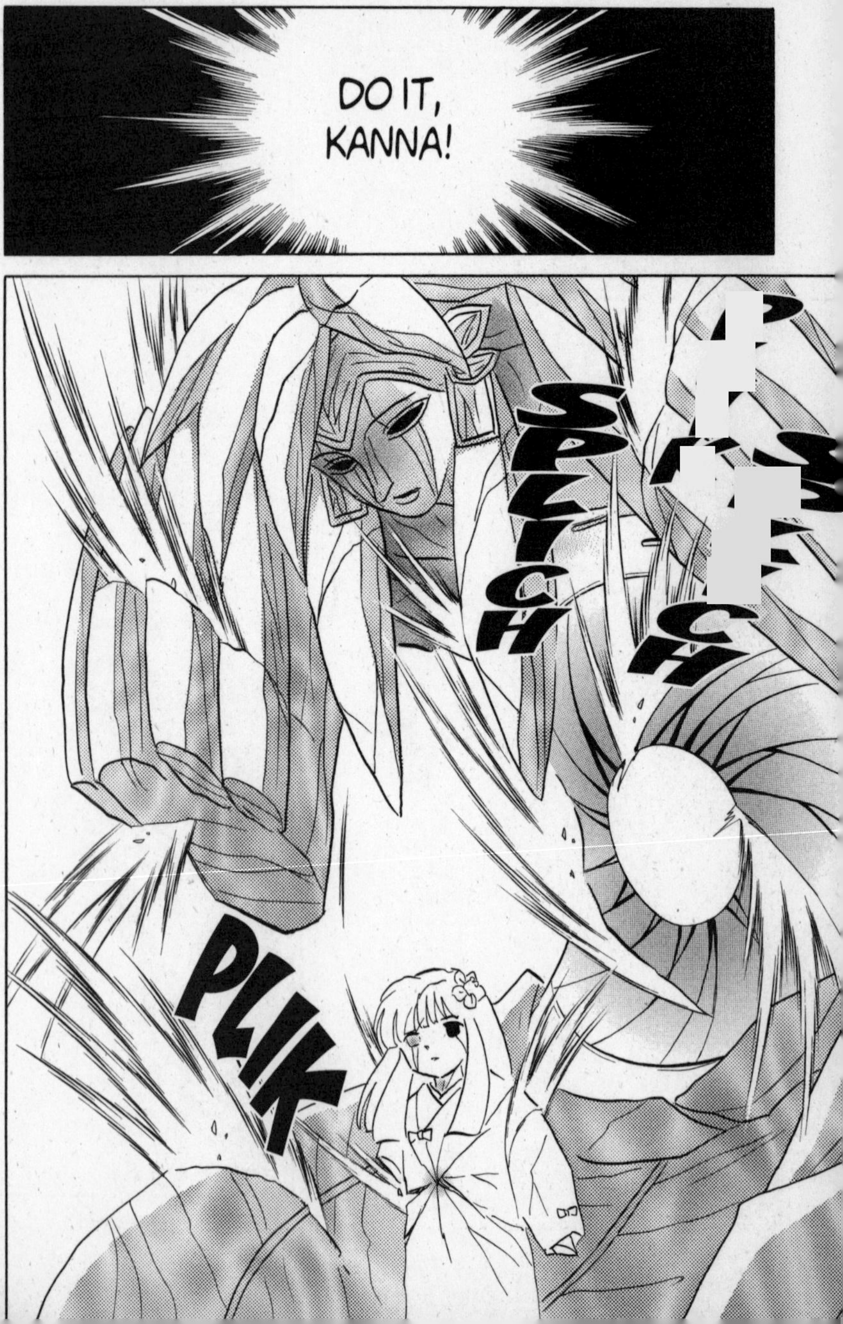
DO IT, KANNA!
SPLICH
PLIK

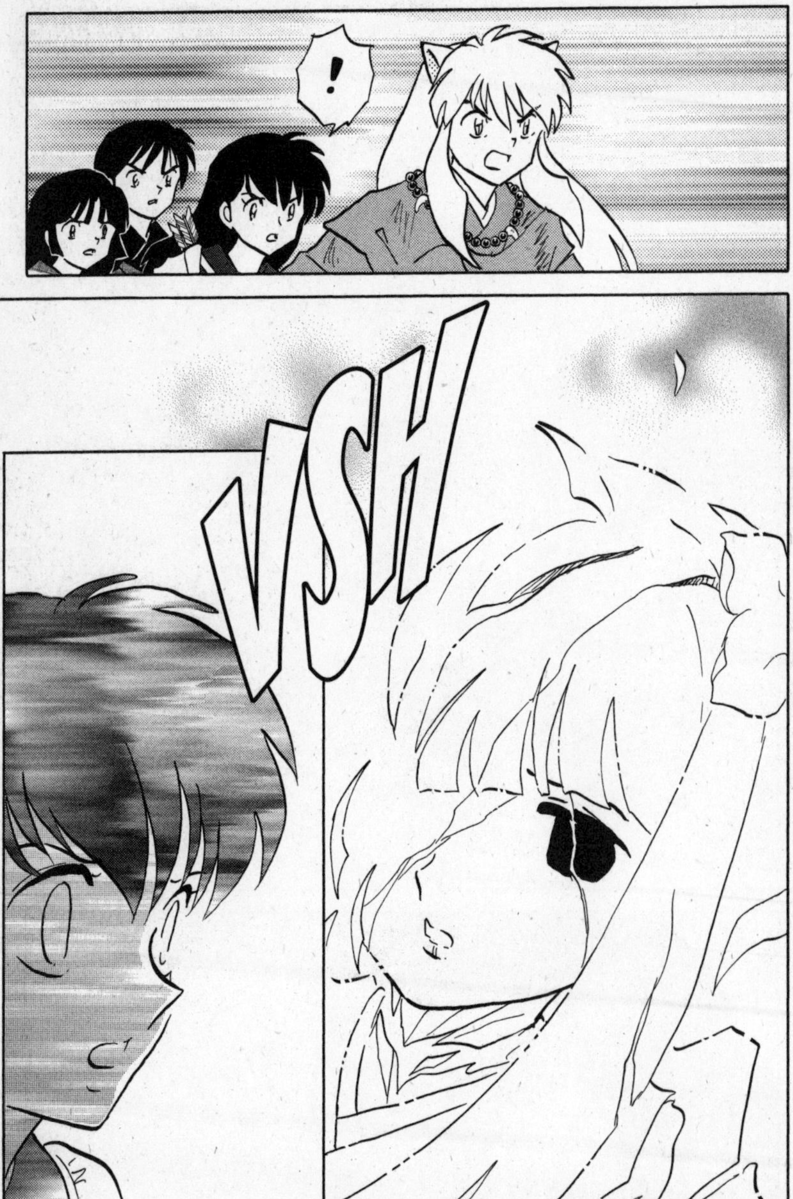
!
VSH

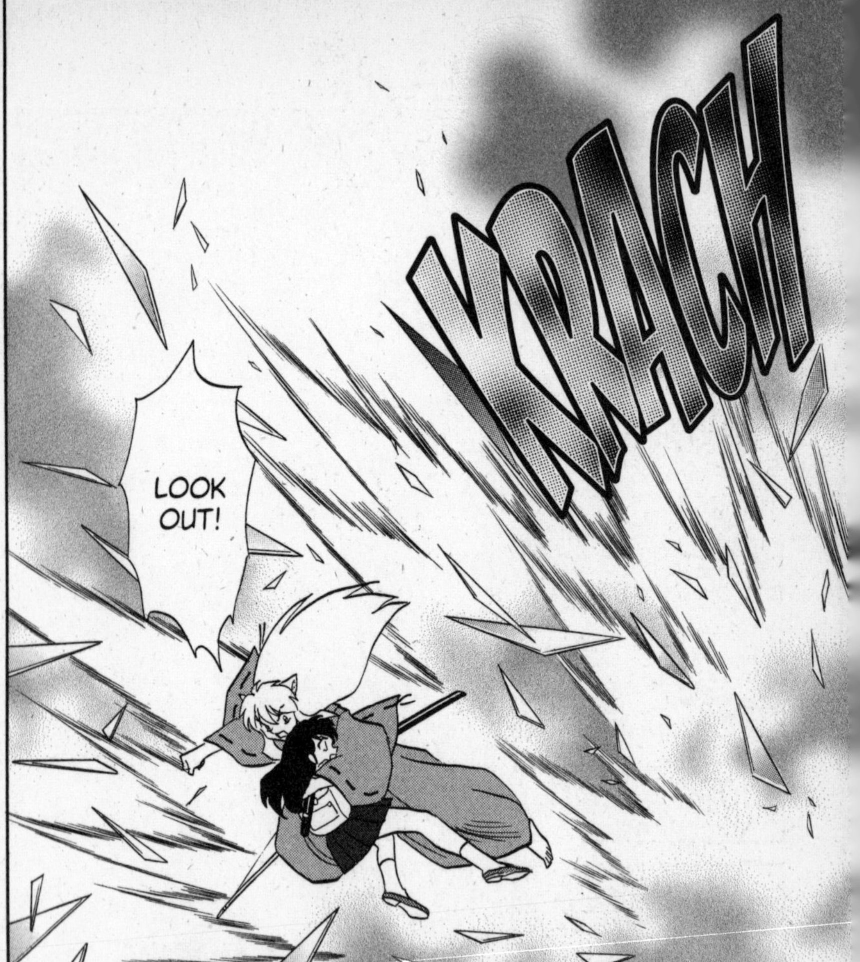
KRACH
LOOK OUT!
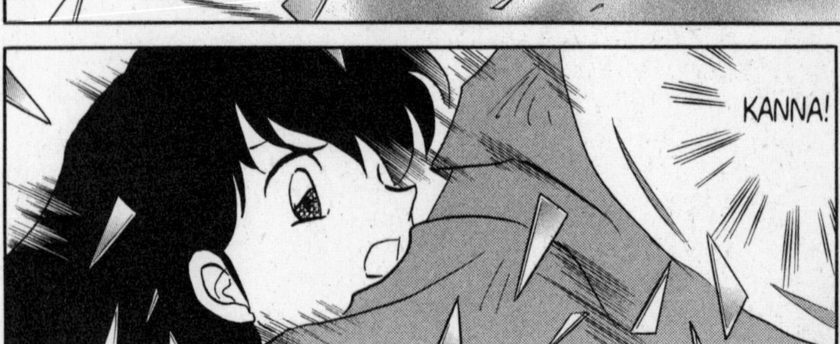
KANNA!

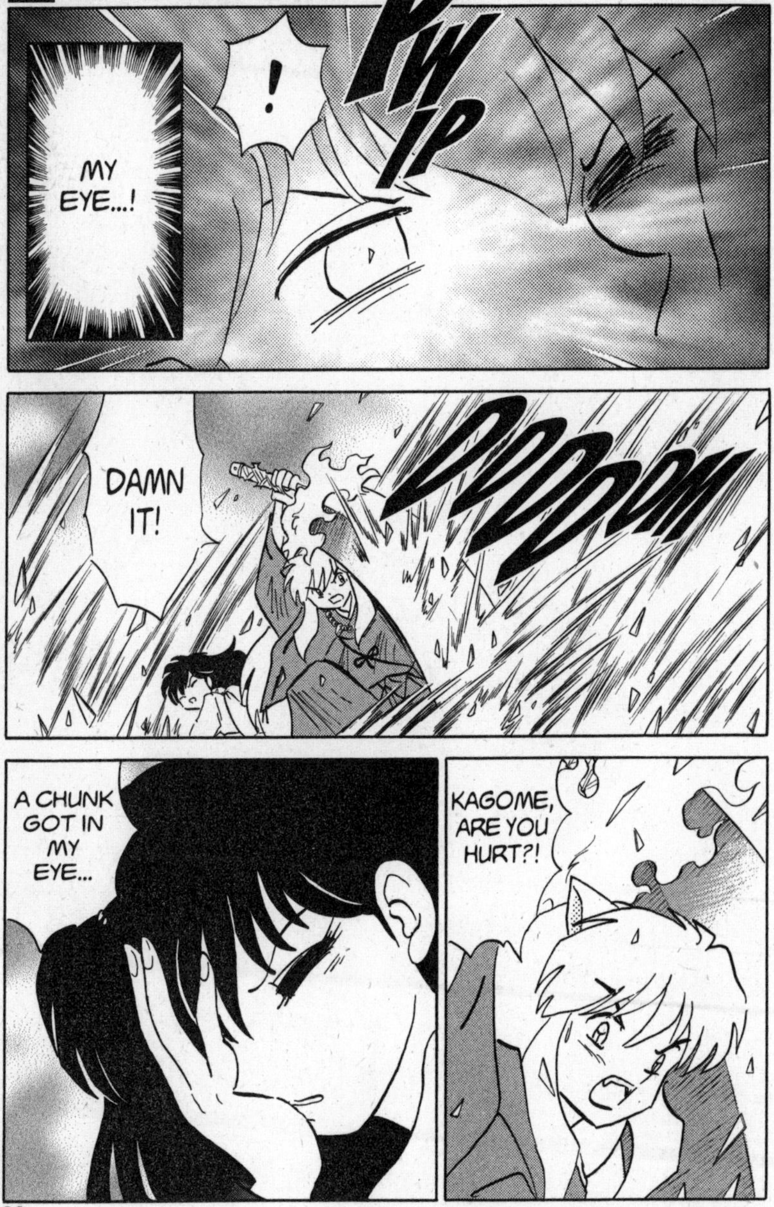
PWIP
!
MY EYE...!
DOOOOM
DAMN IT!
KAGOME, ARE YOU HURT?!
A CHUNK GOT IN MY EYE...

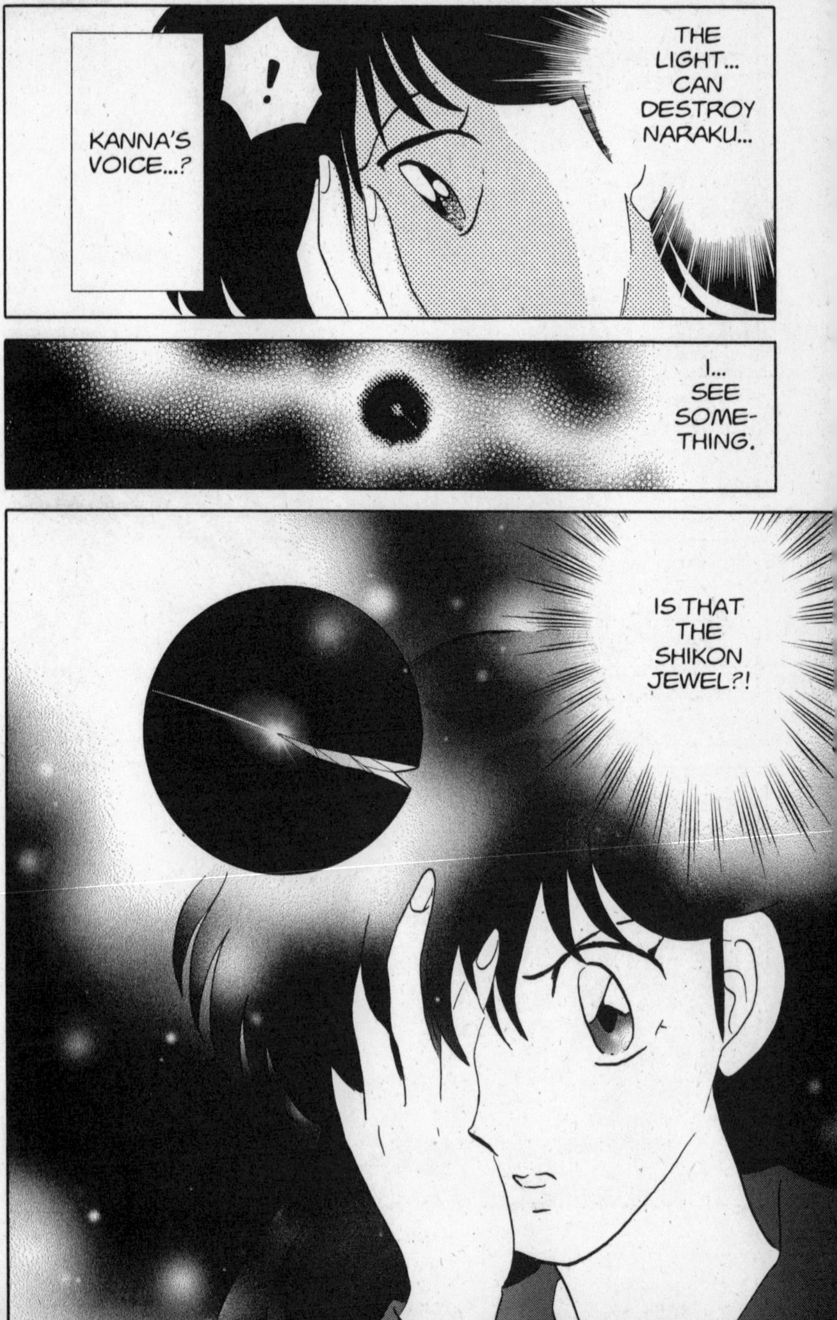
THE LIGHT... CAN DESTROY NARAKU...
!
KANNA'S VOICE...?
I... SEE SOME-THING.
IS THAT THE SHIKON JEWEL?!

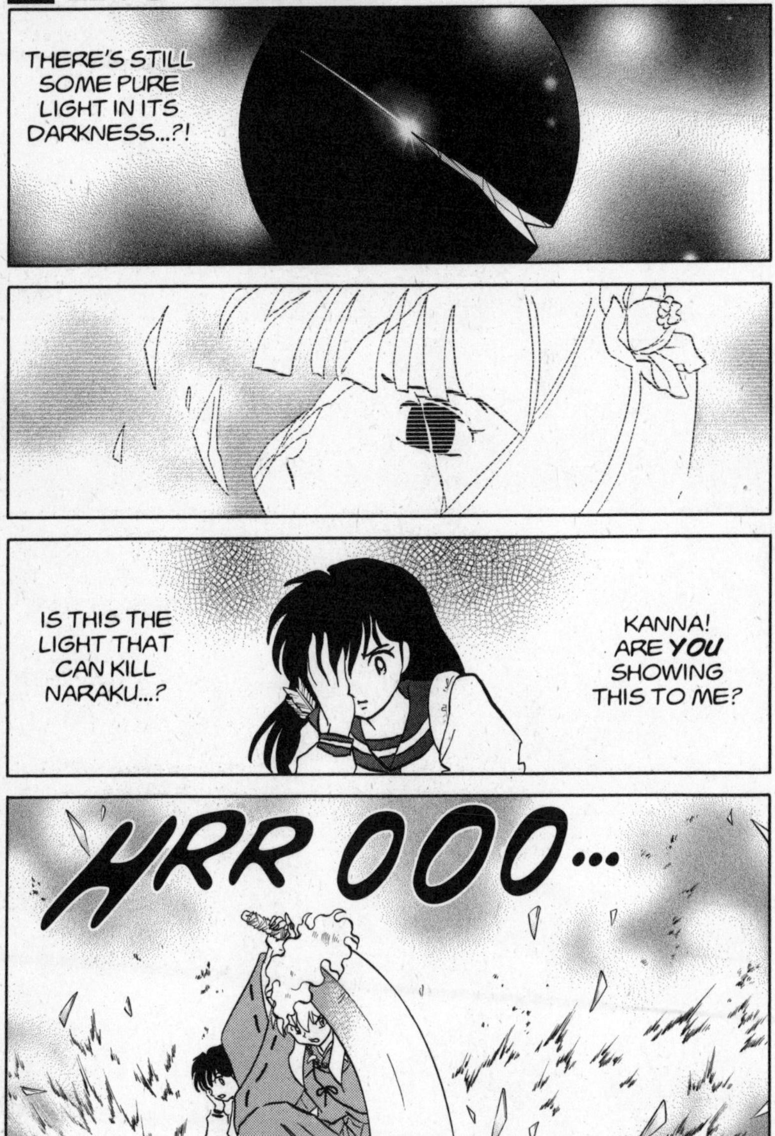
THERE'S STILL SOME PURE LIGHT IN ITS DARKNESS...?!
KANNA! ARE *YOU* SHOWING THIS TO ME?
IS THIS THE LIGHT THAT CAN KILL NARAKU...?
HRR OOO...

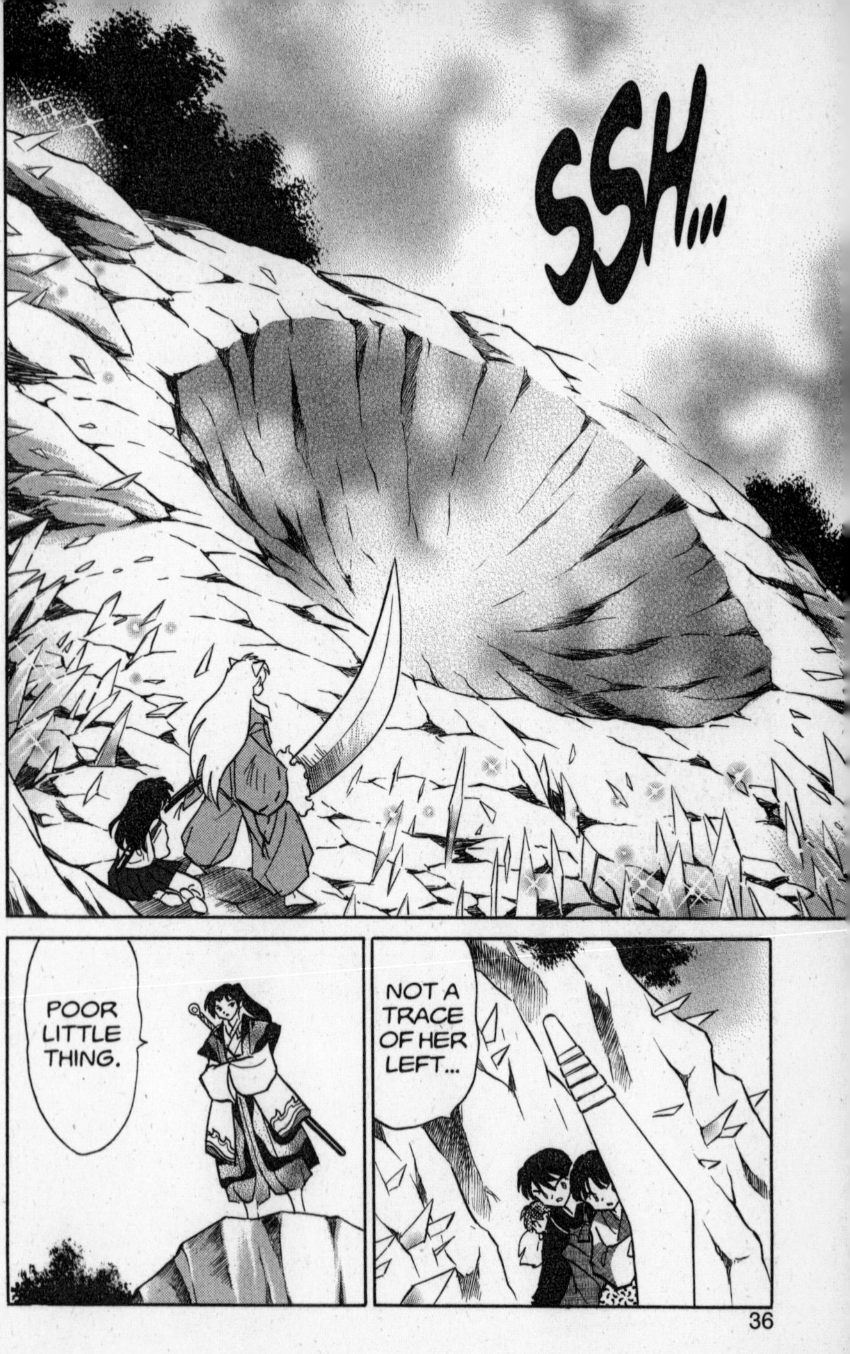
SSH...
NOT A TRACE OF HER LEFT...
POOR LITTLE THING.

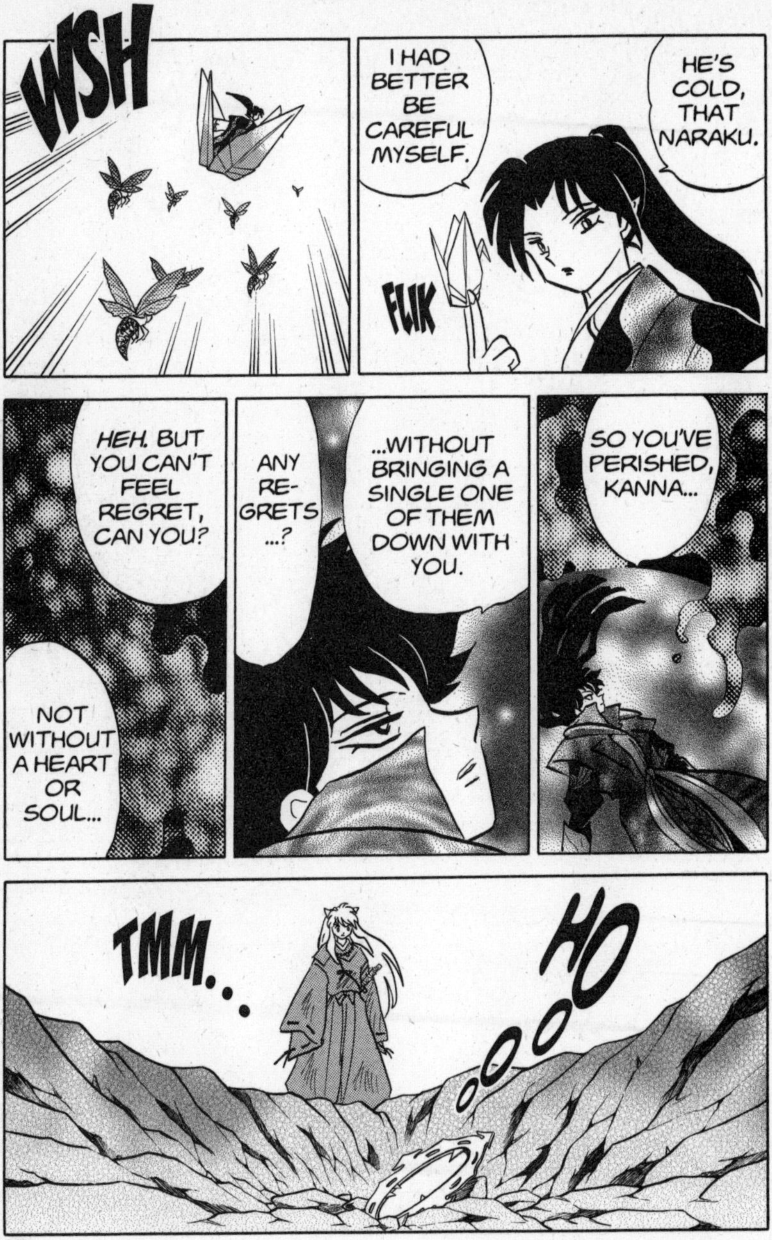
HE'S COLD, THAT NARAKU.
I HAD BETTER BE CAREFUL MYSELF.
FLIK
WSH
SO YOU'VE PERISHED, KANNA...
...WITHOUT BRINGING A SINGLE ONE OF THEM DOWN WITH YOU.
ANY RE-GRETS ...?
HEH. BUT YOU CAN'T FEEL REGRET, CAN YOU?
NOT WITHOUT A HEART OR SOUL...
HOOOOO
TMM...

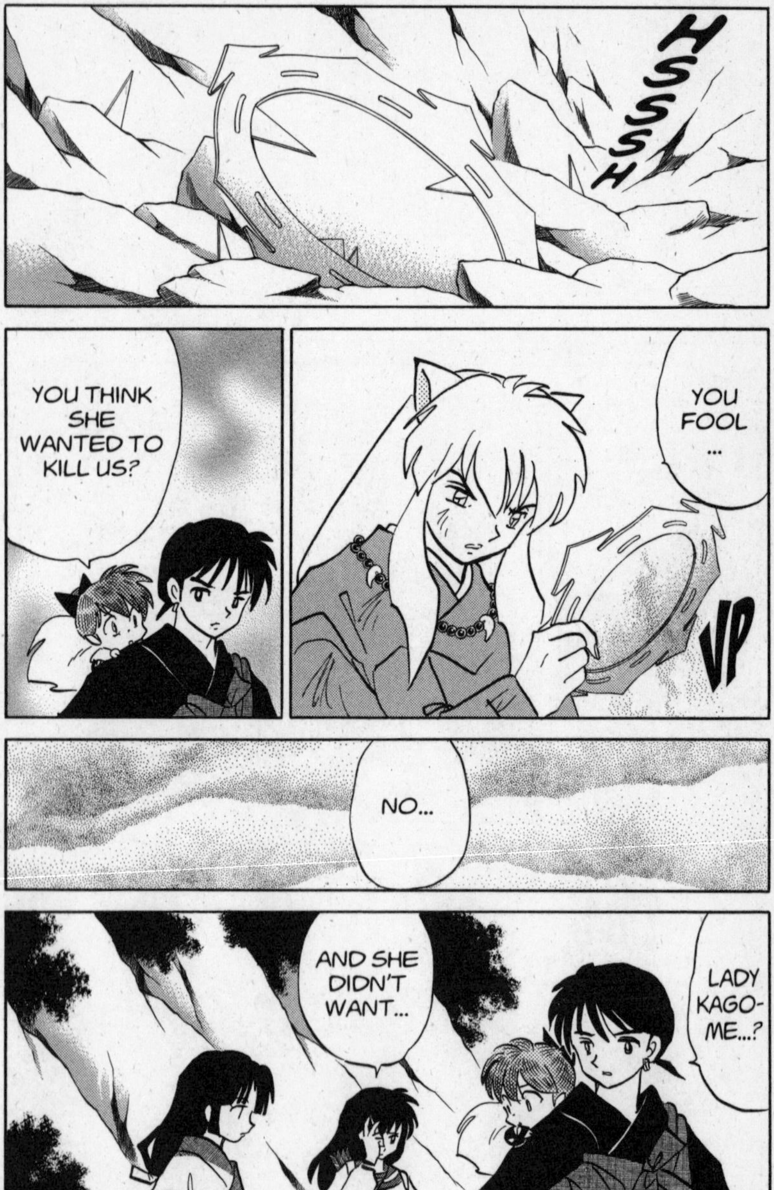
HSSSH
YOU FOOL ...
VP
YOU THINK SHE WANTED TO KILL US?
NO...
LADY KAGO-ME...?
AND SHE DIDN'T WANT...

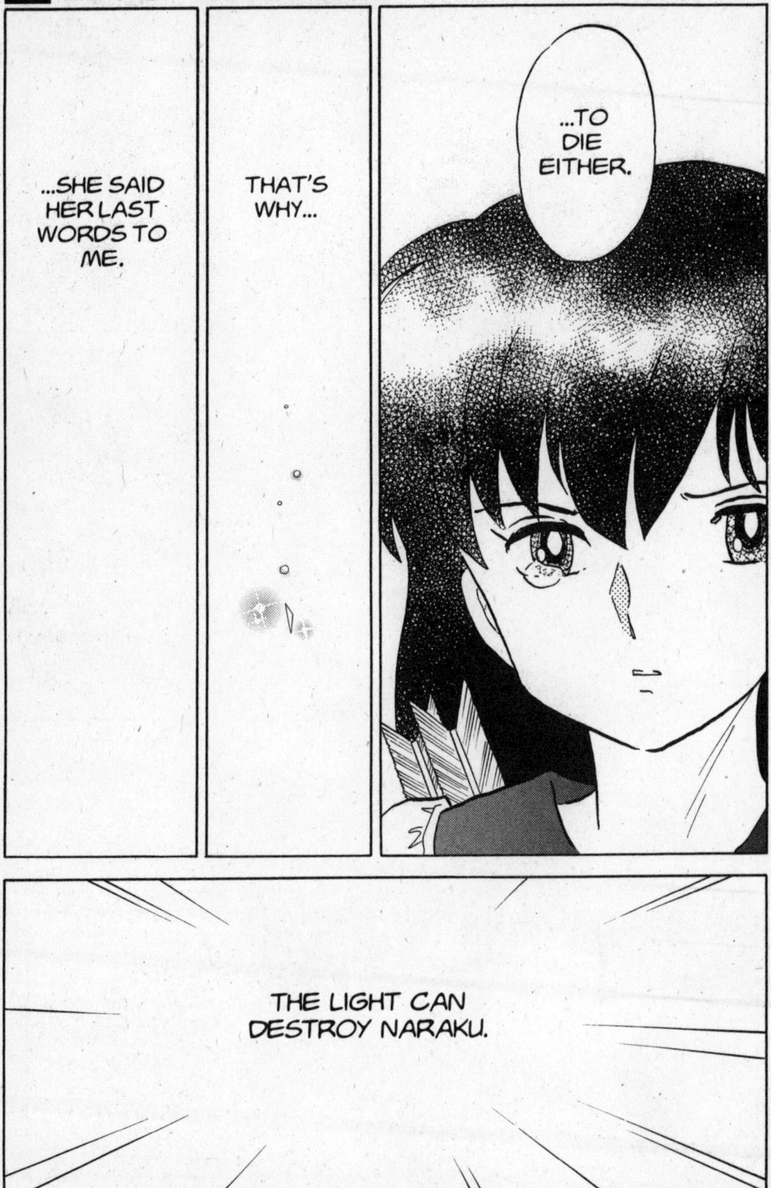
...TO DIE EITHER.
THAT'S WHY...
...SHE SAID HER LAST WORDS TO ME.
THE LIGHT CAN DESTROY NARAKU.

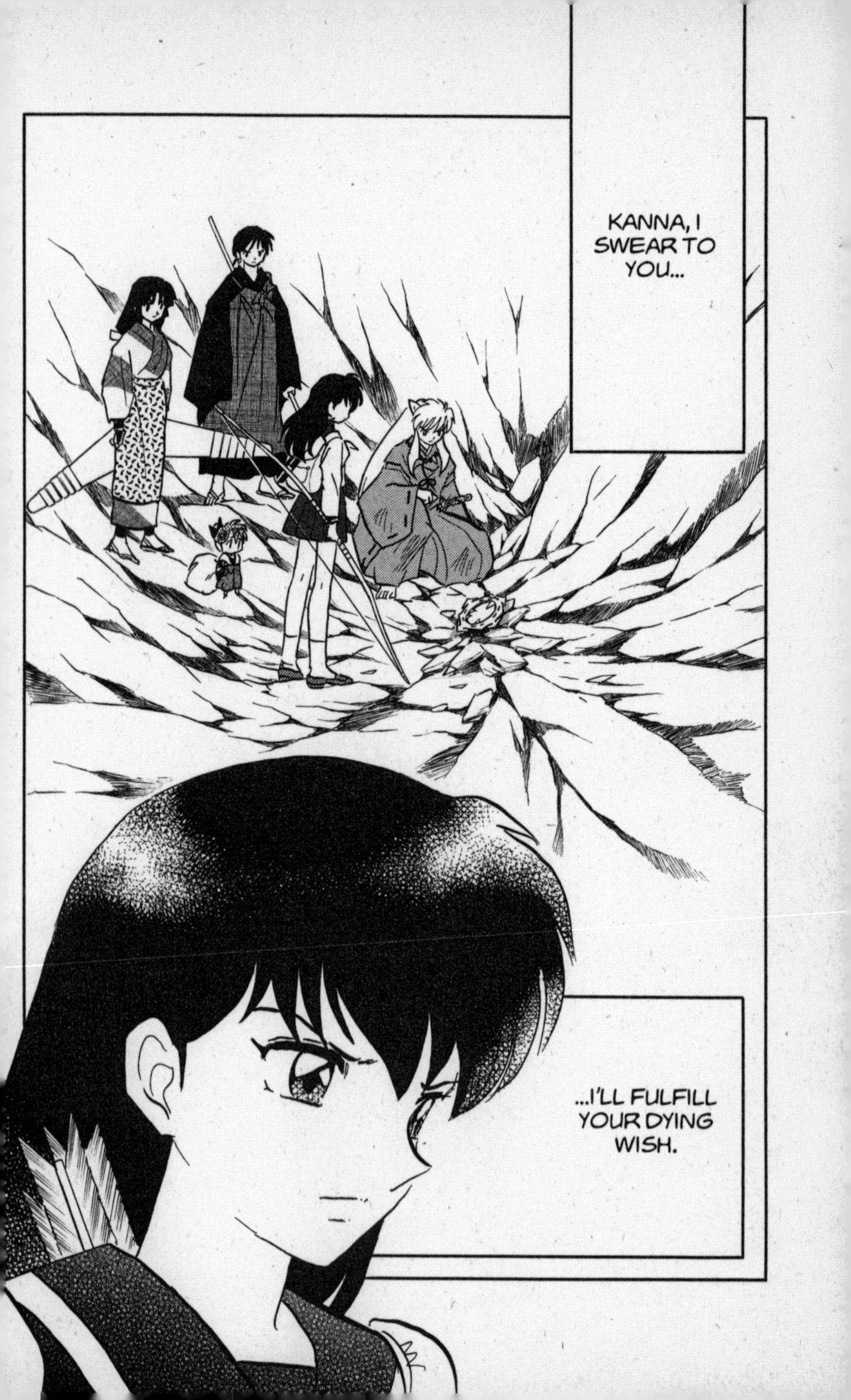
KANNA, I SWEAR TO YOU...
...I'LL FULFILL YOUR DYING WISH.

SCROLL 3
BONES

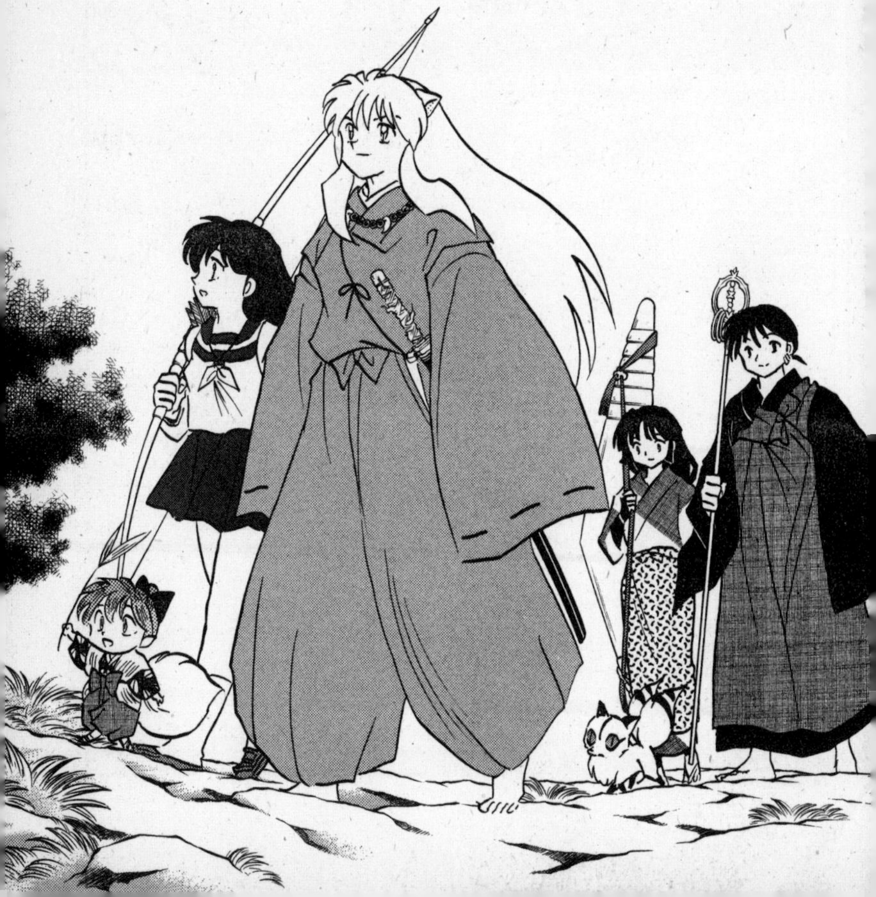

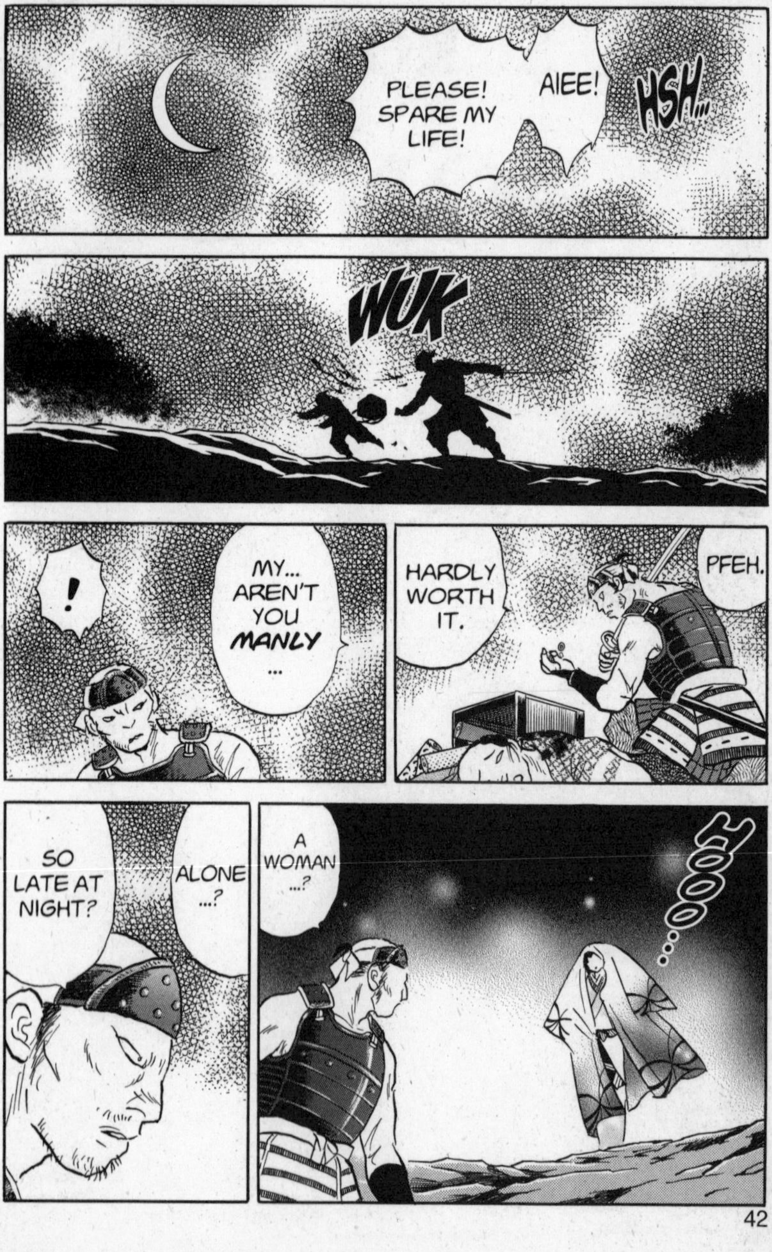
HSH...
AIEE!
PLEASE! SPARE MY LIFE!
WUK
PFEH.
HARDLY WORTH IT.
MY... AREN'T YOU MANLY ...
!
HOOOO...
A WOMAN ...?
ALONE ...?
SO LATE AT NIGHT?

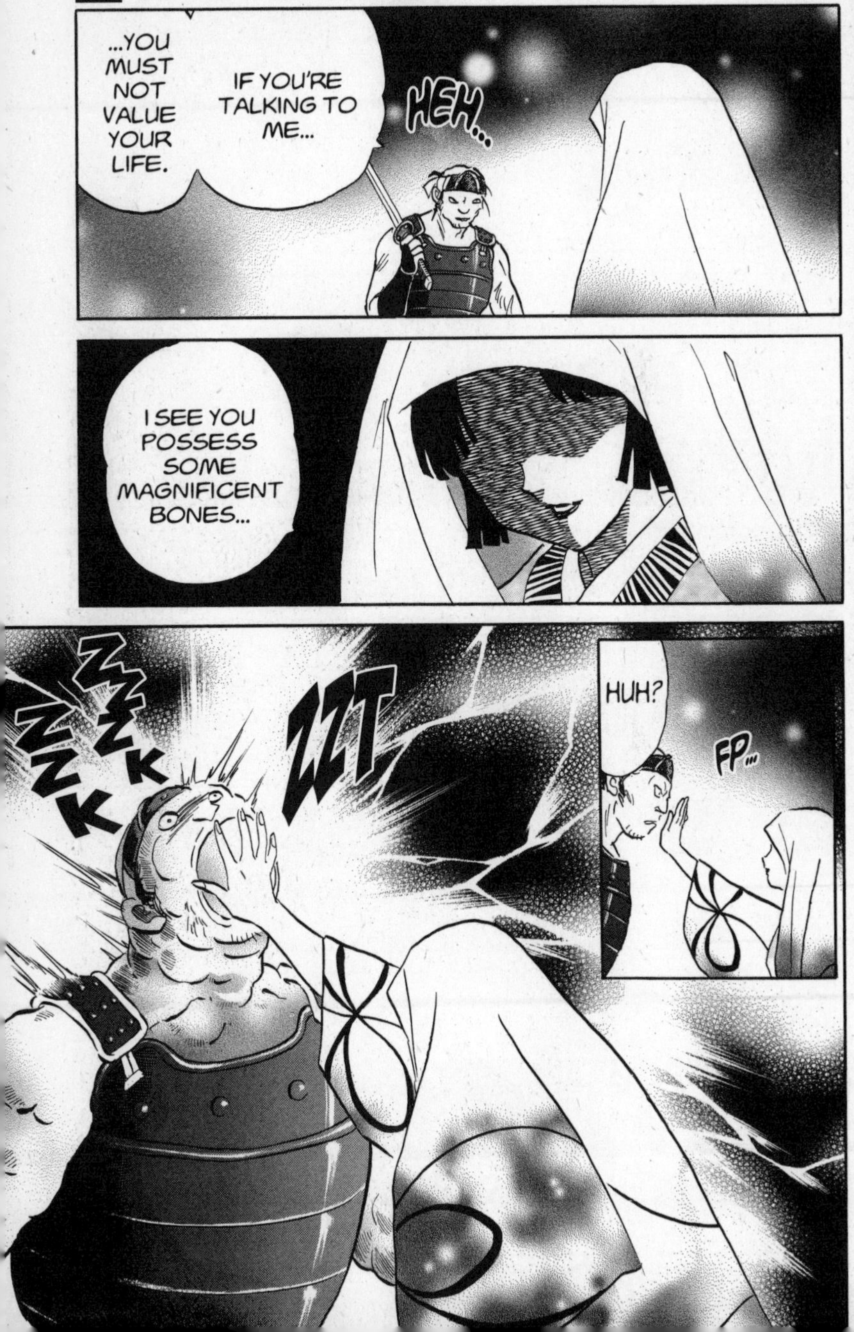
HEH...
IF YOU'RE TALKING TO ME...
...YOU MUST NOT VALUE YOUR LIFE.
I SEE YOU POSSESS SOME MAGNIFICENT BONES...
HUH?
FP...
ZZZT
ZZZK
ZZZK

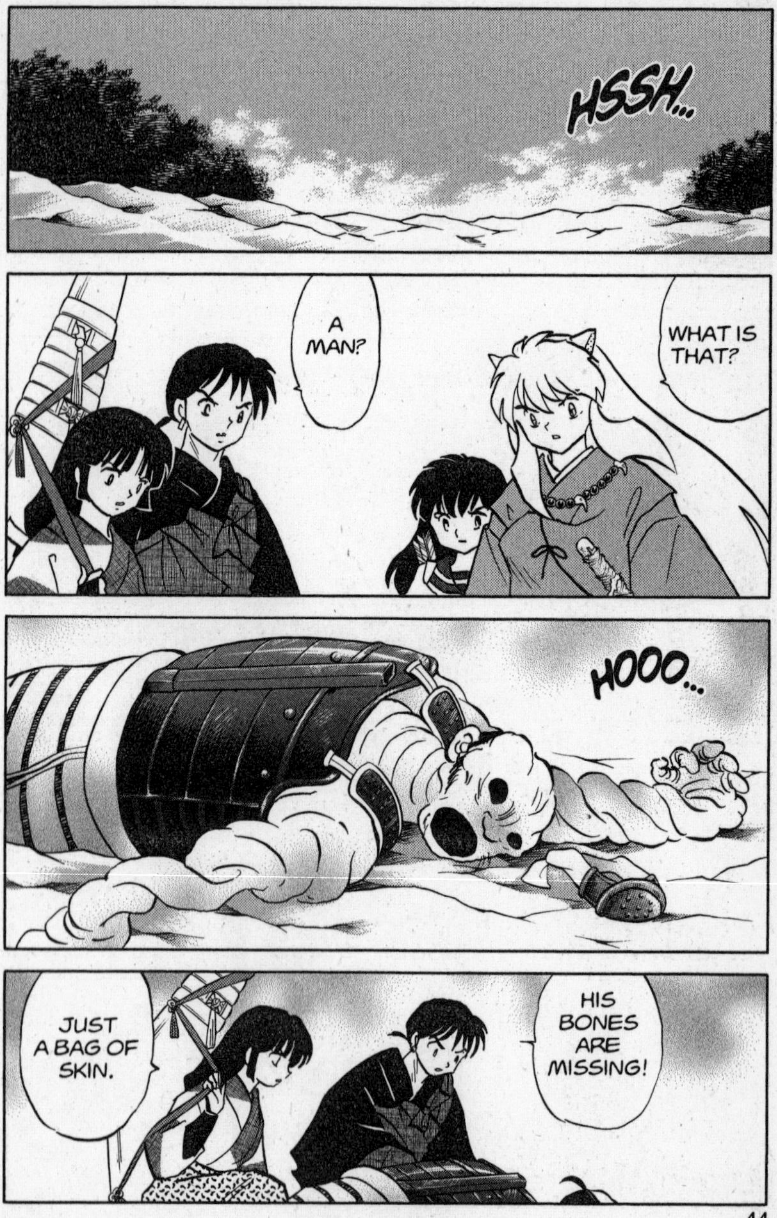
HSSH...
WHAT IS THAT?
A MAN?
HOOO...
HIS BONES ARE MISSING!
JUST A BAG OF SKIN.

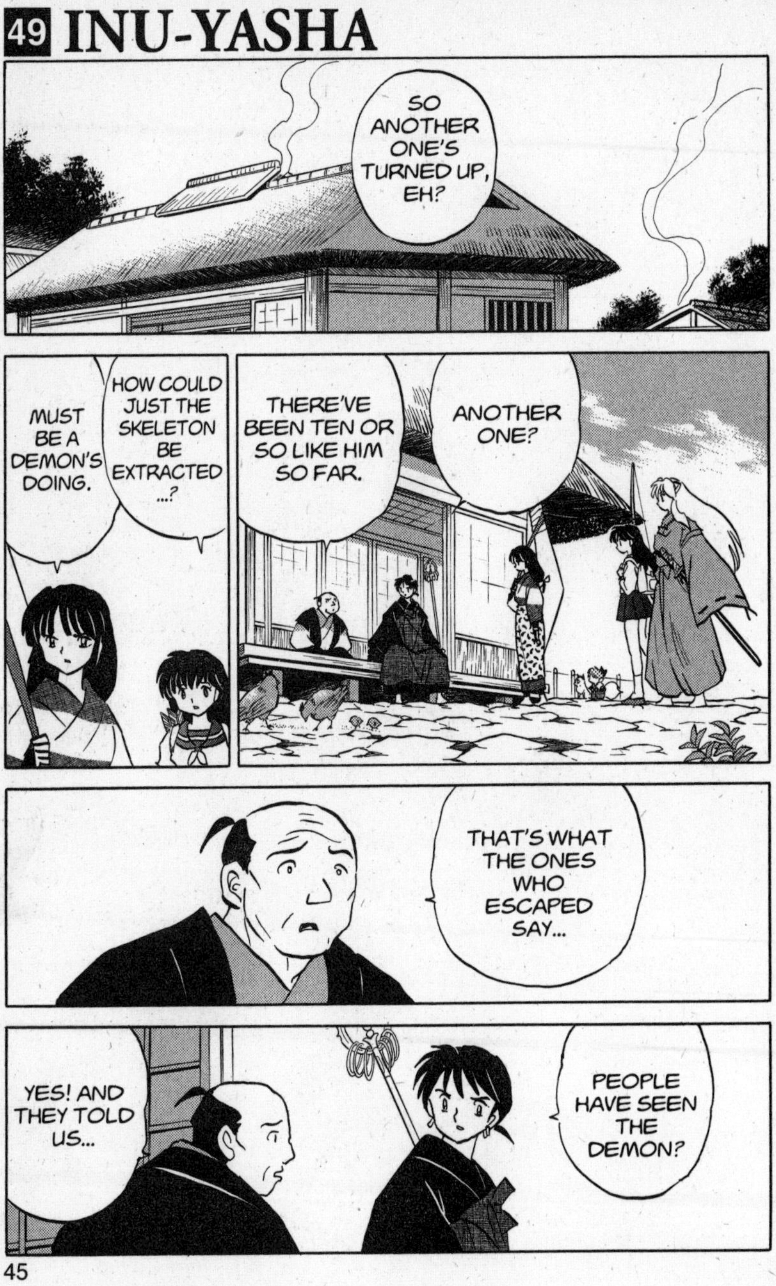
SO ANOTHER ONE'S TURNED UP, EH?
ANOTHER ONE?
THERE'VE BEEN TEN OR SO LIKE HIM SO FAR.
HOW COULD JUST THE SKELETON BE EXTRACTED ...?
MUST BE A DEMON'S DOING.
THAT'S WHAT THE ONES WHO ESCAPED SAY...
PEOPLE HAVE SEEN THE DEMON?
YES! AND THEY TOLD US...

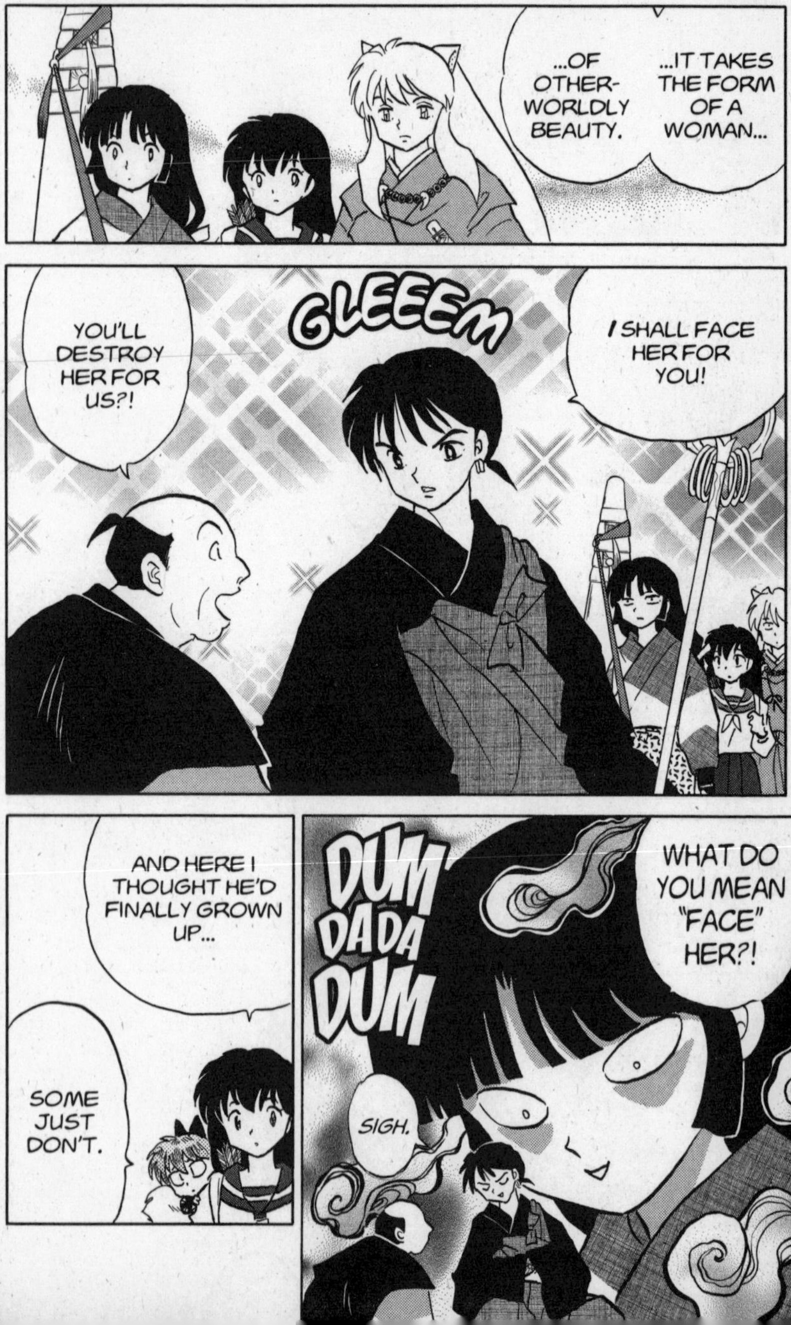
...IT TAKES THE FORM OF A WOMAN...
...OF OTHER-WORLDLY BEAUTY.
I SHALL FACE HER FOR YOU!
GLEEEM
YOU'LL DESTROY HER FOR US?!
WHAT DO YOU MEAN "FACE" HER?!
DUM DA DA DUM
SIGH.
AND HERE I THOUGHT HE'D FINALLY GROWN UP...
SOME JUST DON'T.

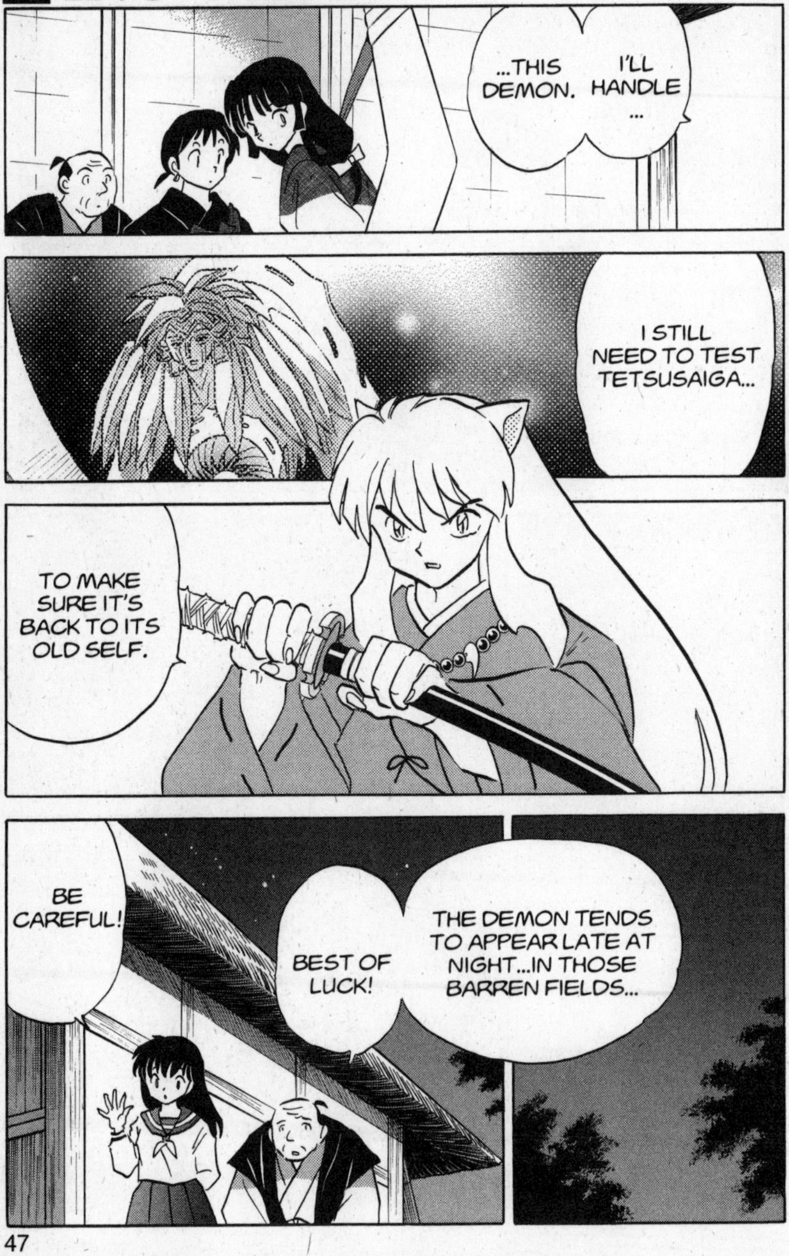
I'LL HANDLE ...
...THIS DEMON.
I STILL NEED TO TEST TETSUSAIGA...
TO MAKE SURE IT'S BACK TO ITS OLD SELF.
THE DEMON TENDS TO APPEAR LATE AT NIGHT...IN THOSE BARREN FIELDS...
BEST OF LUCK!
BE CAREFUL!

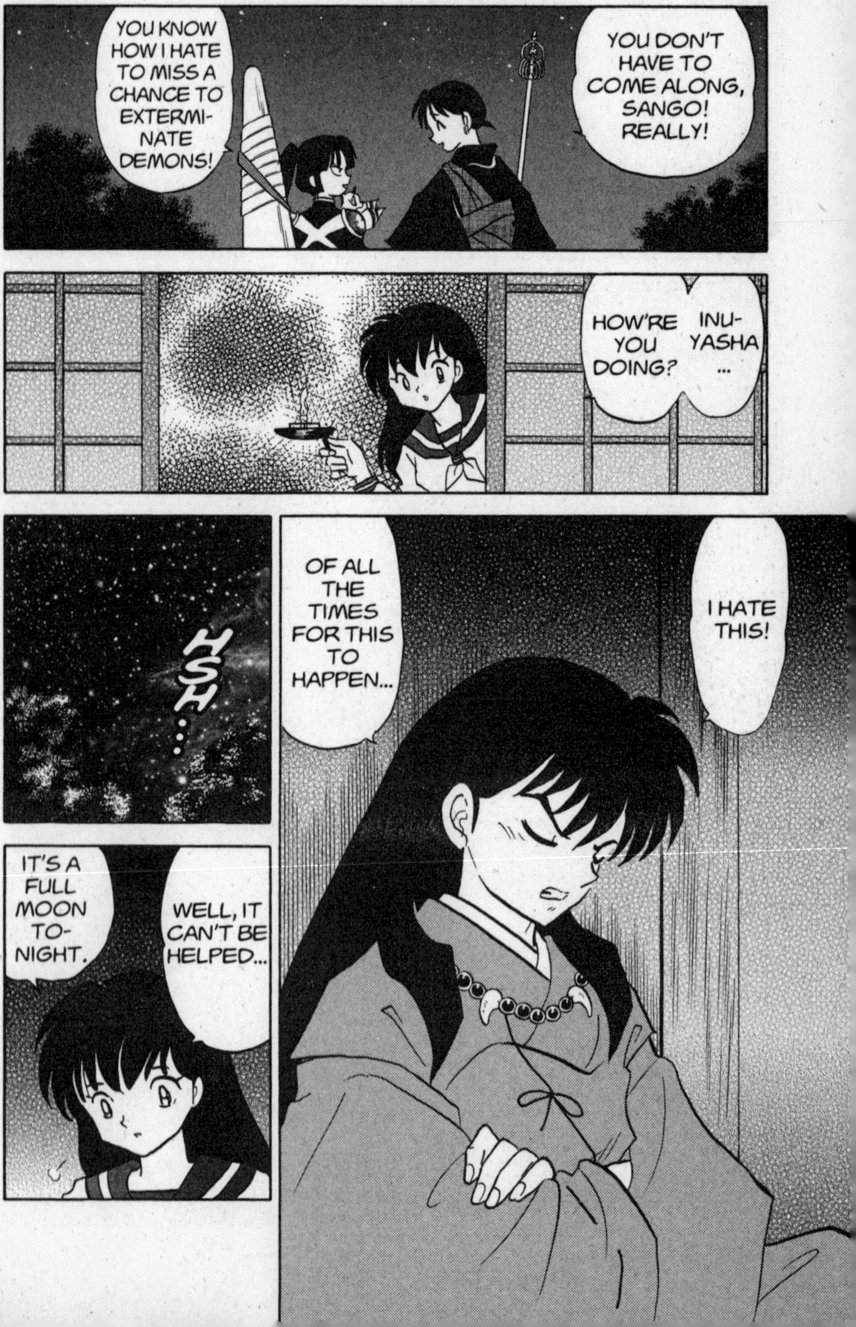
YOU DON'T HAVE TO COME ALONG, SANGO! REALLY!
YOU KNOW HOW I HATE TO MISS A CHANCE TO EXTERMI-NATE DEMONS!
INU-YASHA ...
HOW'RE YOU DOING?
I HATE THIS!
OF ALL THE TIMES FOR THIS TO HAPPEN...
HSH...
WELL, IT CAN'T BE HELPED...
IT'S A FULL MOON TO-NIGHT.

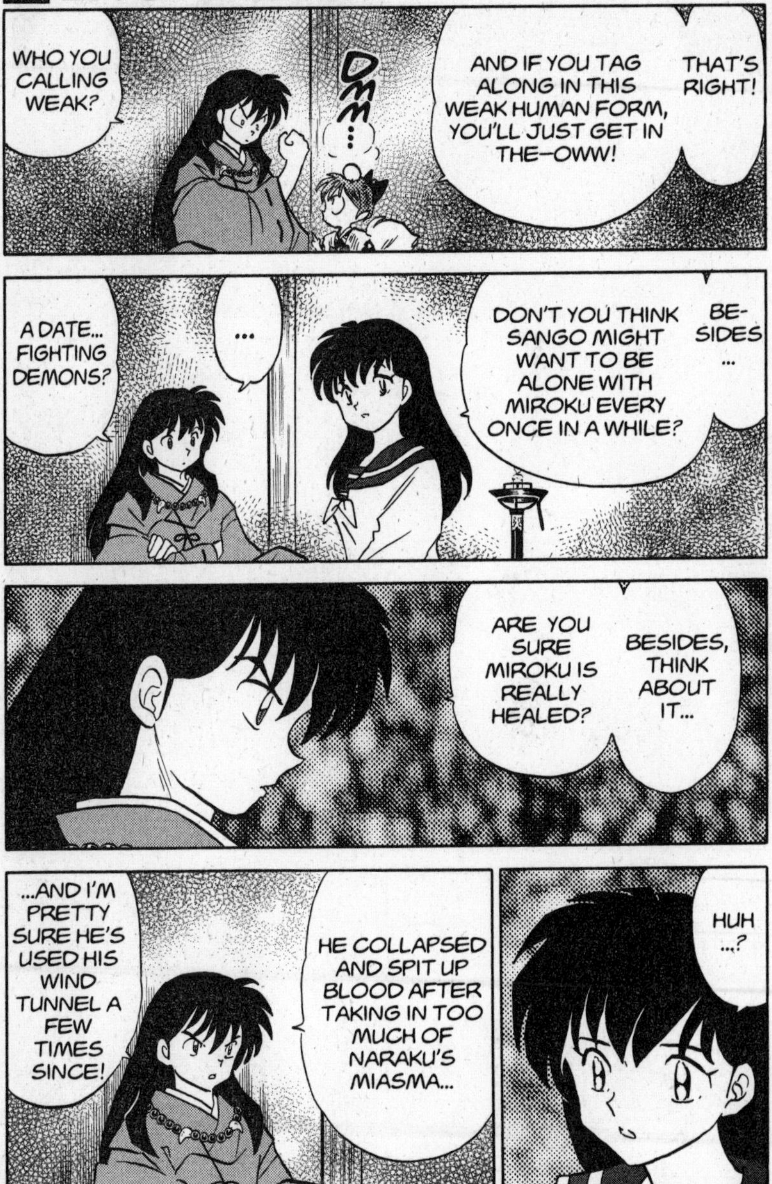
THAT'S RIGHT!
AND IF YOU TAG ALONG IN THIS WEAK HUMAN FORM, YOU'LL JUST GET IN THE—OWW!
DMM...
WHO YOU CALLING WEAK?
BE- SIDES ...
DON'T YOU THINK SANGO MIGHT WANT TO BE ALONE WITH MIROKU EVERY ONCE IN A WHILE?
...
A DATE... FIGHTING DEMONS?
BESIDES, THINK ABOUT IT...
ARE YOU SURE MIROKU IS REALLY HEALED?
HUH ...?
HE COLLAPSED AND SPIT UP BLOOD AFTER TAKING IN TOO MUCH OF NARAKU'S MIASMA...
...AND I'M PRETTY SURE HE'S USED HIS WIND TUNNEL A FEW TIMES SINCE!

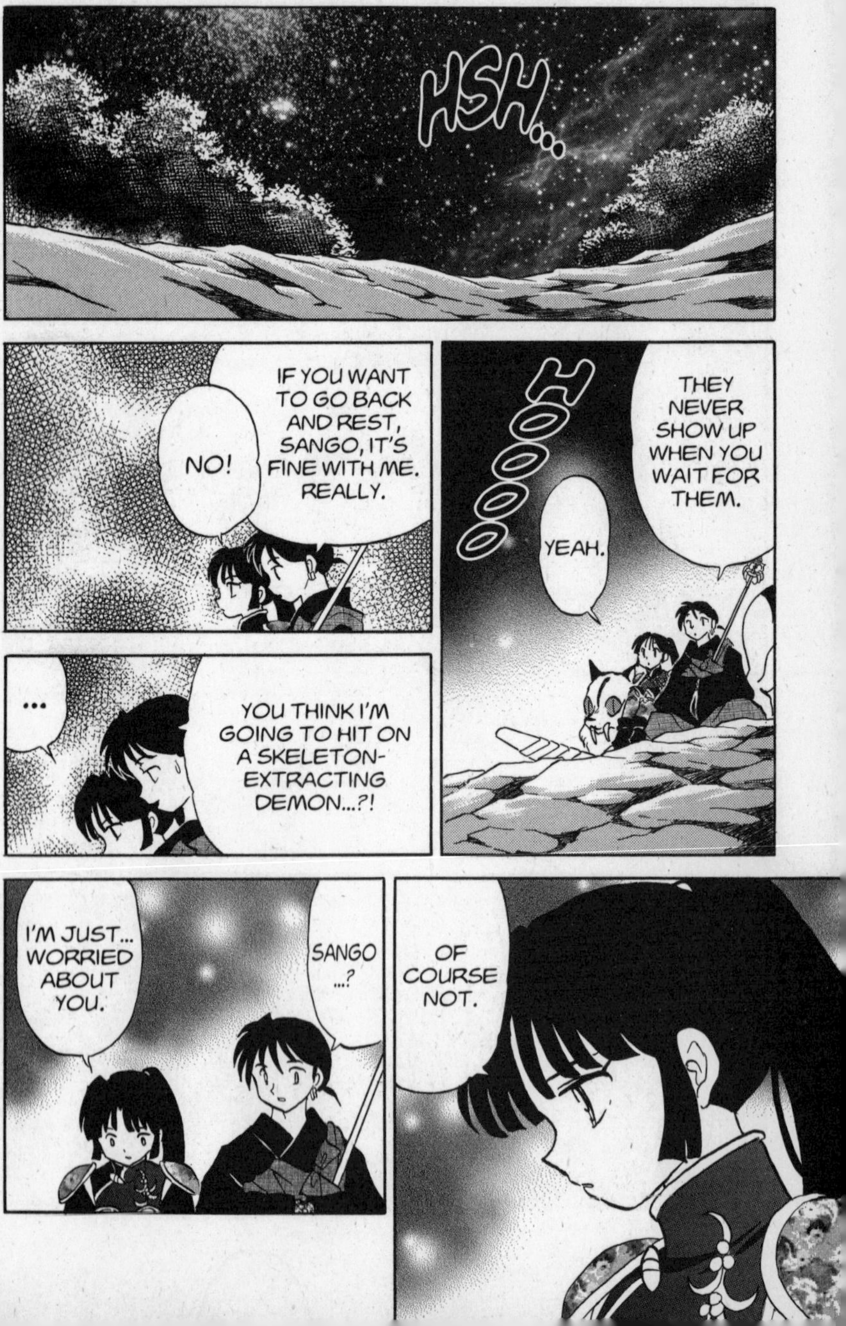
HSH...
THEY NEVER SHOW UP WHEN YOU WAIT FOR THEM.
YEAH.
HOOOOO
IF YOU WANT TO GO BACK AND REST, SANGO, IT'S FINE WITH ME. REALLY.
NO!
YOU THINK I'M GOING TO HIT ON A SKELETON-EXTRACTING DEMON...?!
...
OF COURSE NOT.
SANGO ...?
I'M JUST... WORRIED ABOUT YOU.

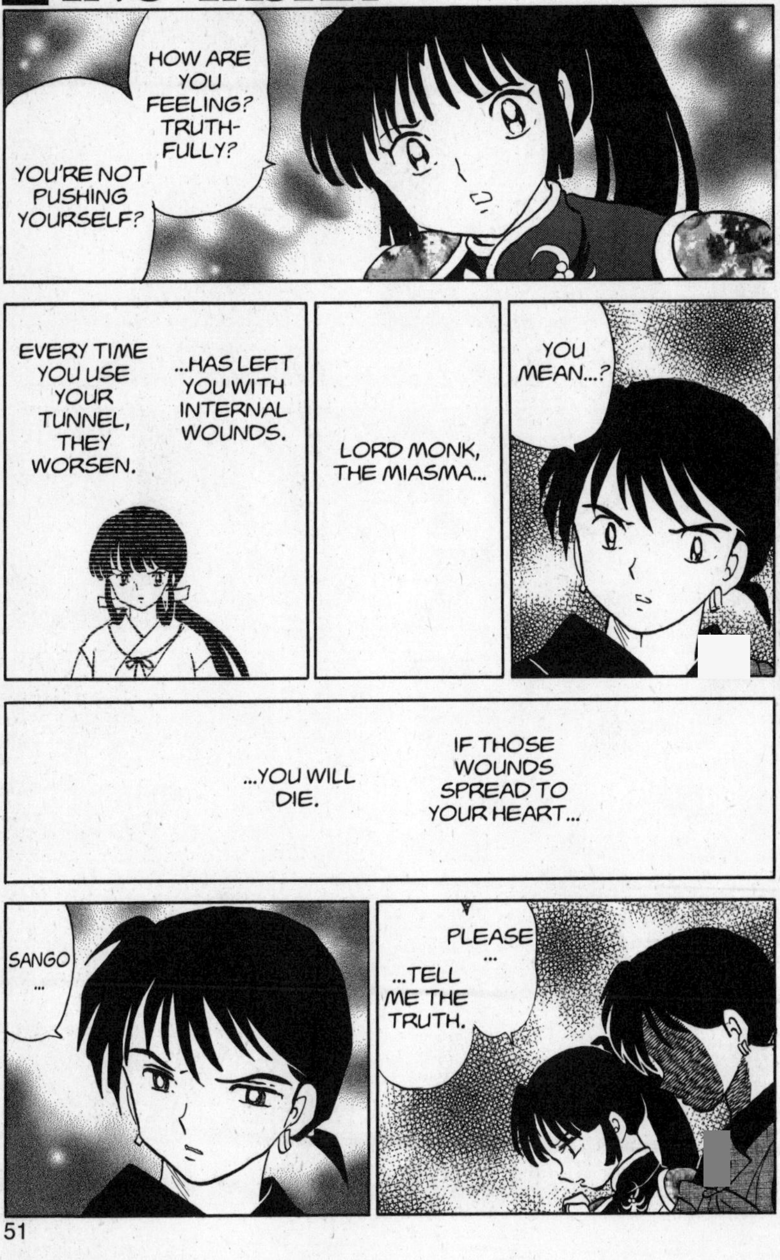
HOW ARE YOU FEELING? TRUTH-FULLY?
YOU'RE NOT PUSHING YOURSELF?
YOU MEAN...?
LORD MONK, THE MIASMA...
...HAS LEFT YOU WITH INTERNAL WOUNDS.
EVERY TIME YOU USE YOUR TUNNEL, THEY WORSEN.
IF THOSE WOUNDS SPREAD TO YOUR HEART...
...YOU WILL DIE.
PLEASE...
...TELL ME THE TRUTH.
SANGO...

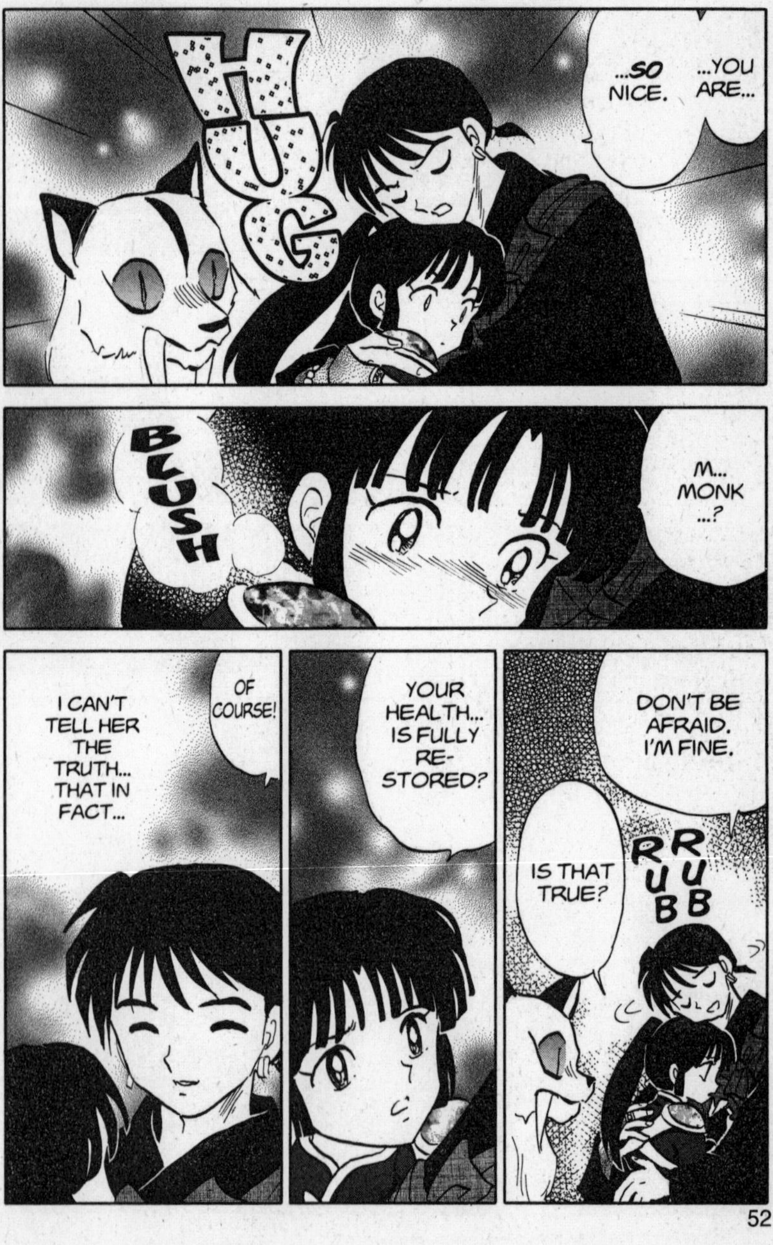
...YOU ARE...
...SO NICE.
HUG
M... MONK ...?
BLUSH
DON'T BE AFRAID. I'M FINE.
RUB RUB
IS THAT TRUE?
YOUR HEALTH... IS FULLY RE-STORED?
OF COURSE!
I CAN'T TELL HER THE TRUTH... THAT IN FACT...

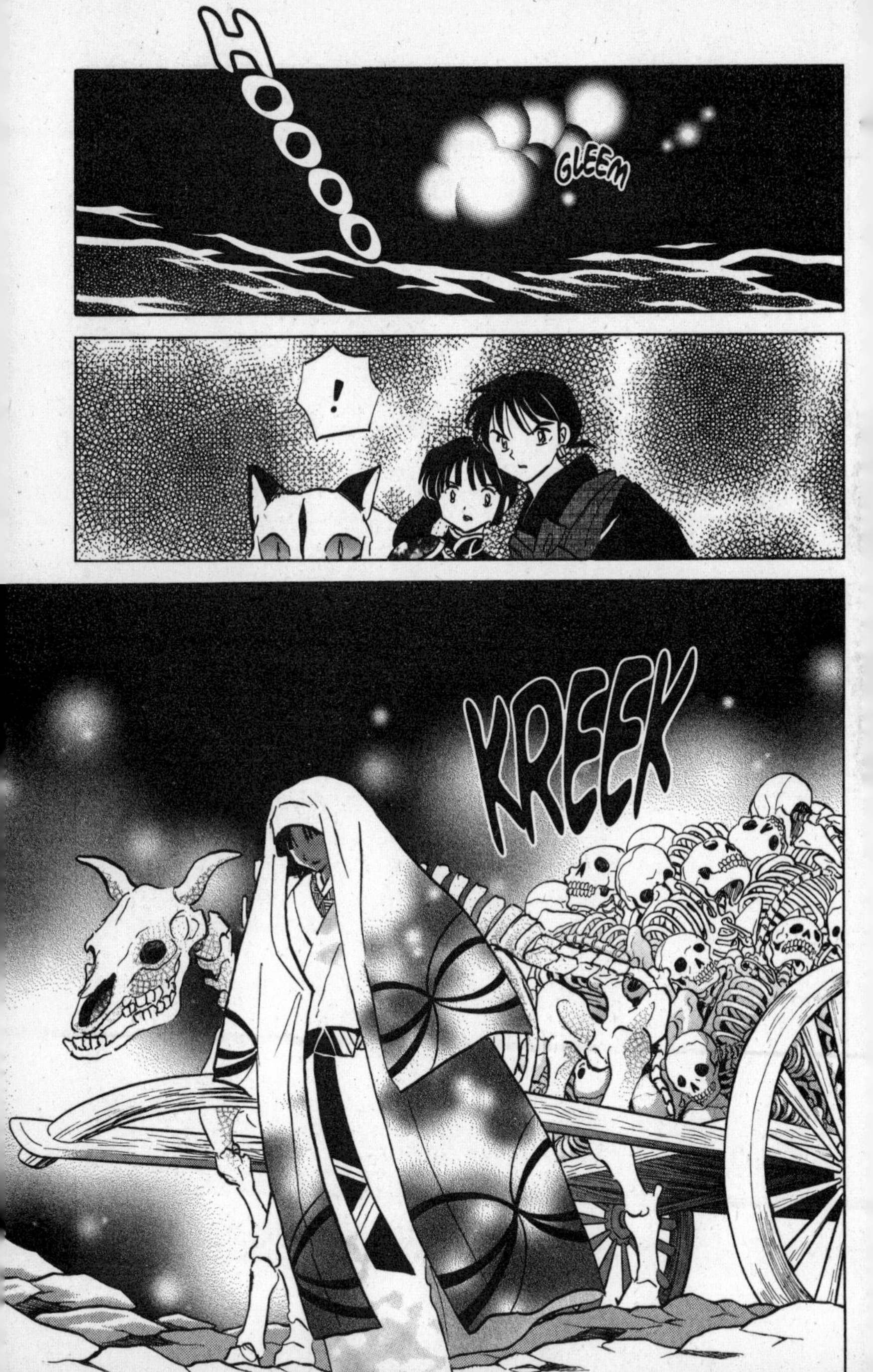
HOOOO
GLEEM
!
KREEK

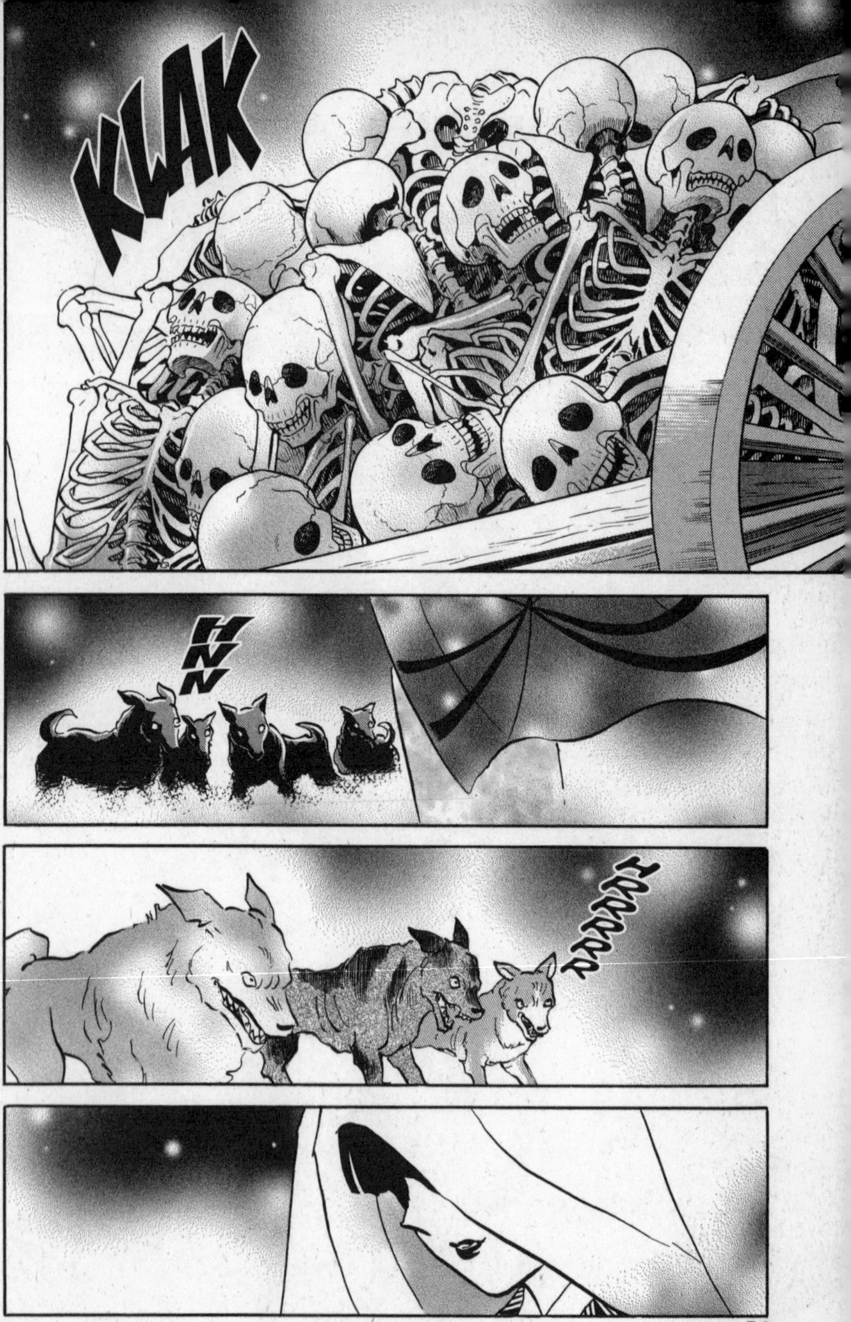
KLAK
HNN
RRRRRR

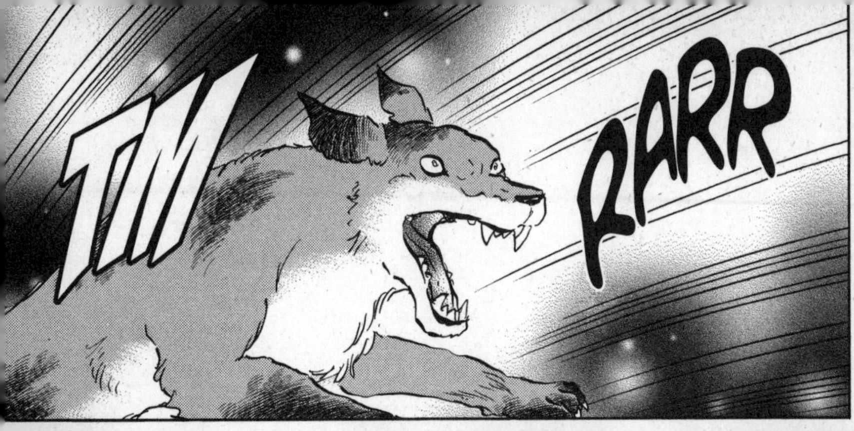
RARR
TM
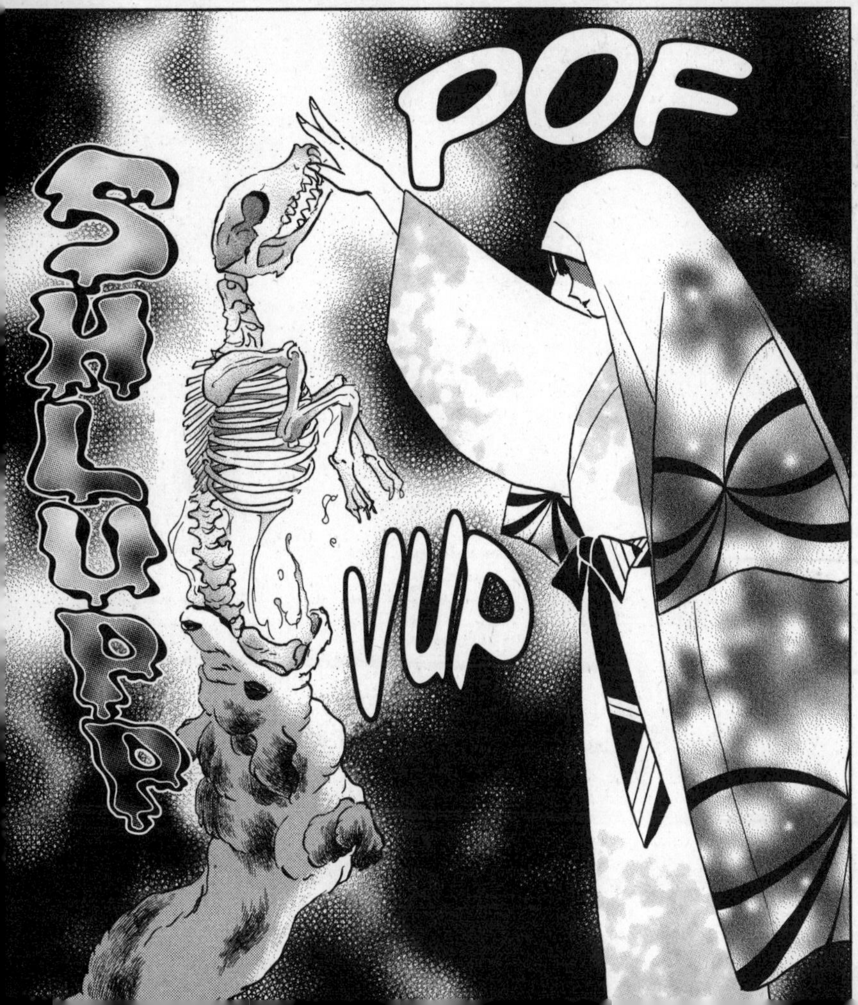
POF
VUP
SHLUPP

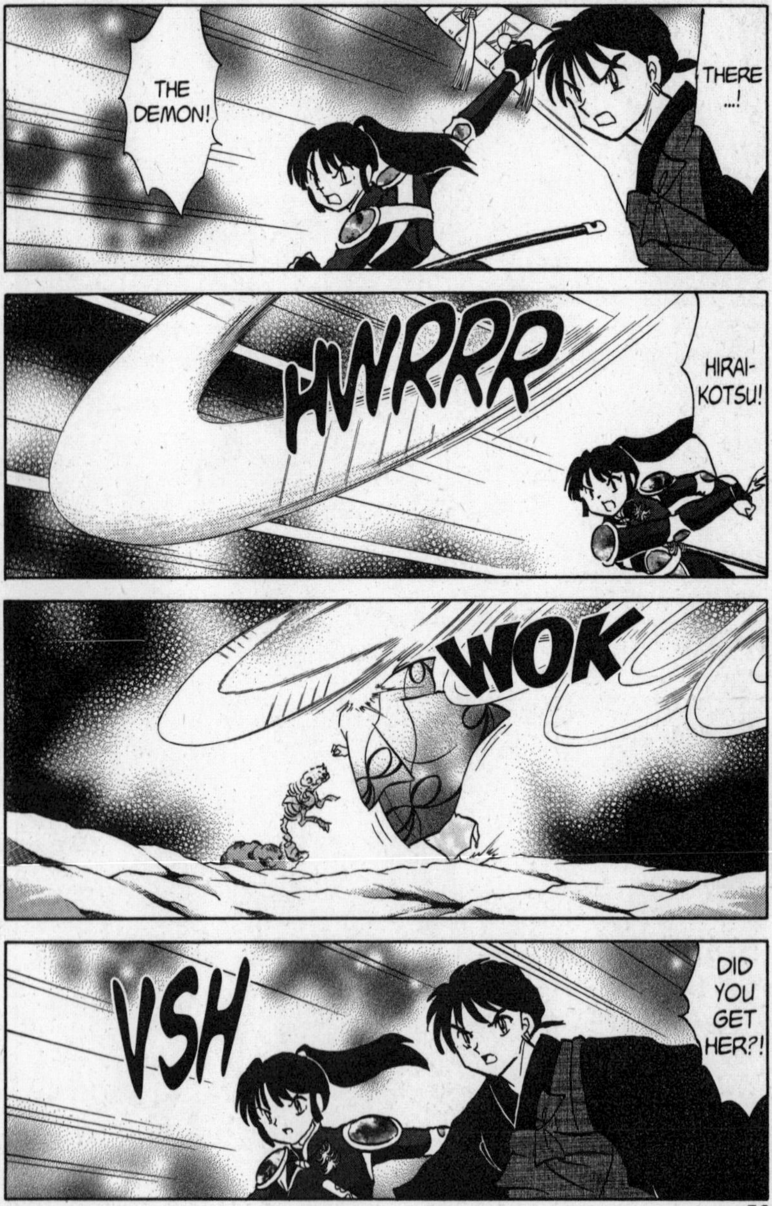
THERE ...!
THE DEMON!
HIRAI-KOTSU!
HWRRR
WOK
DID YOU GET HER?!
VSH

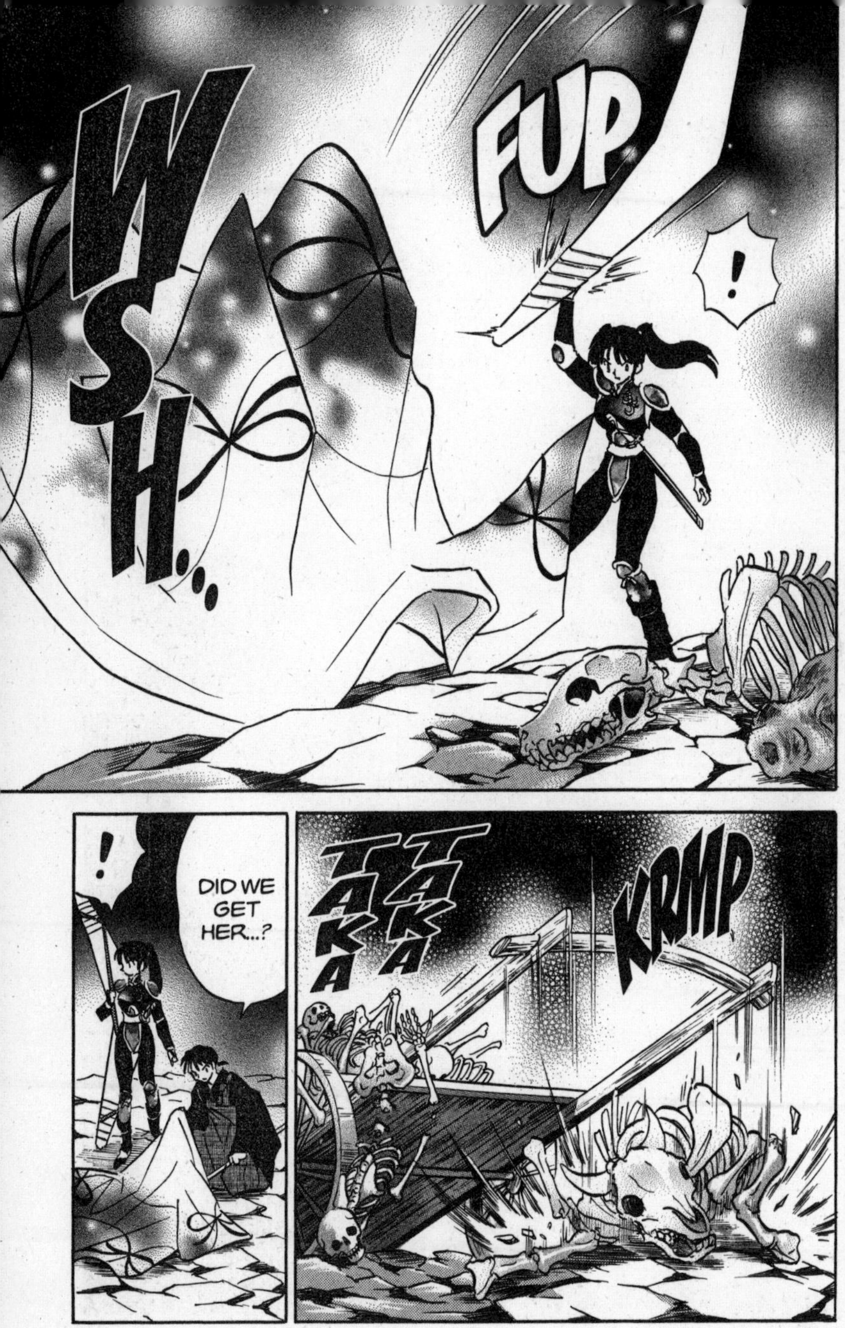
FUP
!
WSH...
KRMP
TAKA
TAKA
!
DID WE GET HER...?

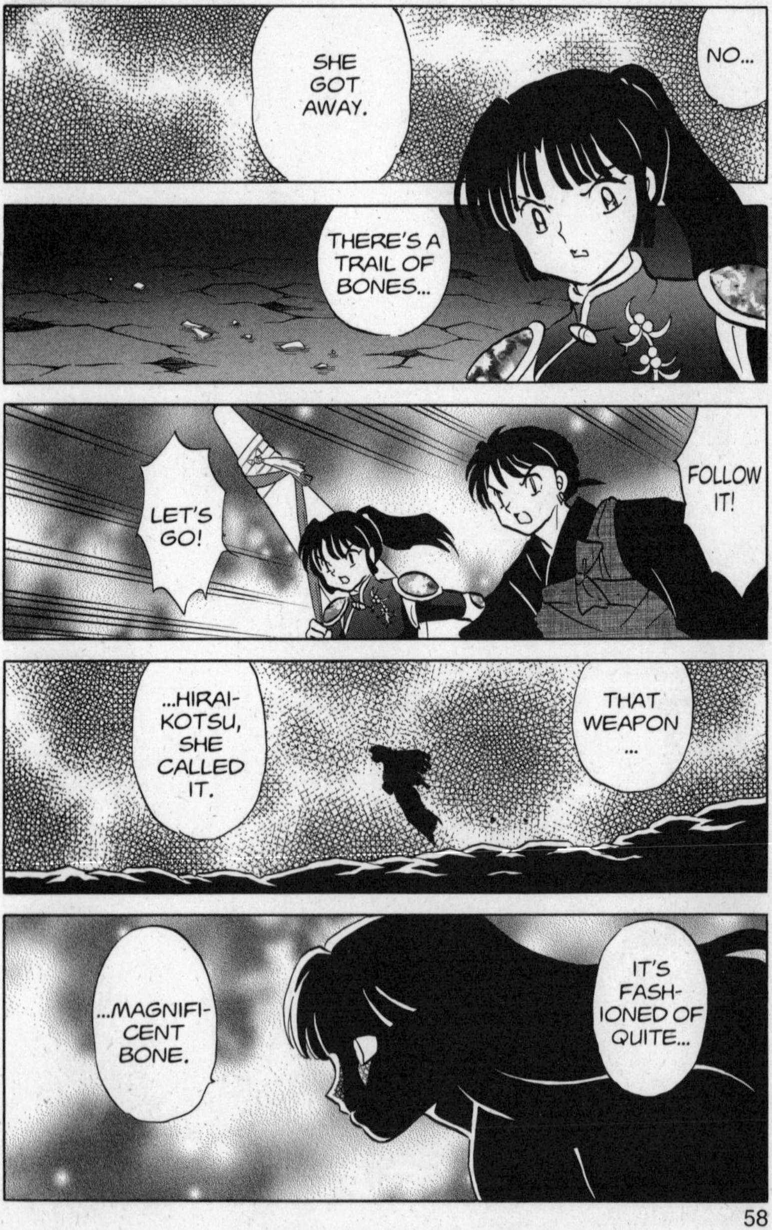
NO...
SHE GOT AWAY.
THERE'S A TRAIL OF BONES...
FOLLOW IT!
LET'S GO!
THAT WEAPON ...
...HIRAI-KOTSU, SHE CALLED IT.
IT'S FASH-IONED OF QUITE...
...MAGNIFI-CENT BONE.

SCROLL 4

WANTED: BOOMERANG BONE

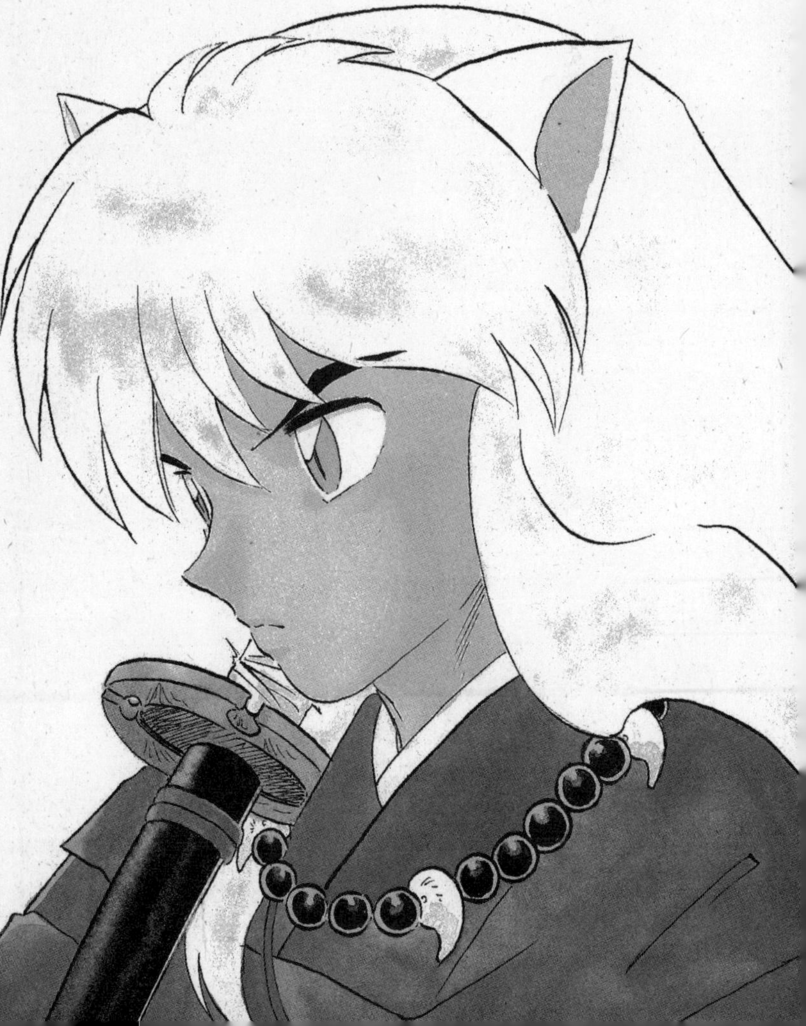

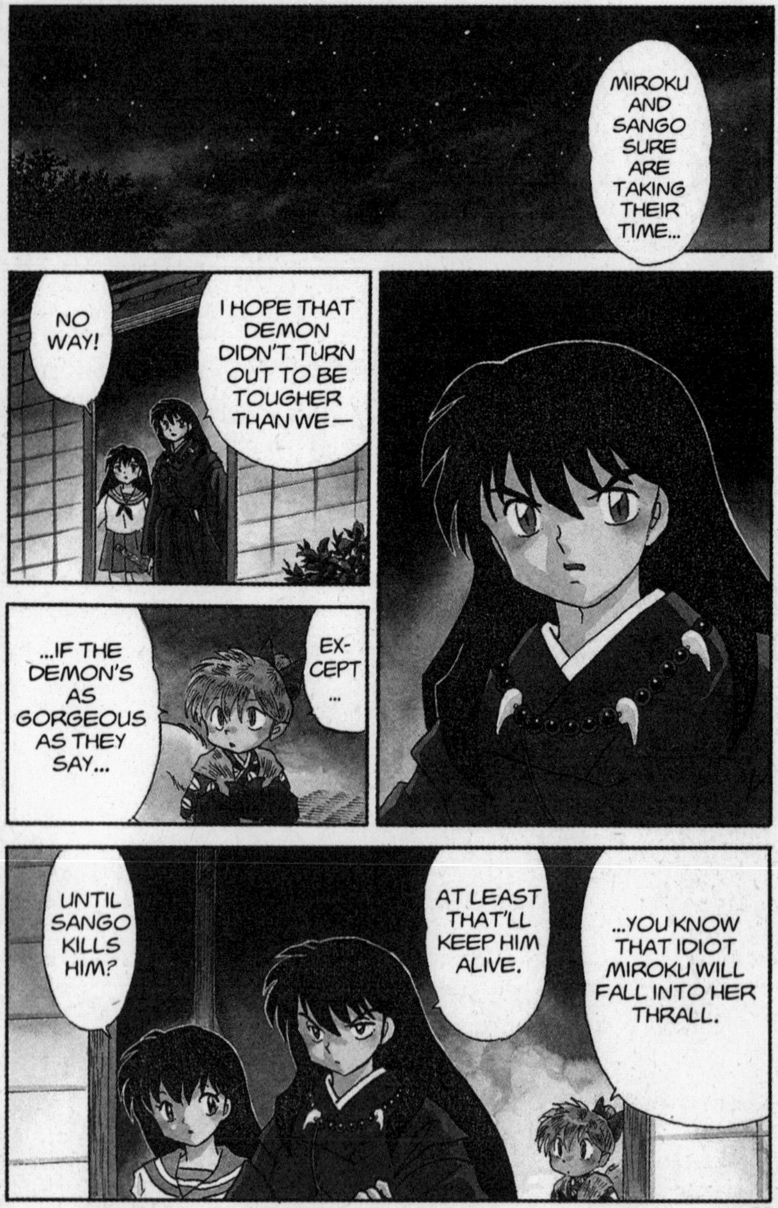
MIROKU AND SANGO SURE ARE TAKING THEIR TIME...
I HOPE THAT DEMON DIDN'T TURN OUT TO BE TOUGHER THAN WE—
NO WAY!
EX-CEPT...
...IF THE DEMON'S AS GORGEOUS AS THEY SAY...
...YOU KNOW THAT IDIOT MIROKU WILL FALL INTO HER THRALL.
AT LEAST THAT'LL KEEP HIM ALIVE.
UNTIL SANGO KILLS HIM?

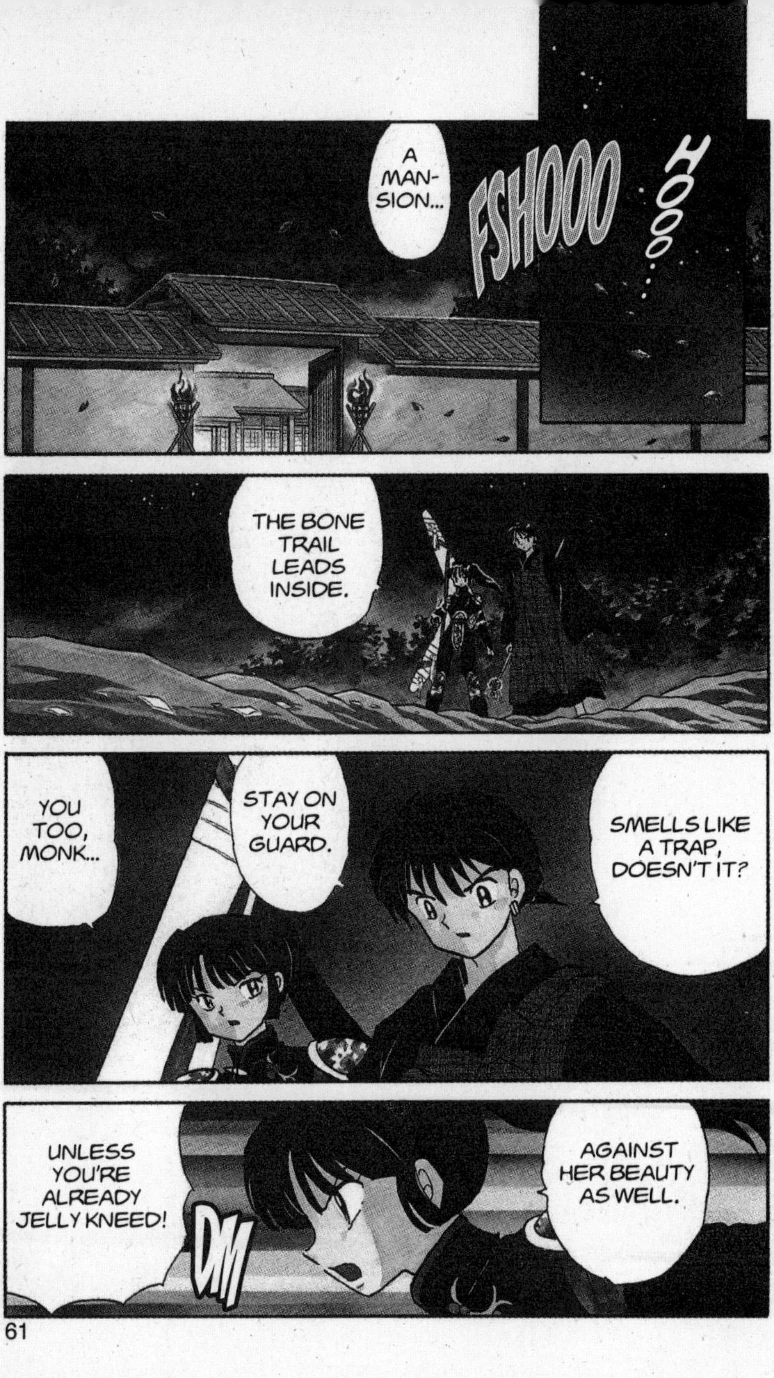
FSHOOO HOOOO...
A MAN-SION...
THE BONE TRAIL LEADS INSIDE.
SMELLS LIKE A TRAP, DOESN'T IT?
STAY ON YOUR GUARD.
YOU TOO, MONK...
AGAINST HER BEAUTY AS WELL.
DM
UNLESS YOU'RE ALREADY JELLY KNEED!

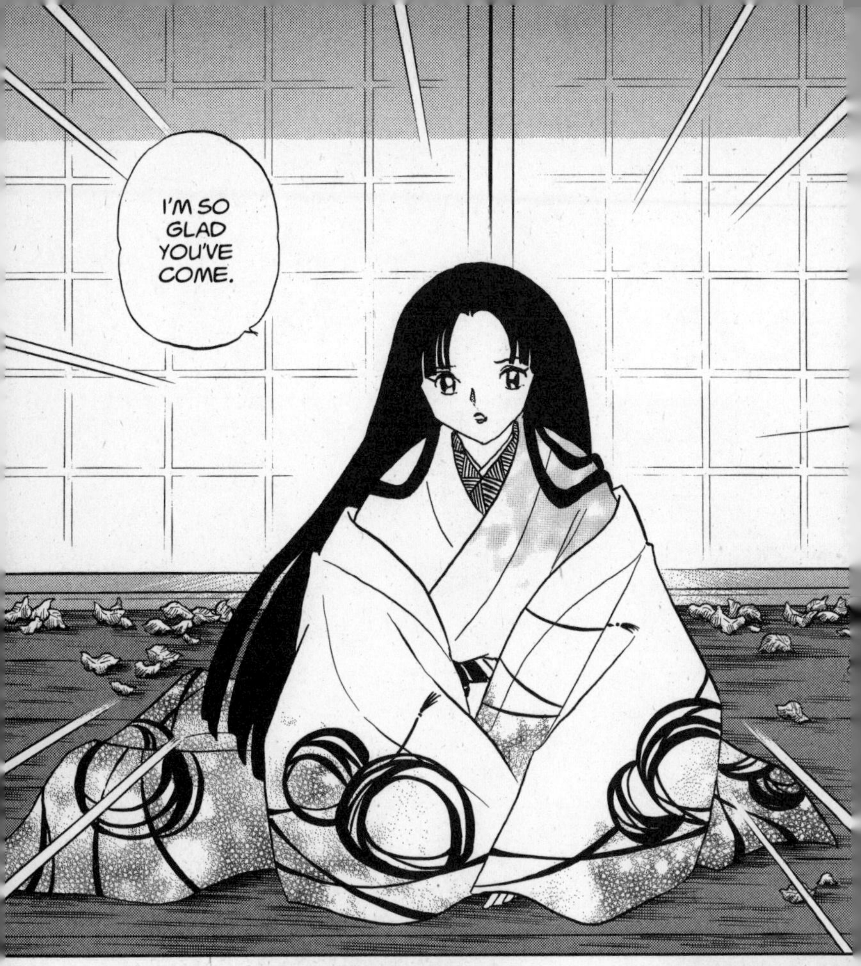
I'M SO GLAD YOU'VE COME.

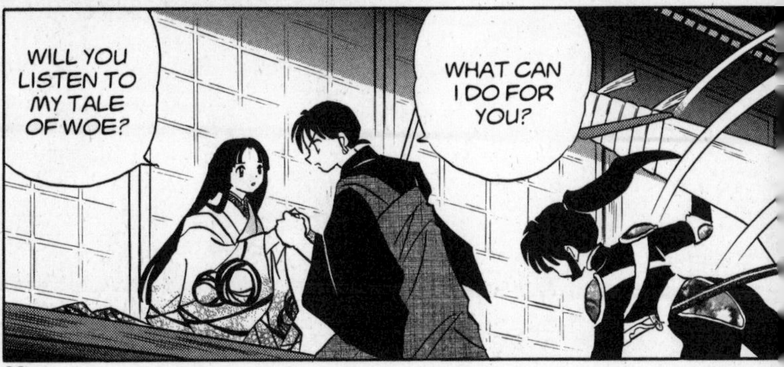
WHAT CAN I DO FOR YOU?
WILL YOU LISTEN TO MY TALE OF WOE?

WHAT HAPPENED TO BEING ON YOUR GUARD?!

YOU SAW...

...WHAT HAPPENED IN THE FIELDS?

!

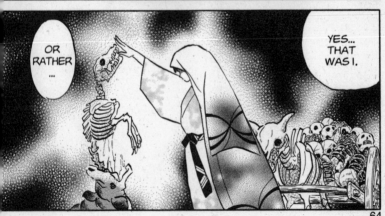

YES... THAT WAS I.

OR RATHER...

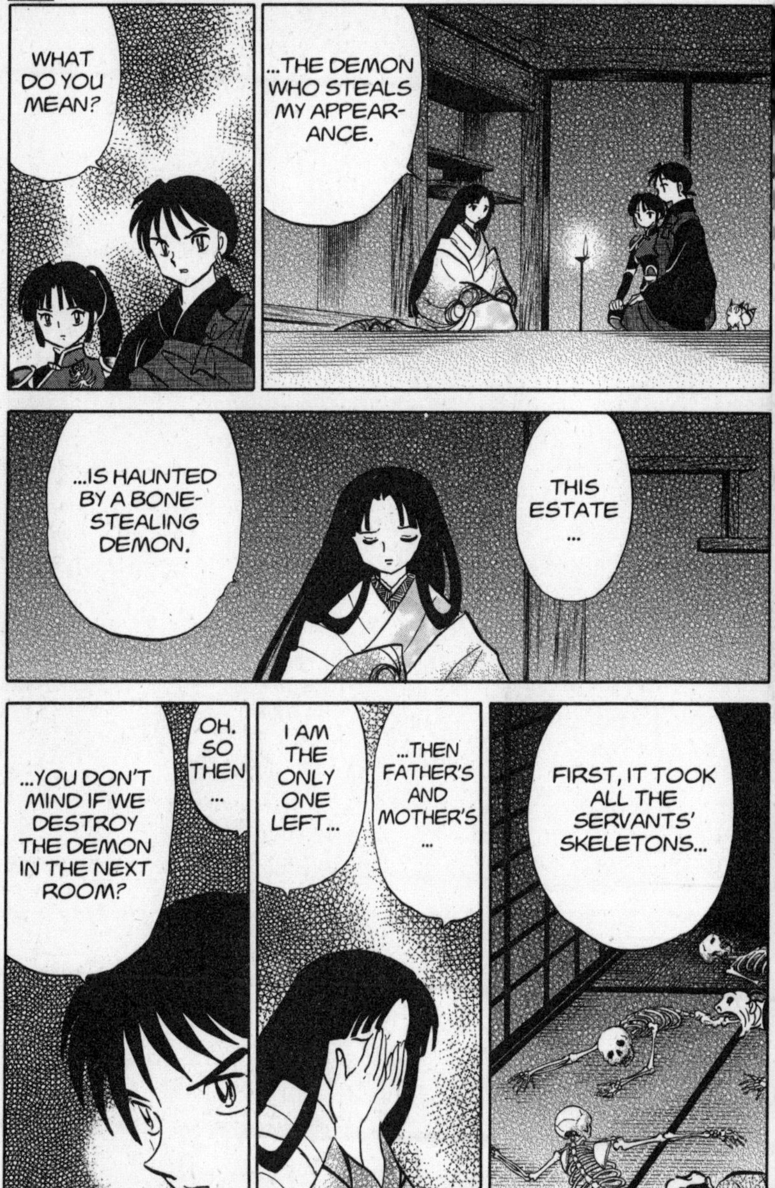
...THE DEMON WHO STEALS MY APPEARANCE.
WHAT DO YOU MEAN?
THIS ESTATE ...
...IS HAUNTED BY A BONE-STEALING DEMON.
FIRST, IT TOOK ALL THE SERVANTS' SKELETONS...
...THEN FATHER'S AND MOTHER'S ...
I AM THE ONLY ONE LEFT...
OH. SO THEN ...
...YOU DON'T MIND IF WE DESTROY THE DEMON IN THE NEXT ROOM?

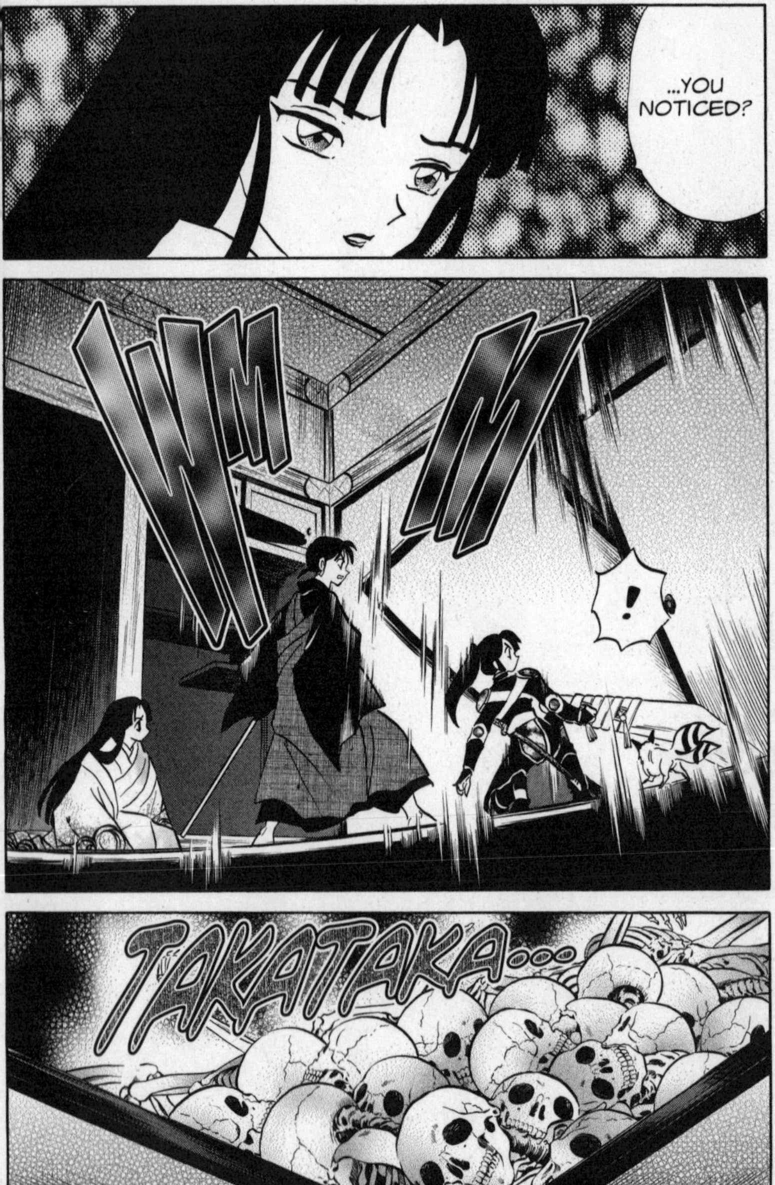
...YOU NOTICED?
WHMM
!
TAKATAKA...

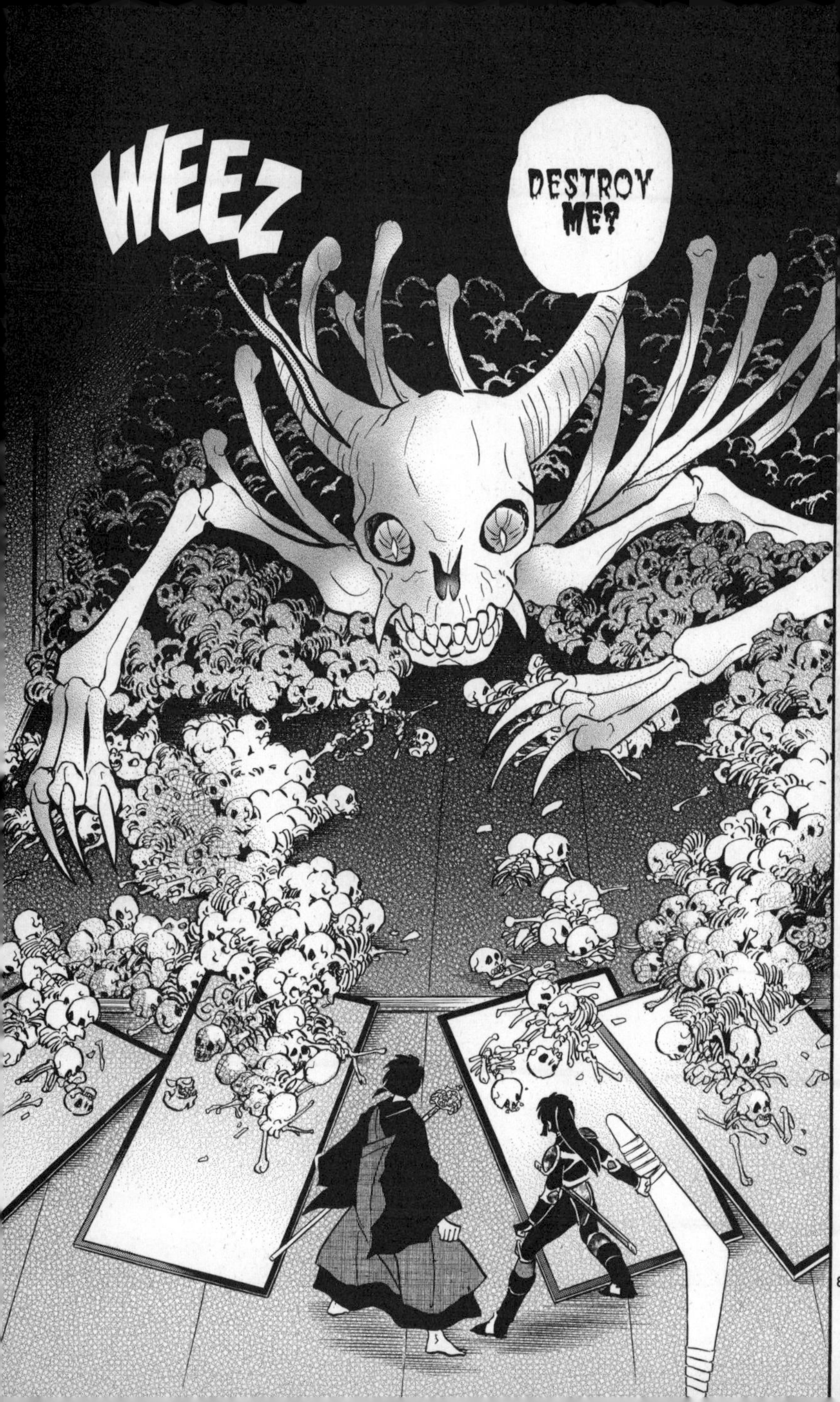
DESTROY ME?
WEEZ

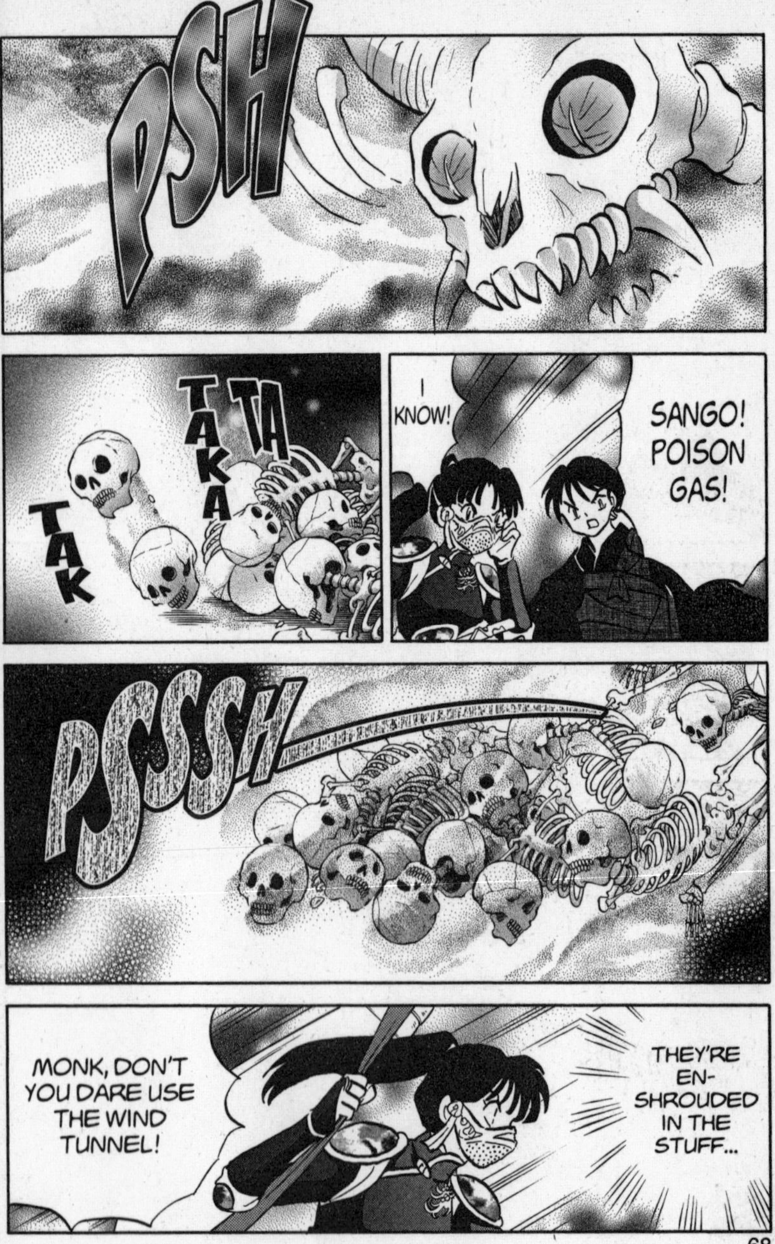
PSH
SANGO! POISON GAS!
I KNOW!
TA
TAKA
TAK
PSSSH
THEY'RE EN-SHROUDED IN THE STUFF...
MONK, DON'T YOU DARE USE THE WIND TUNNEL!

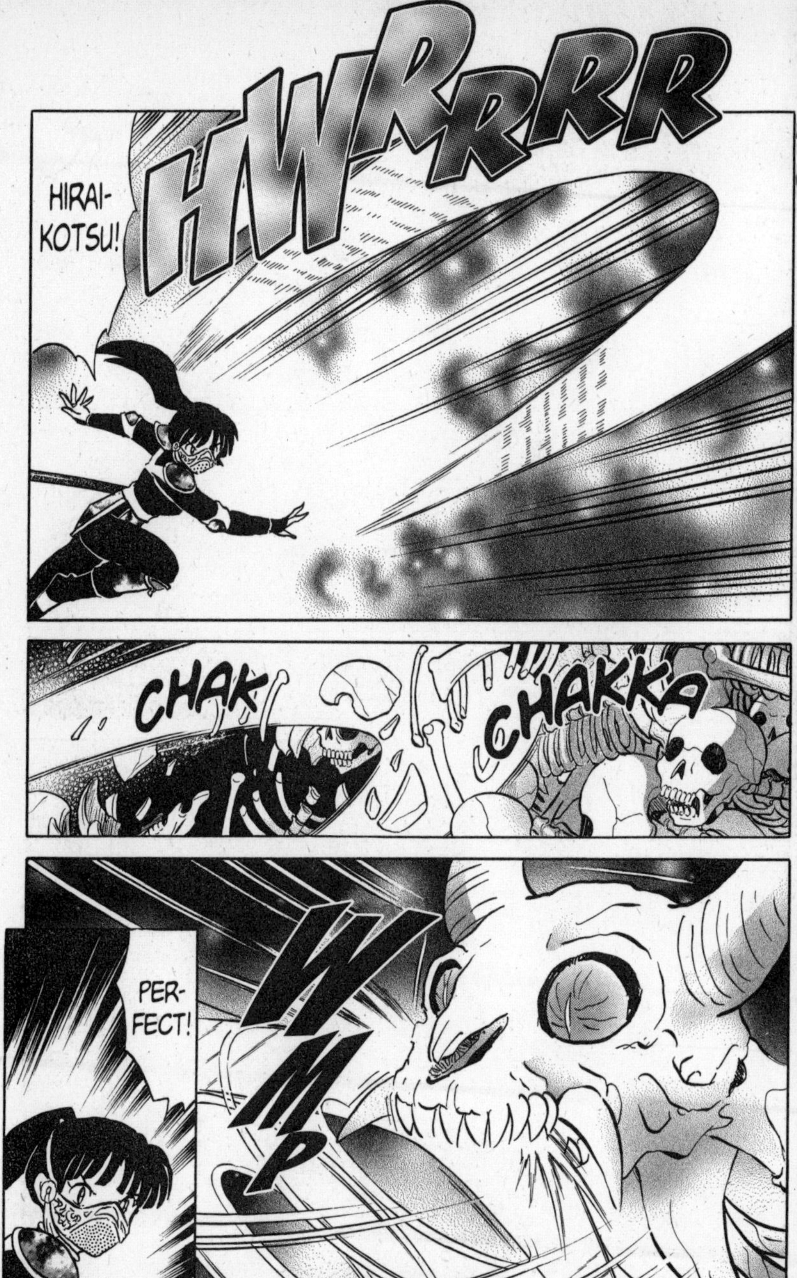
HWRRRRR
HIRAI-
KOTSU!
CHAKKA
CHAK
WMP
PER-
FECT!

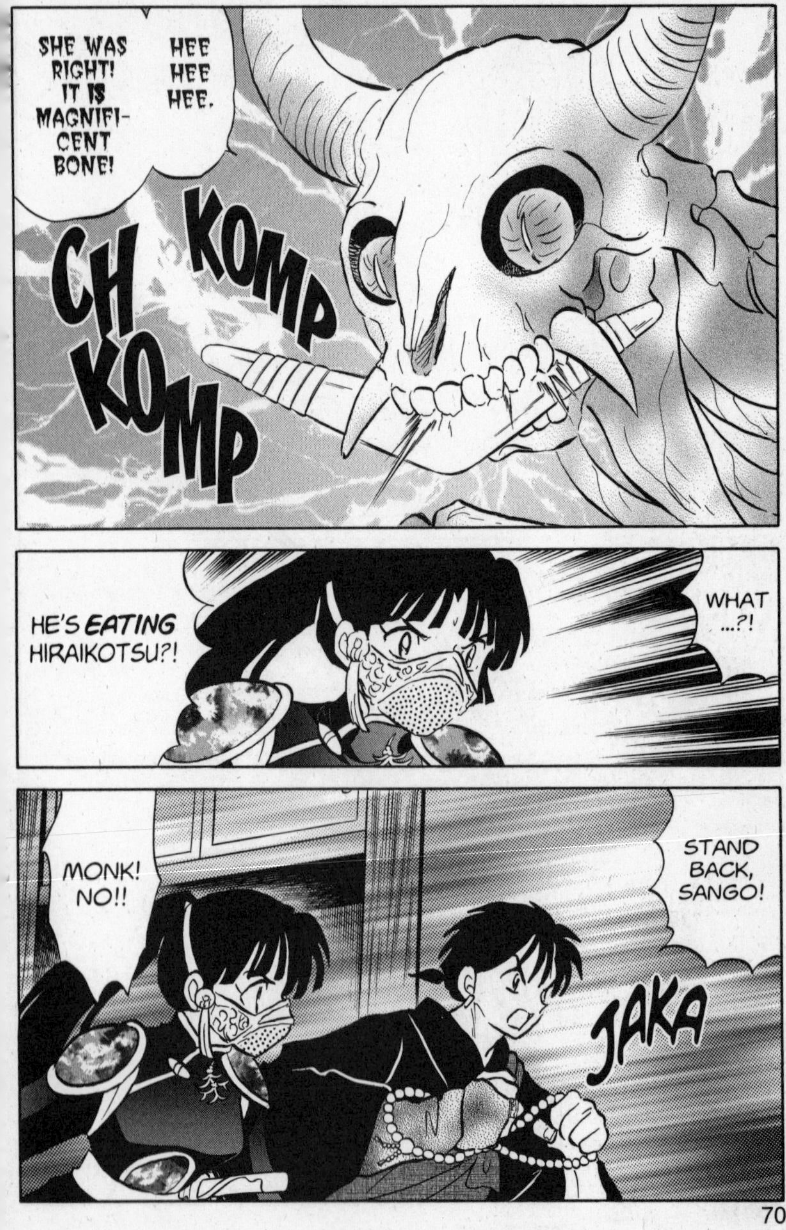
SHE WAS RIGHT! IT IS MAGNIFICENT BONE!
HEE HEE HEE.
CH
KOMP
KOMP
KOMP
WHAT ...?!
HE'S *EATING* HIRAIKOTSU?!
STAND BACK, SANGO!
JAKA
MONK! NO!!

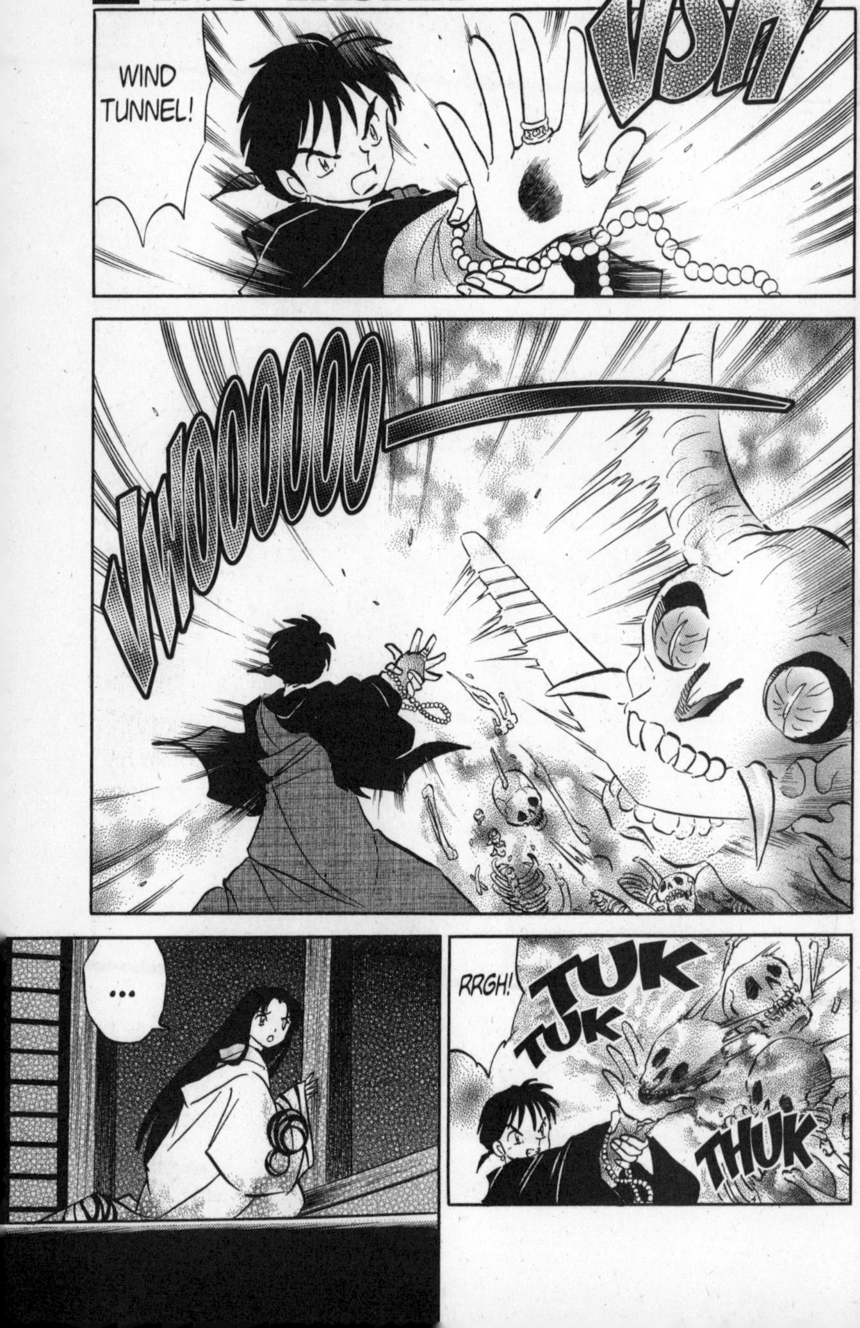
WIND TUNNEL!
VSH
VHOOOOOO
RRGH!
TUK
TUK
THUK
...

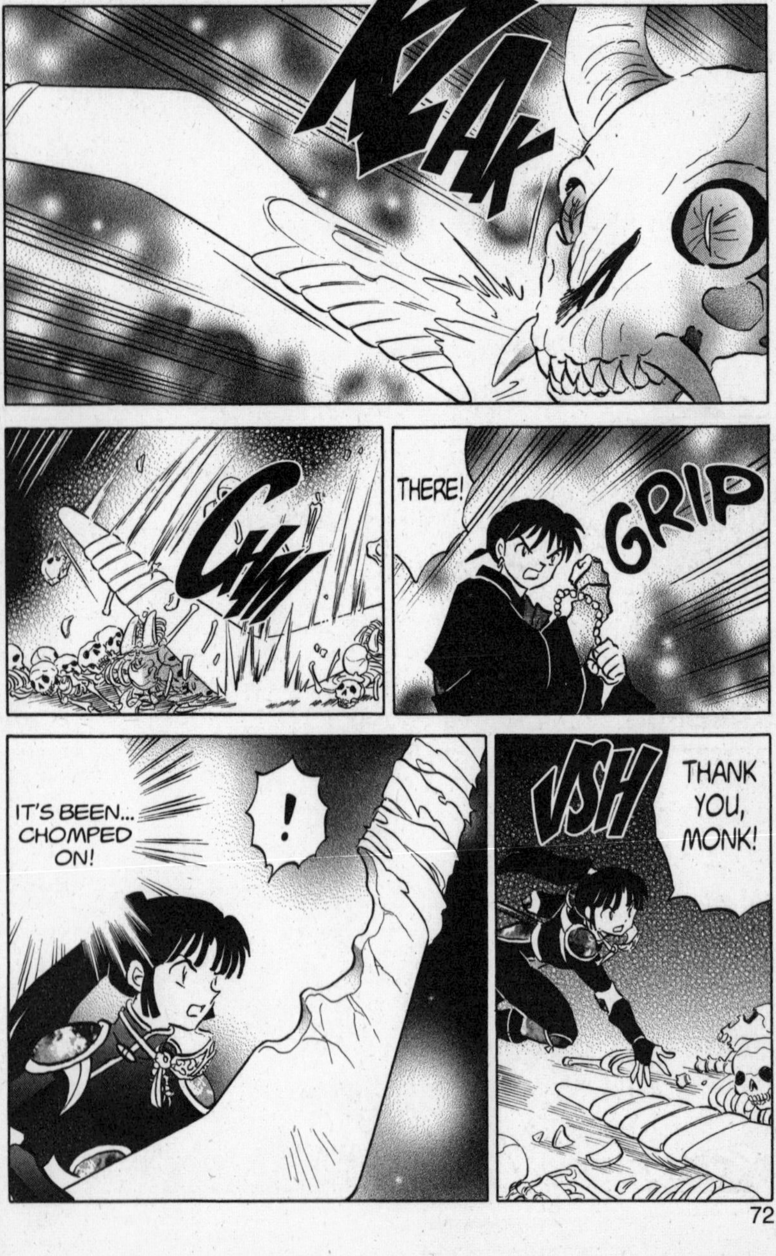
KLAK
THERE!
GRIP
CHM
VSH
THANK YOU, MONK!
!
IT'S BEEN... CHOMPED ON!

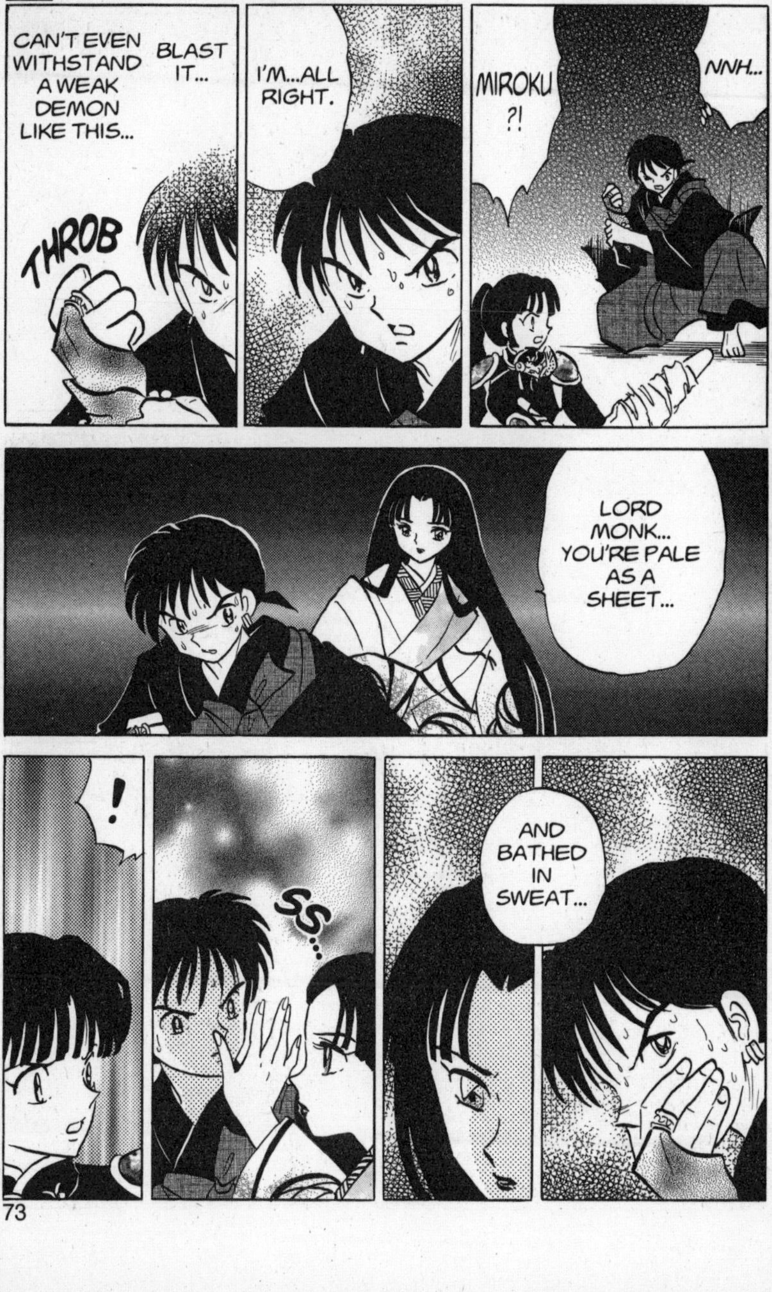
NNH...
MIROKU ?!
I'M...ALL RIGHT.
BLAST IT...
CAN'T EVEN WITHSTAND A WEAK DEMON LIKE THIS...
THROB
LORD MONK... YOU'RE PALE AS A SHEET...
AND BATHED IN SWEAT...
SS...
!

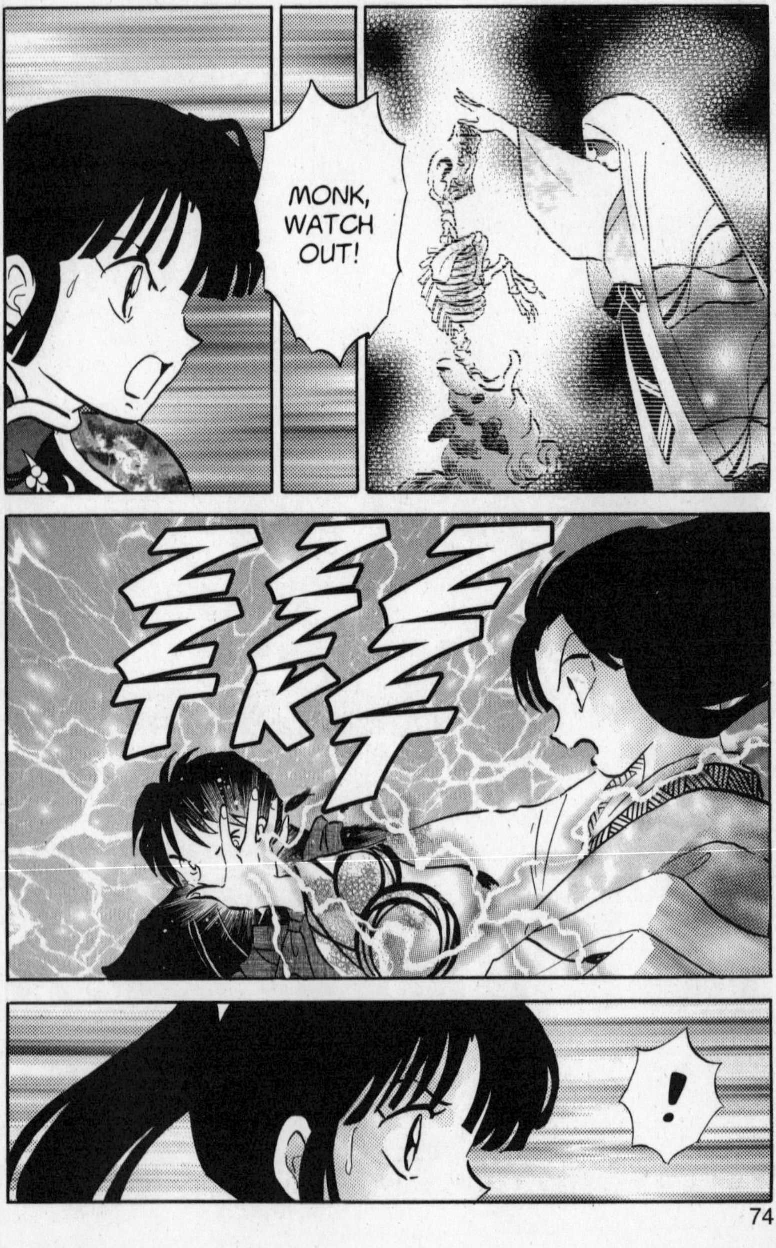
MONK, WATCH OUT!
ZZZT ZZZK ZZZZT
!

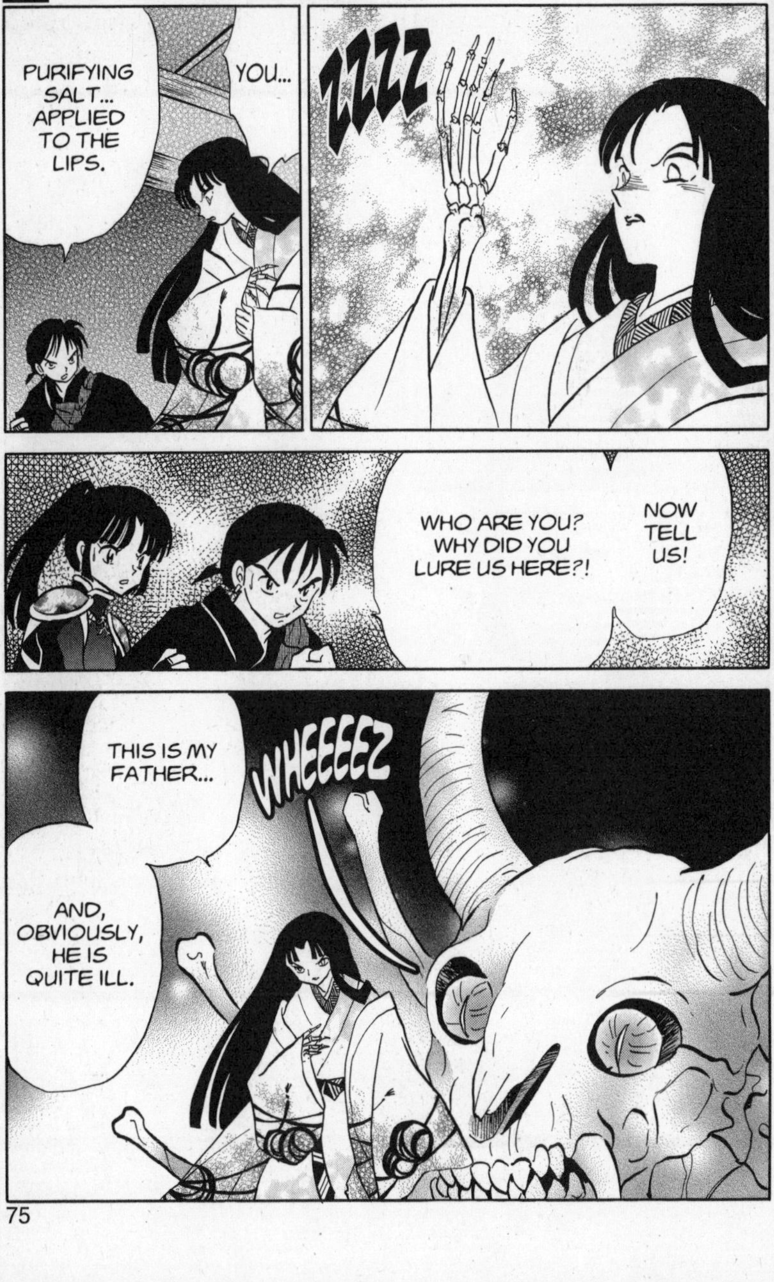
ZZZZ
YOU...
PURIFYING SALT... APPLIED TO THE LIPS.
NOW TELL US!
WHO ARE YOU? WHY DID YOU LURE US HERE?!
WHEEEEZ
THIS IS MY FATHER...
AND, OBVIOUSLY, HE IS QUITE ILL.

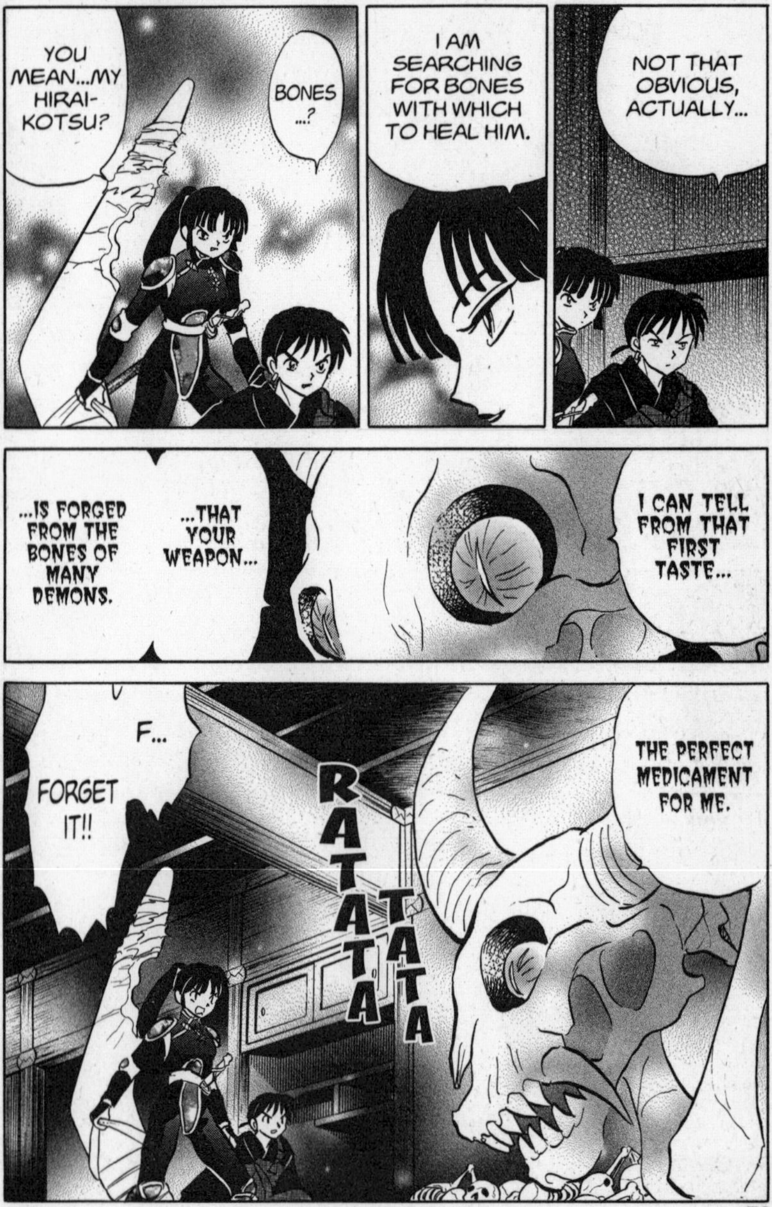
NOT THAT OBVIOUS, ACTUALLY...
I AM SEARCHING FOR BONES WITH WHICH TO HEAL HIM.
BONES ...?
YOU MEAN...MY HIRAI-KOTSU?
I CAN TELL FROM THAT FIRST TASTE...
...THAT YOUR WEAPON...
...IS FORGED FROM THE BONES OF MANY DEMONS.
THE PERFECT MEDICAMENT FOR ME.
RATATA
TATA
F...
FORGET IT!!

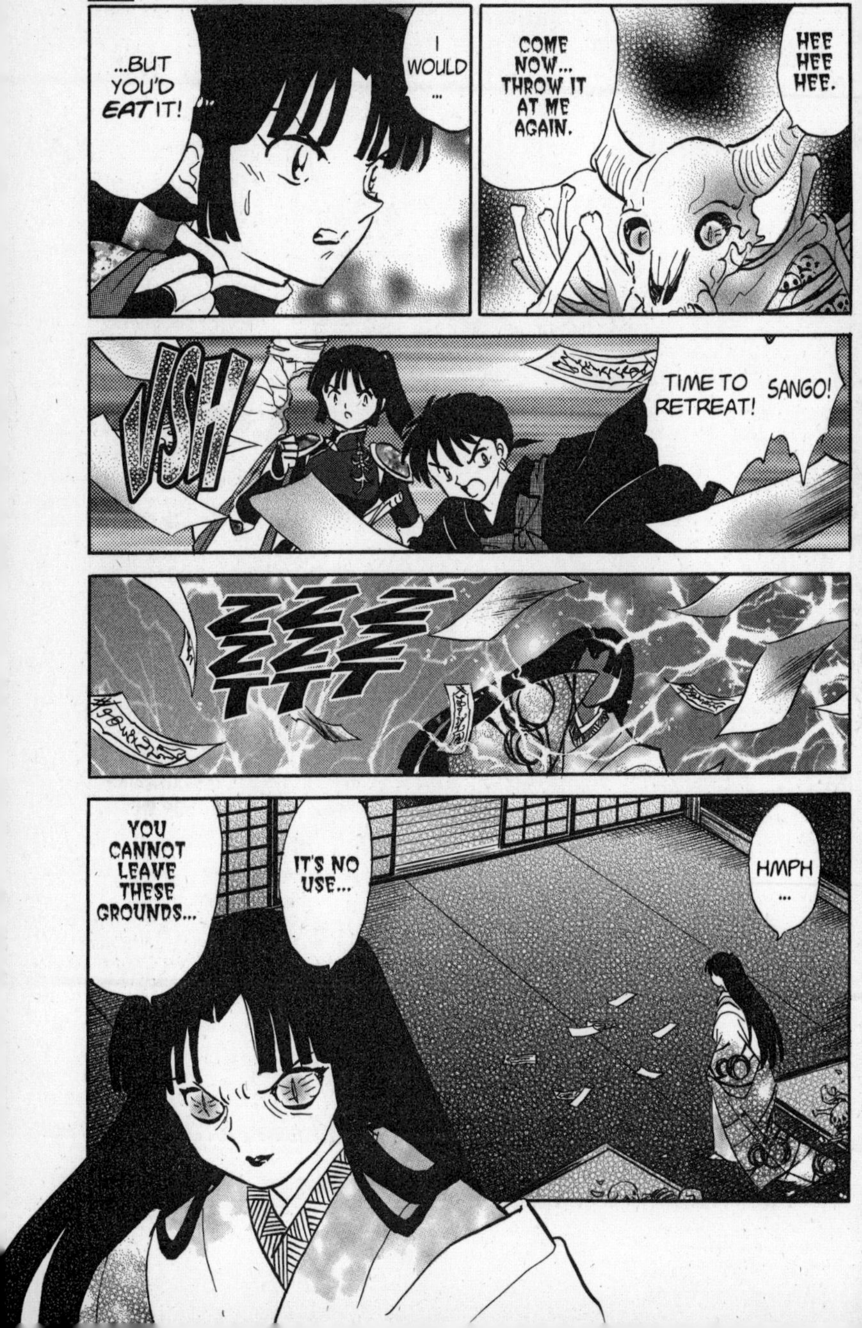
HEE HEE HEE.
COME NOW... THROW IT AT ME AGAIN.
I WOULD...
...BUT YOU'D EAT IT!
SANGO!
TIME TO RETREAT!
VSH
ZZZZZZZTTT
HMPH...
IT'S NO USE...
YOU CANNOT LEAVE THESE GROUNDS...

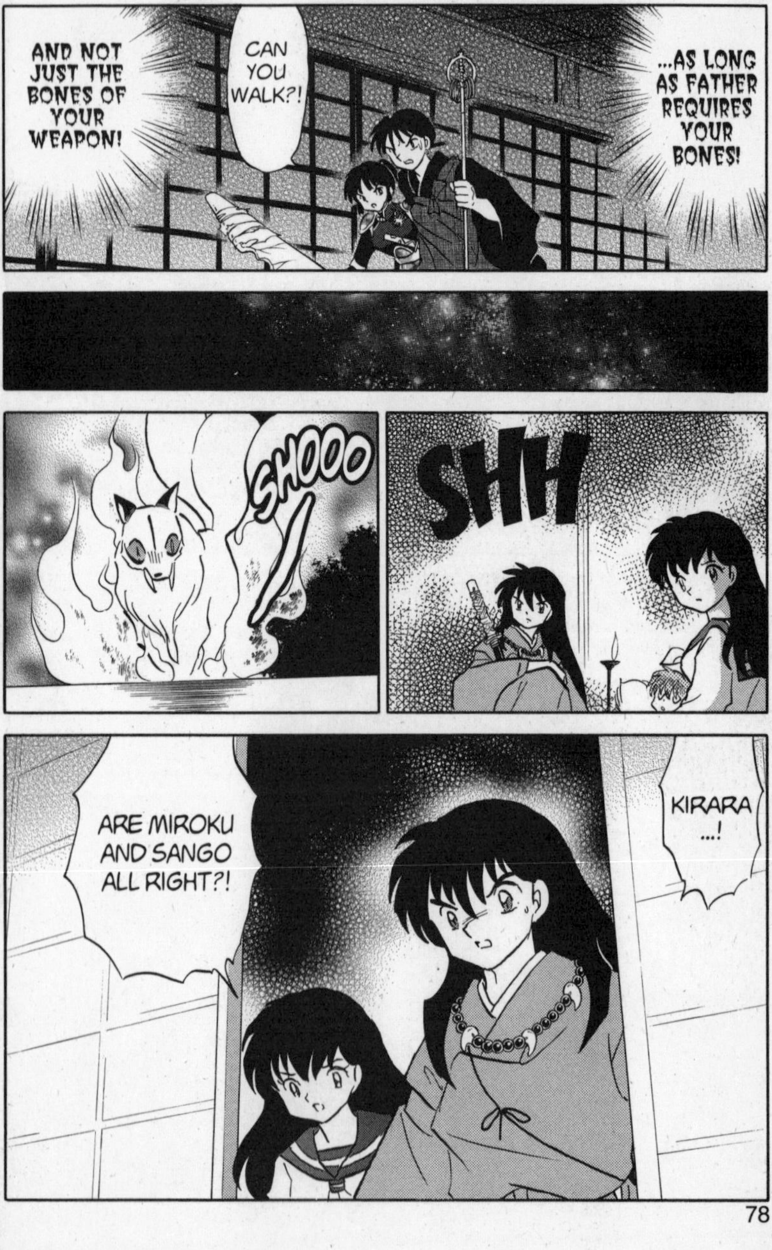
...AS LONG AS FATHER REQUIRES YOUR BONES!
CAN YOU WALK?!
AND NOT JUST THE BONES OF YOUR WEAPON!
SHH
SHOOO
KIRARA ...!
ARE MIROKU AND SANGO ALL RIGHT?!

SCROLL 5

THE CAGE OF BONES

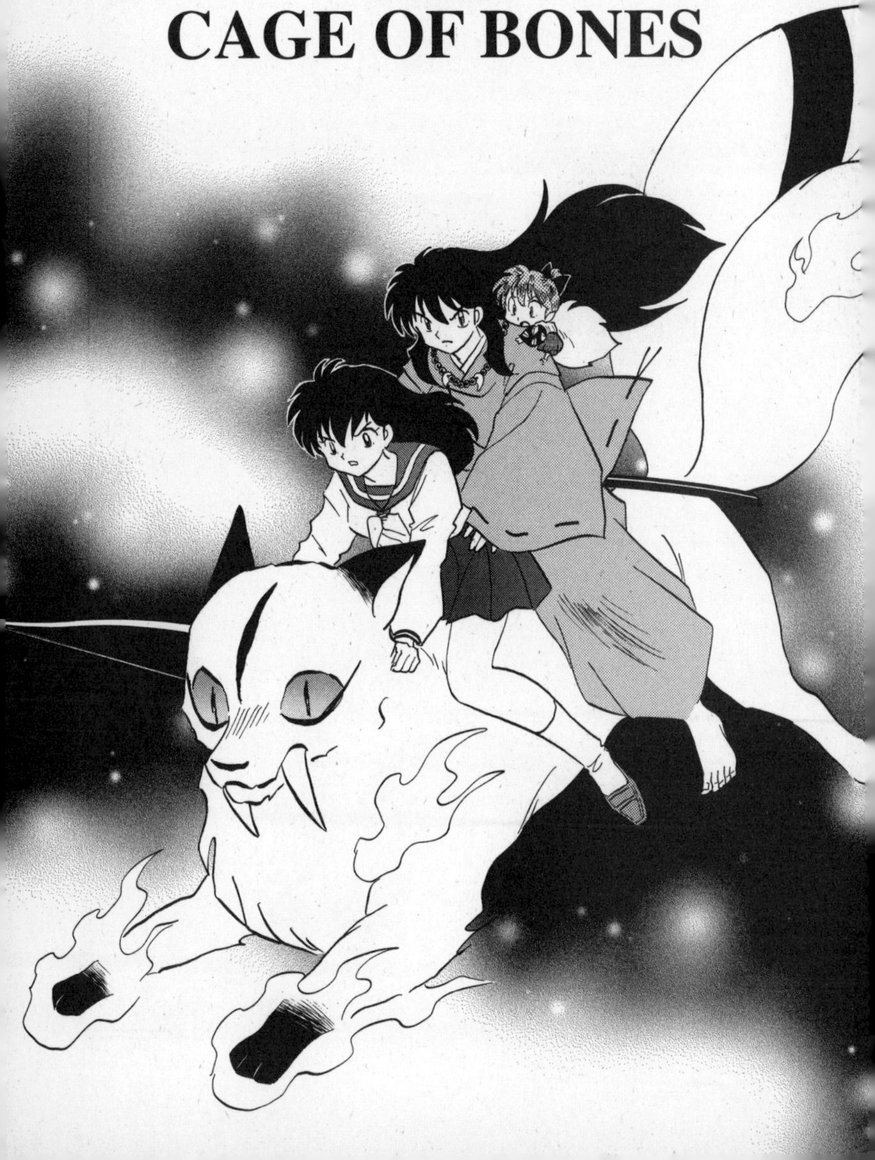

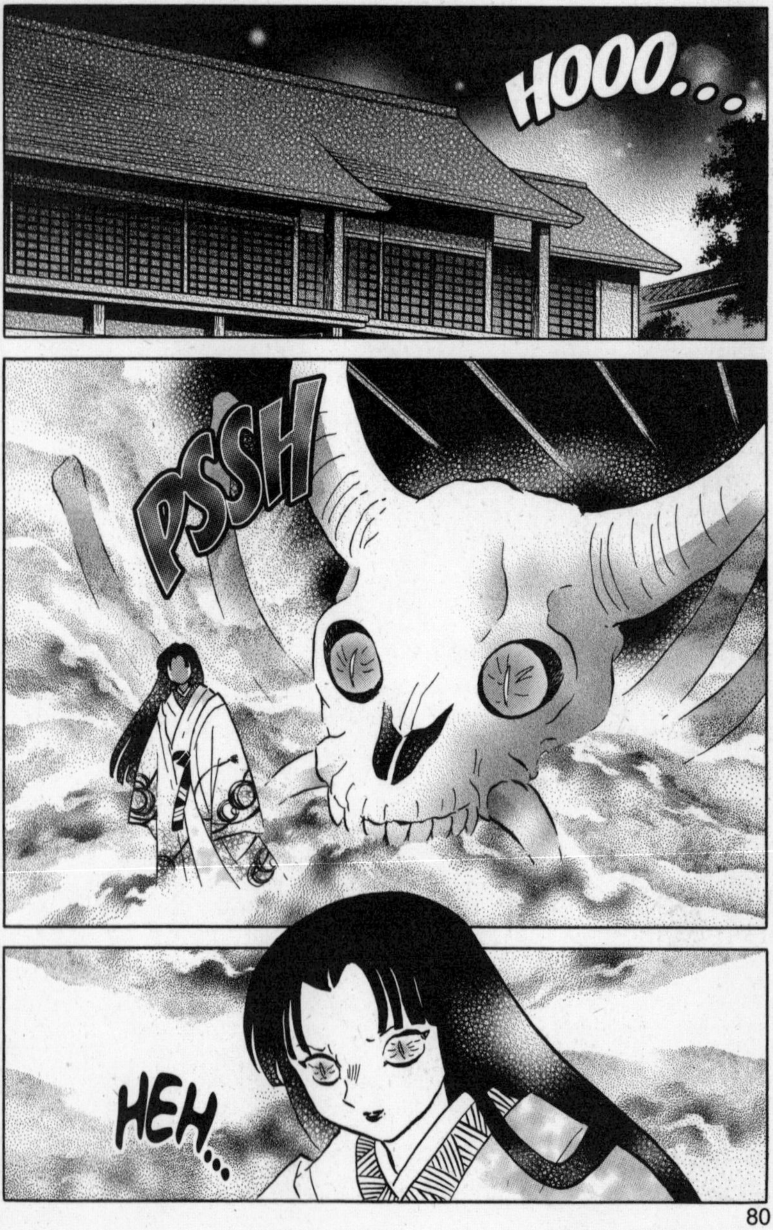
HOOO...
PSSH
HEH...

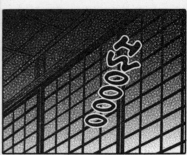

...BREAK THROUGH ANYWHERE. I CAN'T...

...

PSSH...

THE GAS IS SPREADING!

81

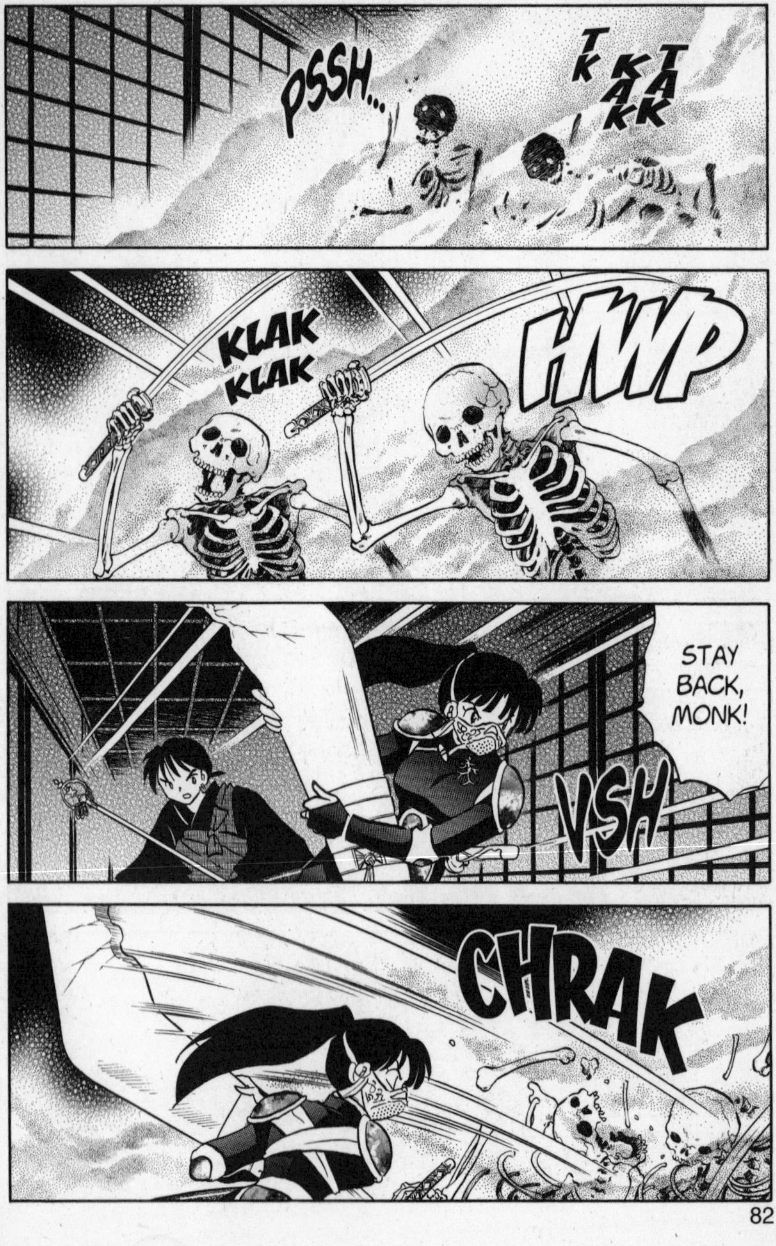
TAKK
KAK
TK
PSSH...
HWP
KLAK KLAK
STAY BACK, MONK!
VSH
CHRAK

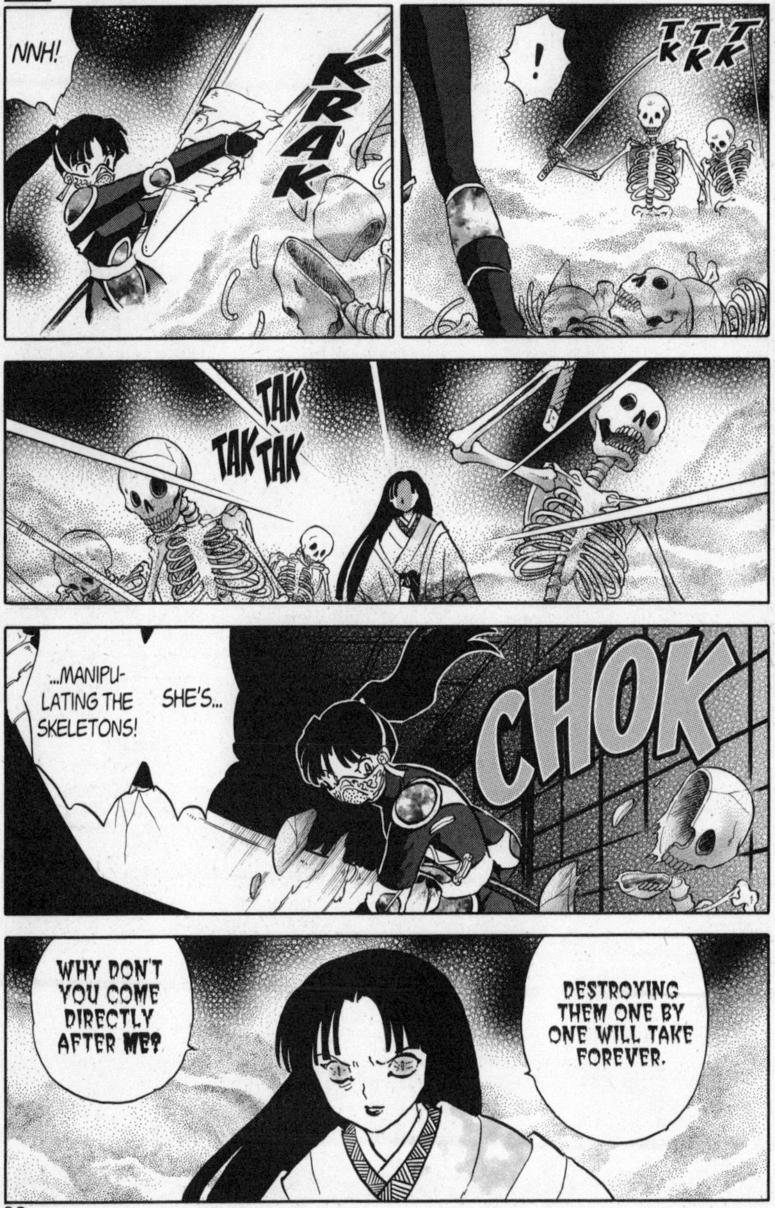
!
TK TK TK
NNH!
KRAK
TAK TAK TAK
CHOK
SHE'S...
...MANIPULATING THE SKELETONS!
DESTROYING THEM ONE BY ONE WILL TAKE FOREVER.
WHY DON'T YOU COME DIRECTLY AFTER ME?

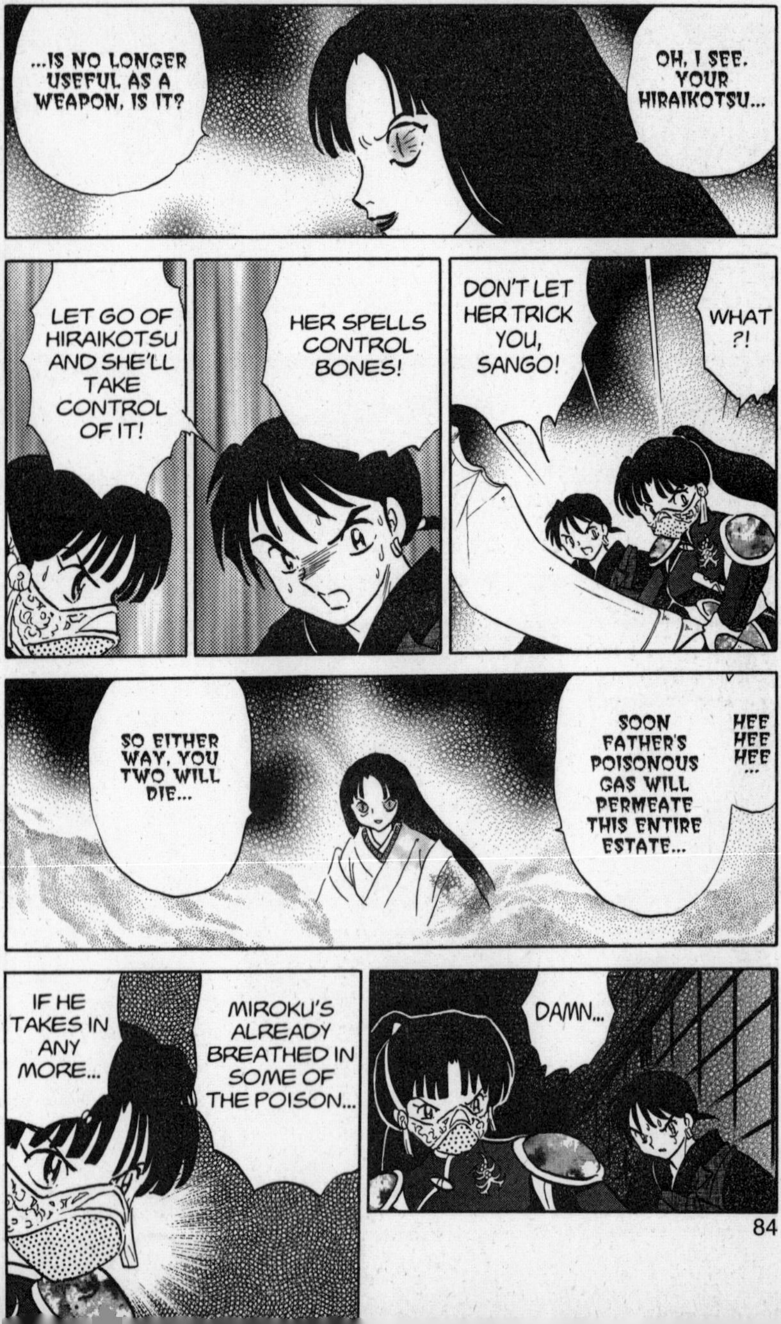
OH, I SEE. YOUR HIRAIKOTSU...
...IS NO LONGER USEFUL AS A WEAPON, IS IT?
WHAT ?!
DON'T LET HER TRICK YOU, SANGO!
HER SPELLS CONTROL BONES!
LET GO OF HIRAIKOTSU AND SHE'LL TAKE CONTROL OF IT!
HEE HEE HEE...
SOON FATHER'S POISONOUS GAS WILL PERMEATE THIS ENTIRE ESTATE...
SO EITHER WAY, YOU TWO WILL DIE...
DAMN...
MIROKU'S ALREADY BREATHED IN SOME OF THE POISON...
IF HE TAKES IN ANY MORE...

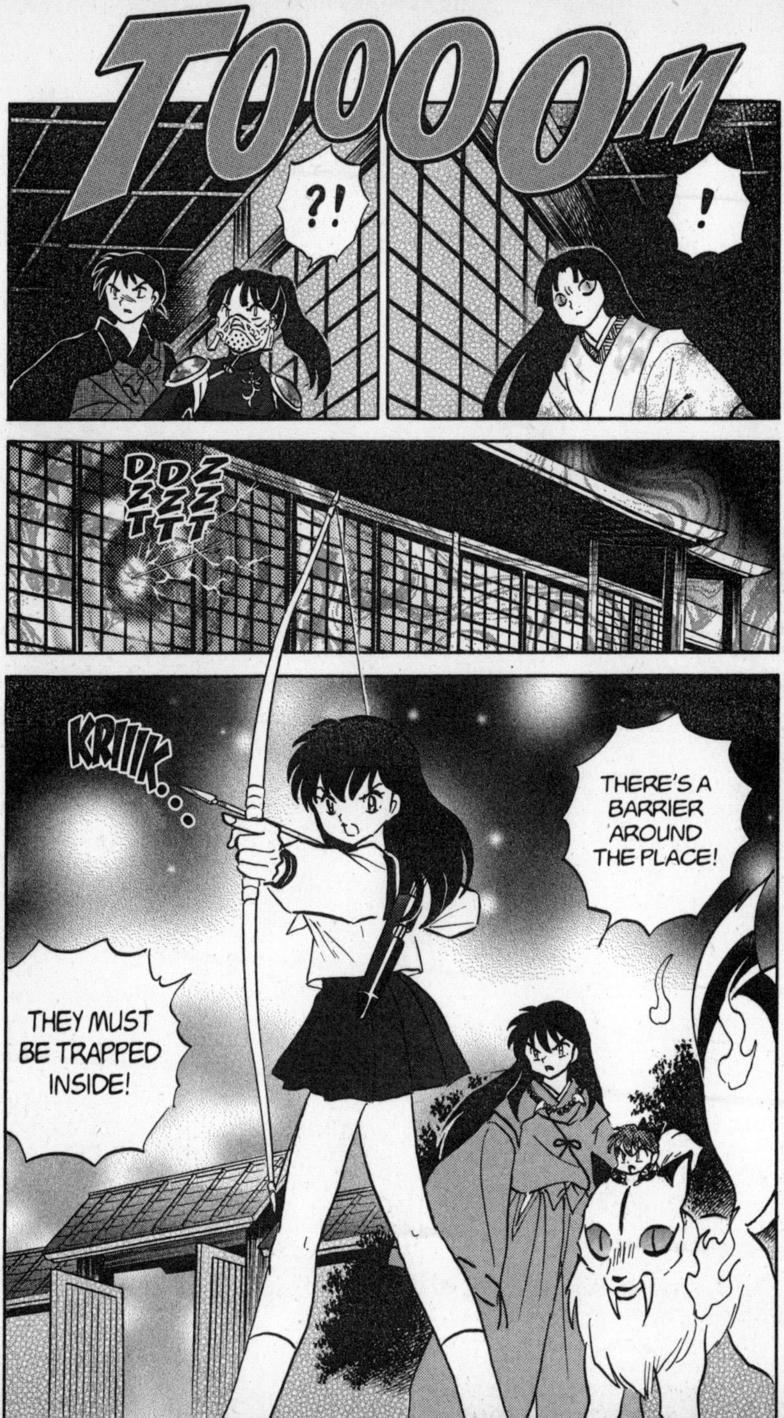
TOOOOM
!
?!
DZZT
THERE'S A BARRIER AROUND THE PLACE!
KRIIIK...
THEY MUST BE TRAPPED INSIDE!

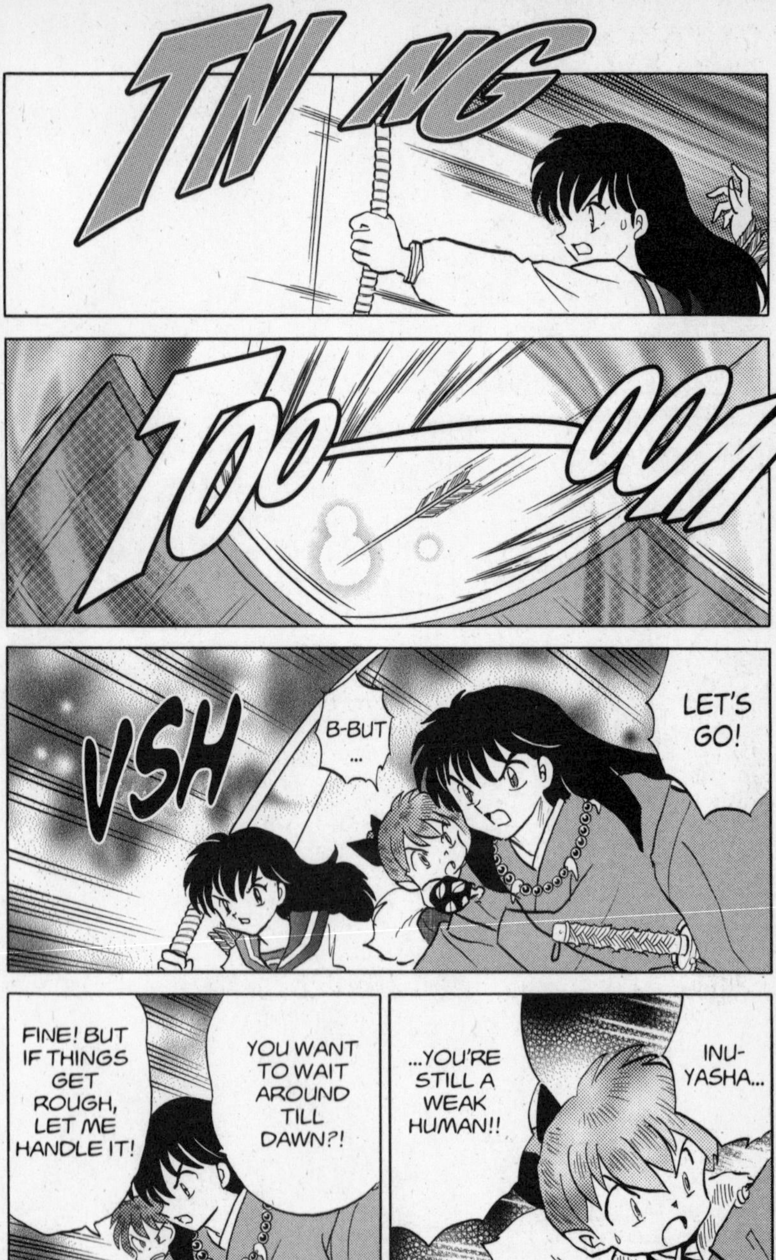
TWNG
TOOO—OOM
LET'S GO!
B-BUT...
VSH
INU-YASHA...
...YOU'RE STILL A WEAK HUMAN!!
YOU WANT TO WAIT AROUND TILL DAWN?!
FINE! BUT IF THINGS GET ROUGH, LET ME HANDLE IT!

SANGO?! MIROKU?!

TMP

YEEEK!

TTTT AAA KK KK

PSSH

CHAK

THIS MUST BE THE PLACE!

FEH!

I'LL PURIFY IT!

KRIK

POISON ?!

PSSH...

!

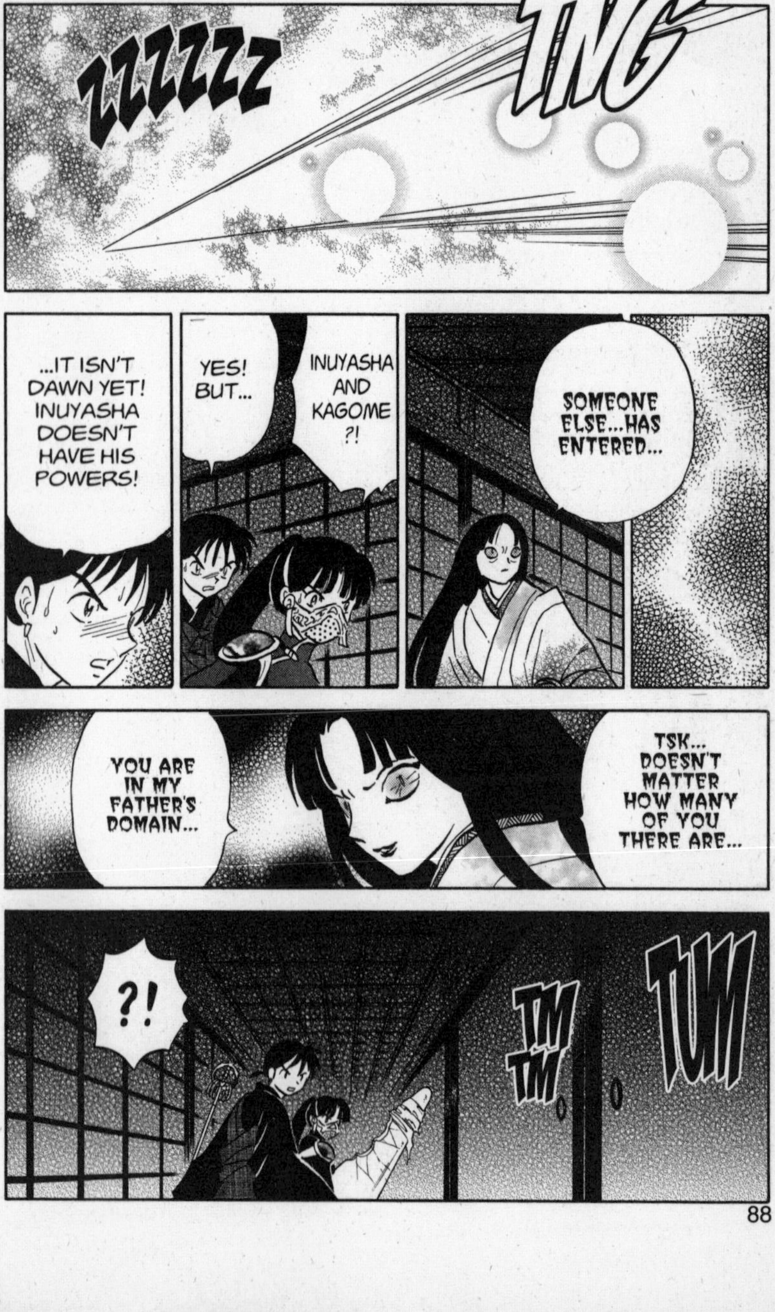
TNG
ZZZZZZ
SOMEONE ELSE...HAS ENTERED...
INUYASHA AND KAGOME ?!
YES! BUT...
...IT ISN'T DAWN YET! INUYASHA DOESN'T HAVE HIS POWERS!
TSK... DOESN'T MATTER HOW MANY OF YOU THERE ARE...
YOU ARE IN MY FATHER'S DOMAIN...
TUM
TM TM
?!

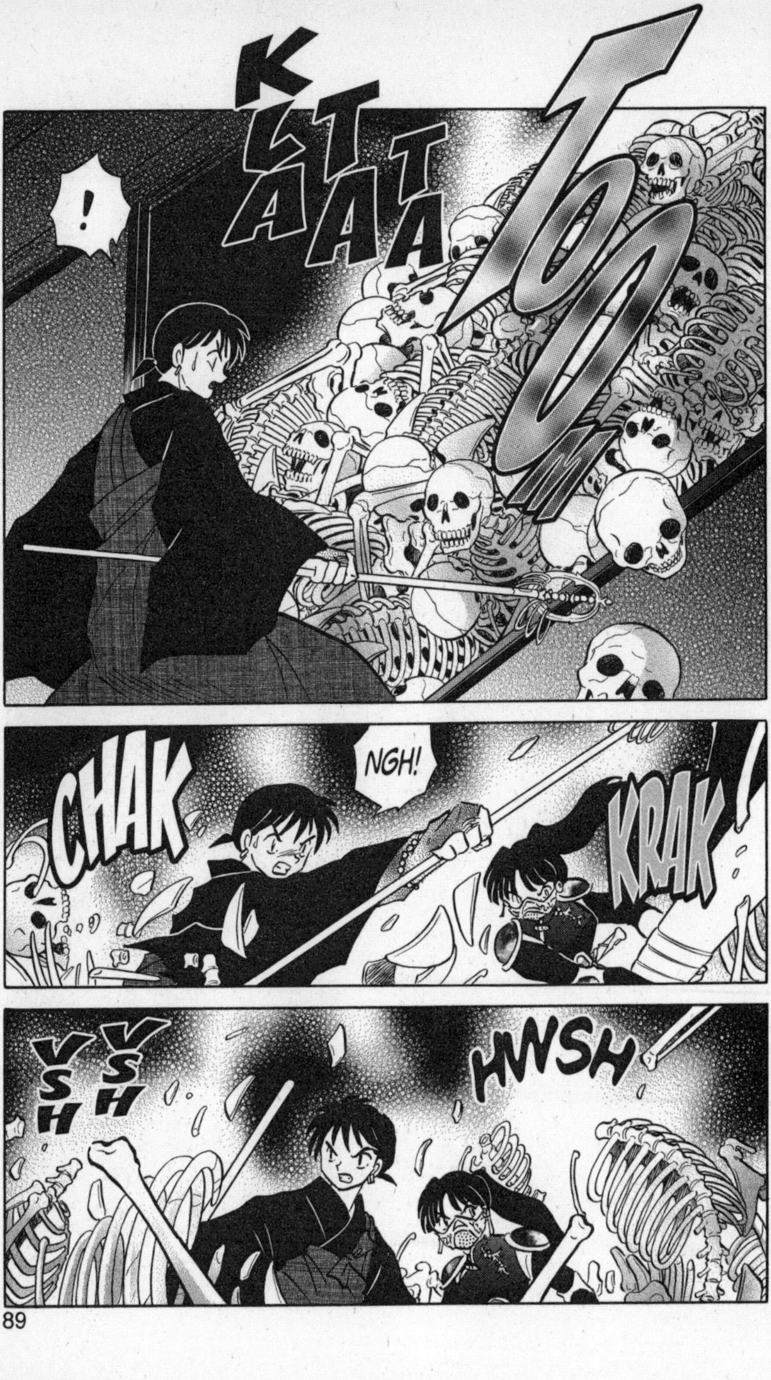
!
KRAK
NGH!
CHAK
HWSH
VSH
VSH

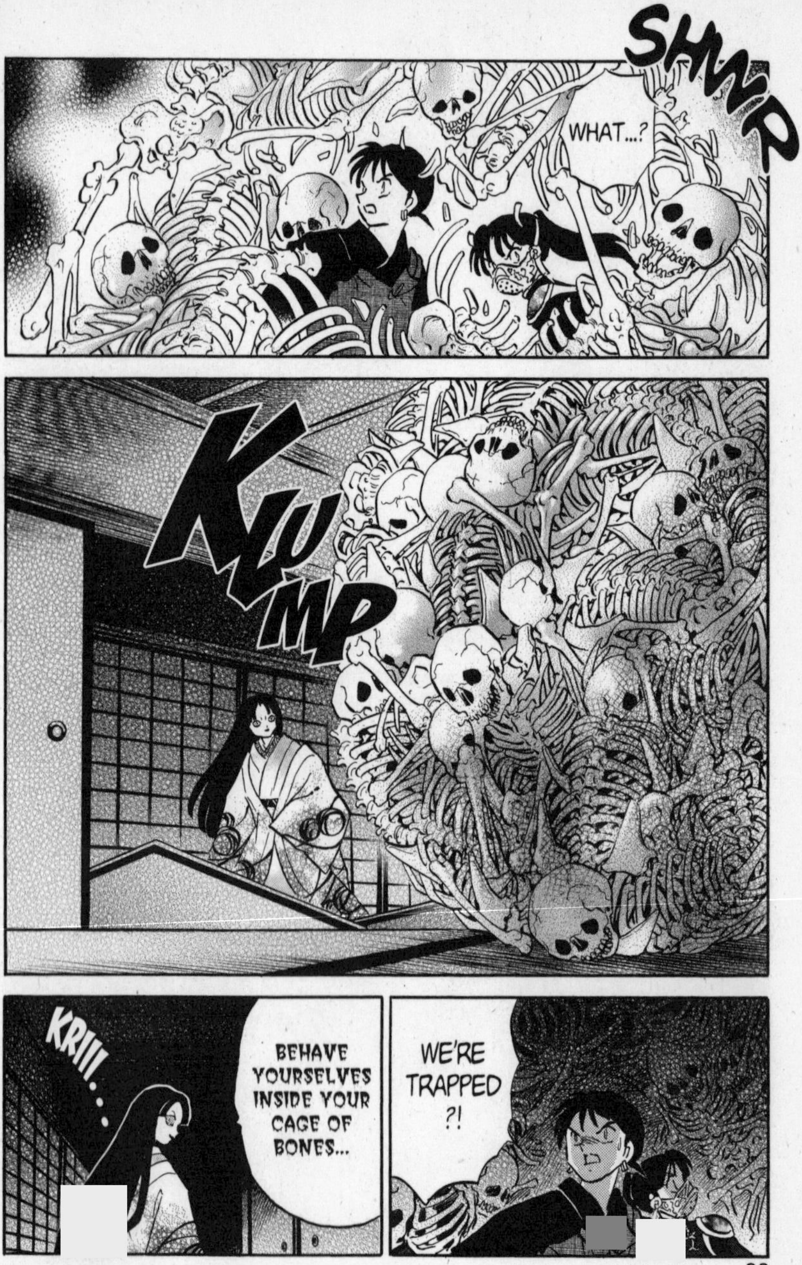
SHWR
WHAT...?
KWUMP
WE'RE TRAPPED ?!
BEHAVE YOURSELVES INSIDE YOUR CAGE OF BONES...
KRIII...

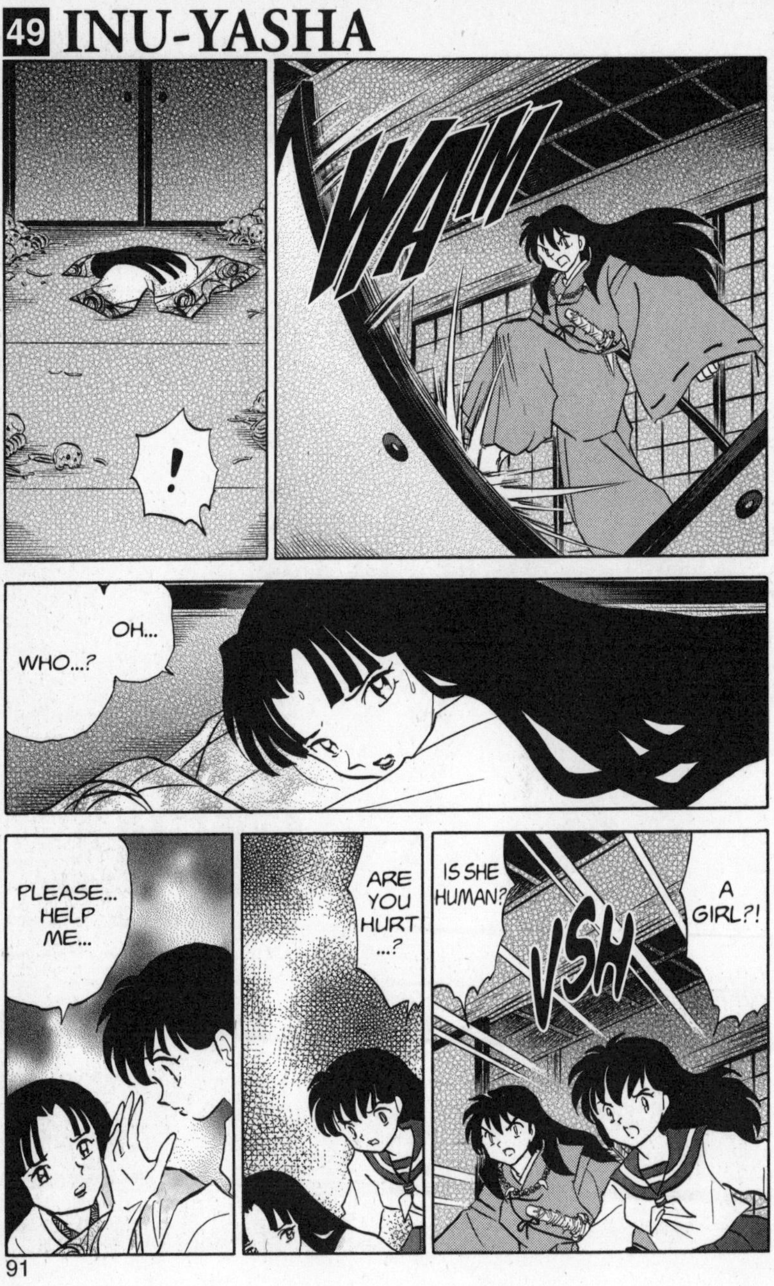
WAM
!
OH...
WHO...?
A GIRL?!
IS SHE HUMAN?
VSH
ARE YOU HURT ...?
PLEASE... HELP ME...

SO I CAN STEAL YOUR BONES!

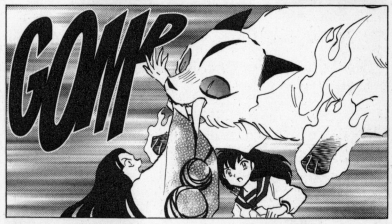

GOMP

SNAP SNAP

FMP

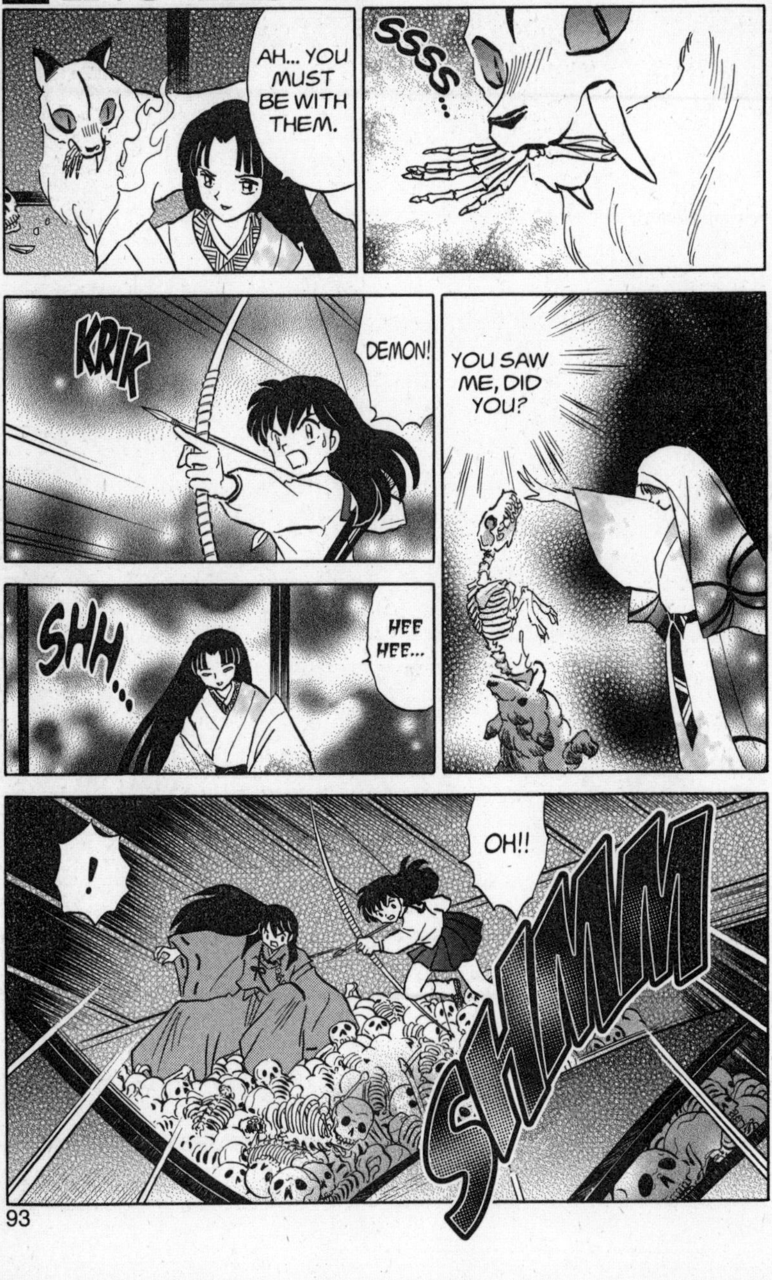
SSSS...
AH... YOU MUST BE WITH THEM.
YOU SAW ME, DID YOU?
DEMON!
KRIK
HEE HEE...
SHH...
OH!!
!
SHMMM

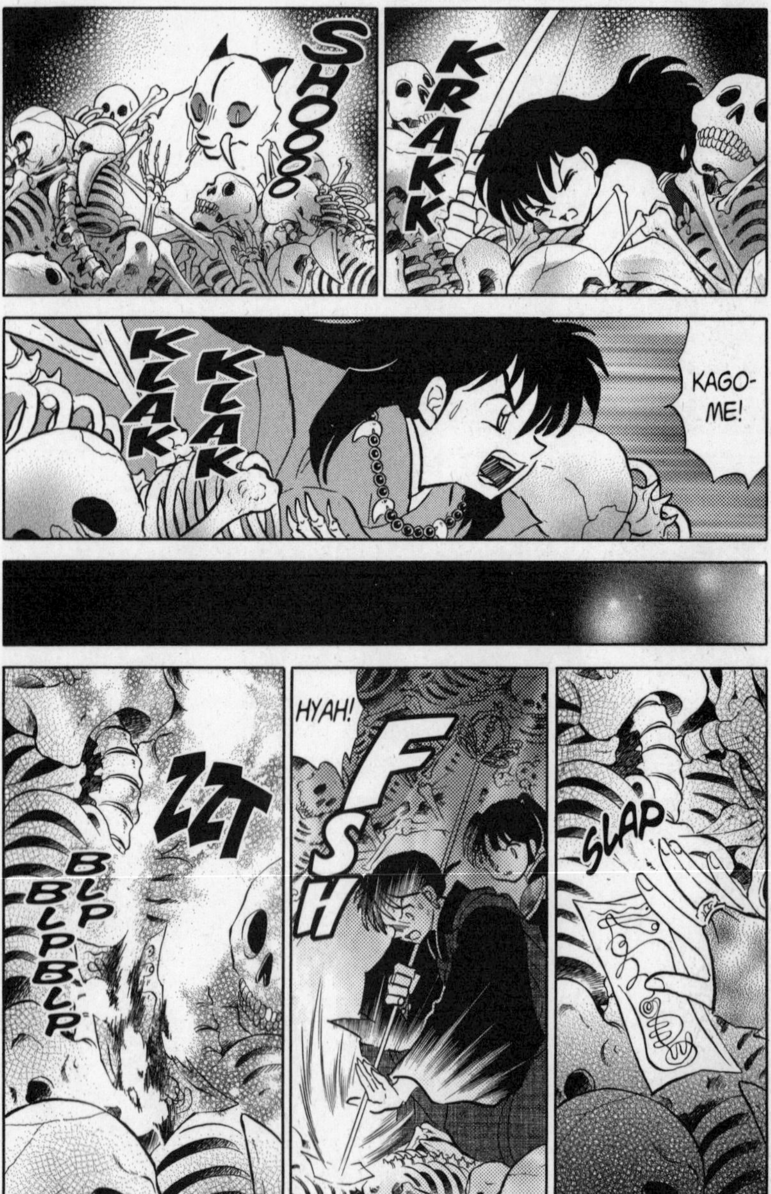
KRAKK
SHOOOOO
KAGO-ME!
KLAK KLAK
SLAP
HYAH!
FSH
ZZT
BLP BLPBLPBLP

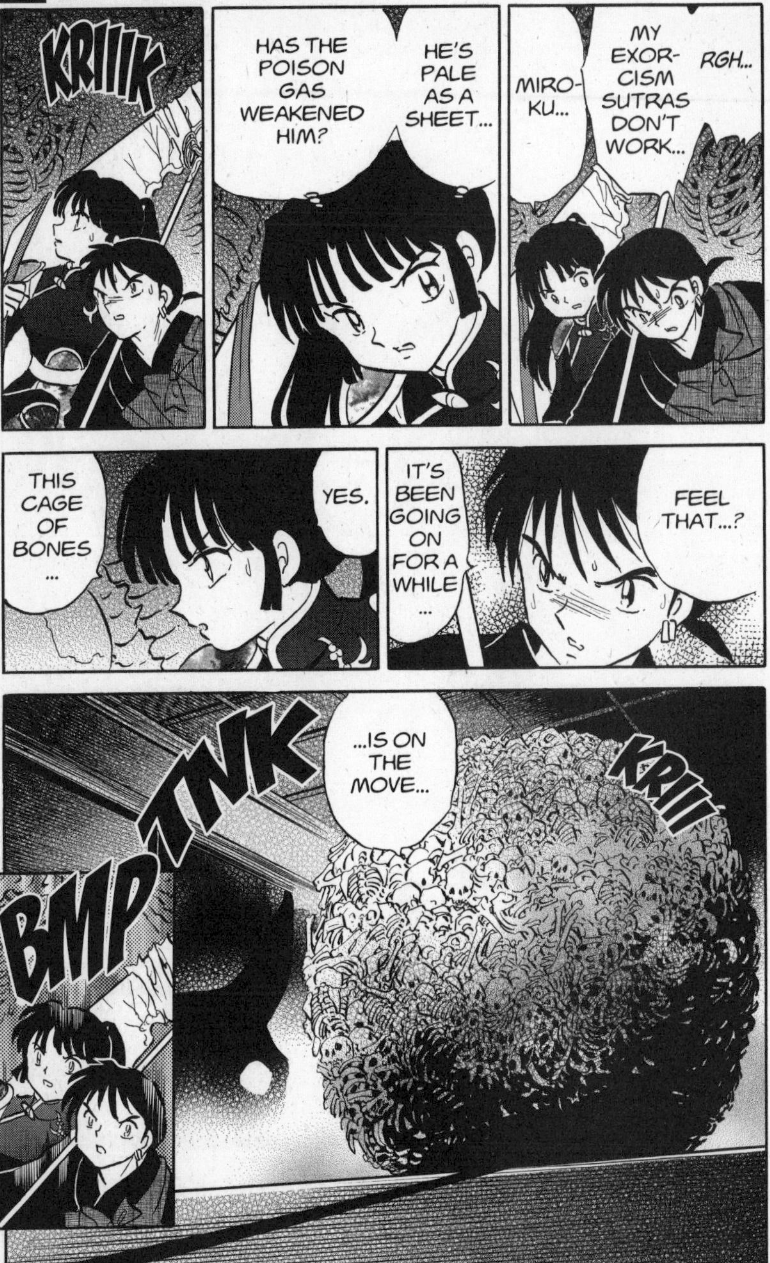
RGH...
MY EXOR-CISM SUTRAS DON'T WORK...
MIRO-KU...
HE'S PALE AS A SHEET...
HAS THE POISON GAS WEAKENED HIM?
KRIIIK
FEEL THAT...?
IT'S BEEN GOING ON FOR A WHILE...
YES.
THIS CAGE OF BONES...
KRIII
...IS ON THE MOVE...
TNK
BMP

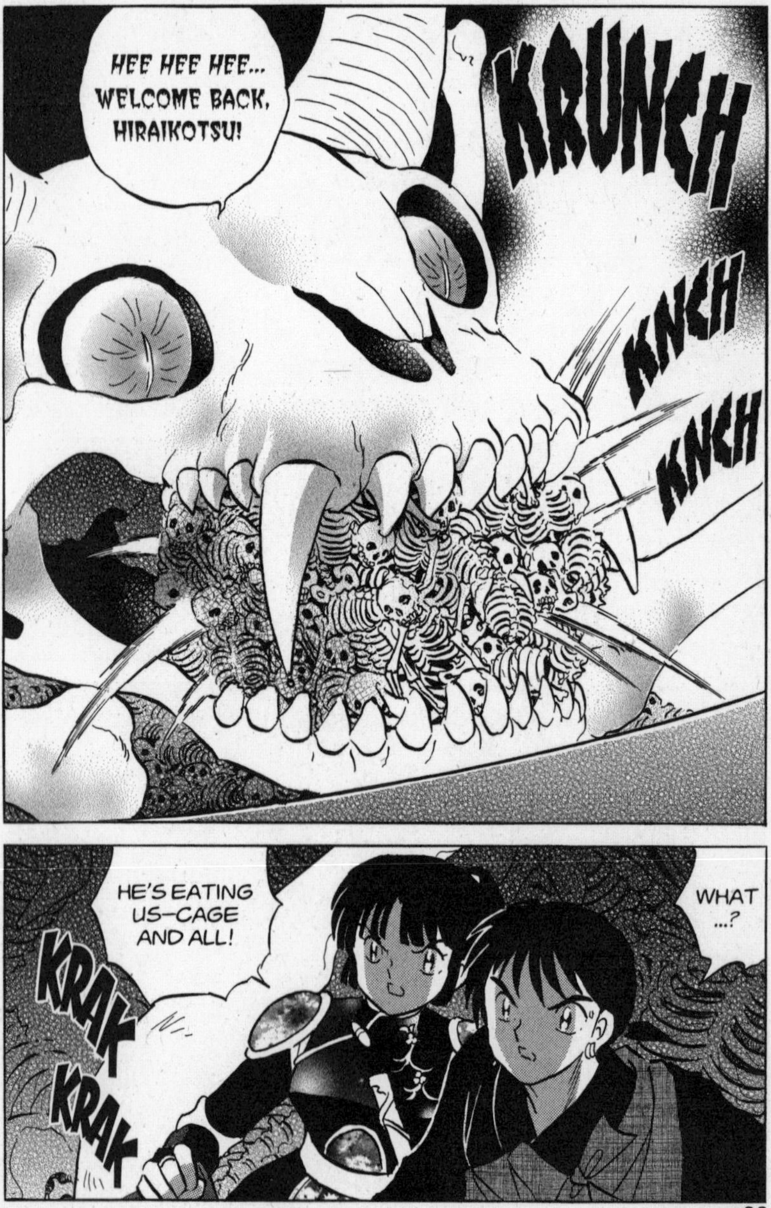
KRUNCH
HEE HEE HEE... WELCOME BACK, HIRAIKOTSU!
KNCH
KNCH
WHAT ...?
HE'S EATING US—CAGE AND ALL!
KRAK
KRAK
KRAK

SCROLL 6

THE POISON SALVE

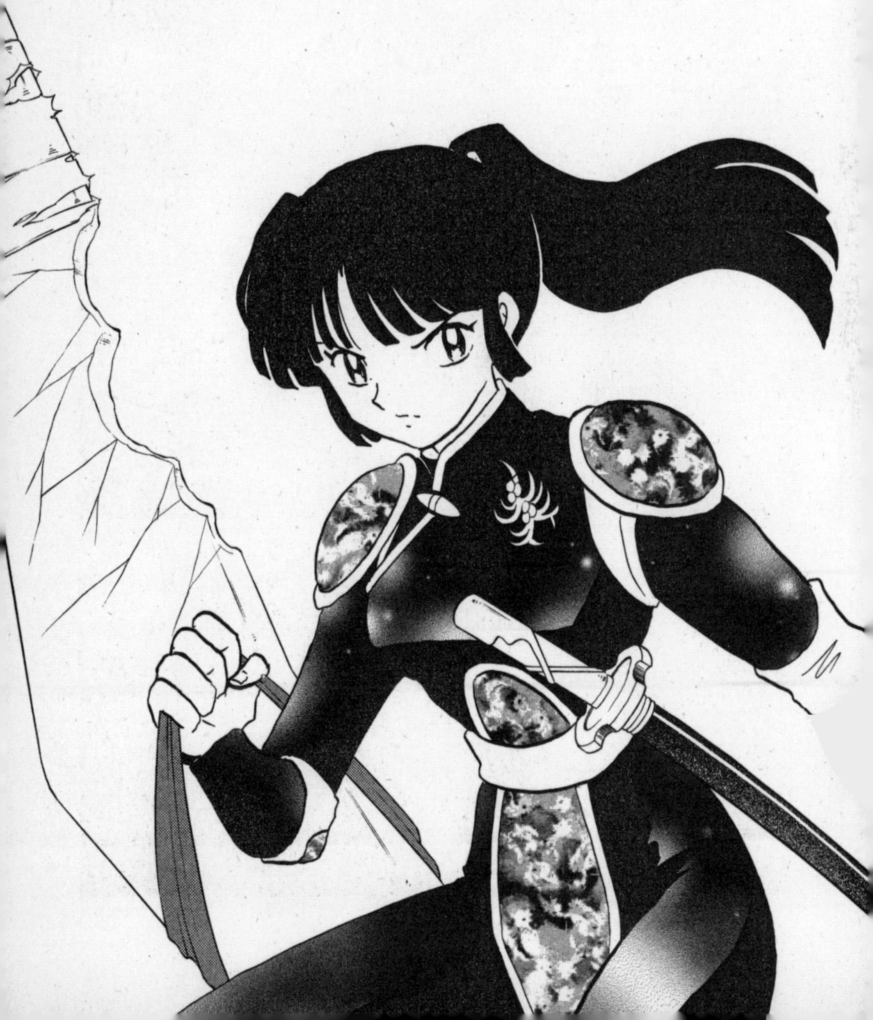

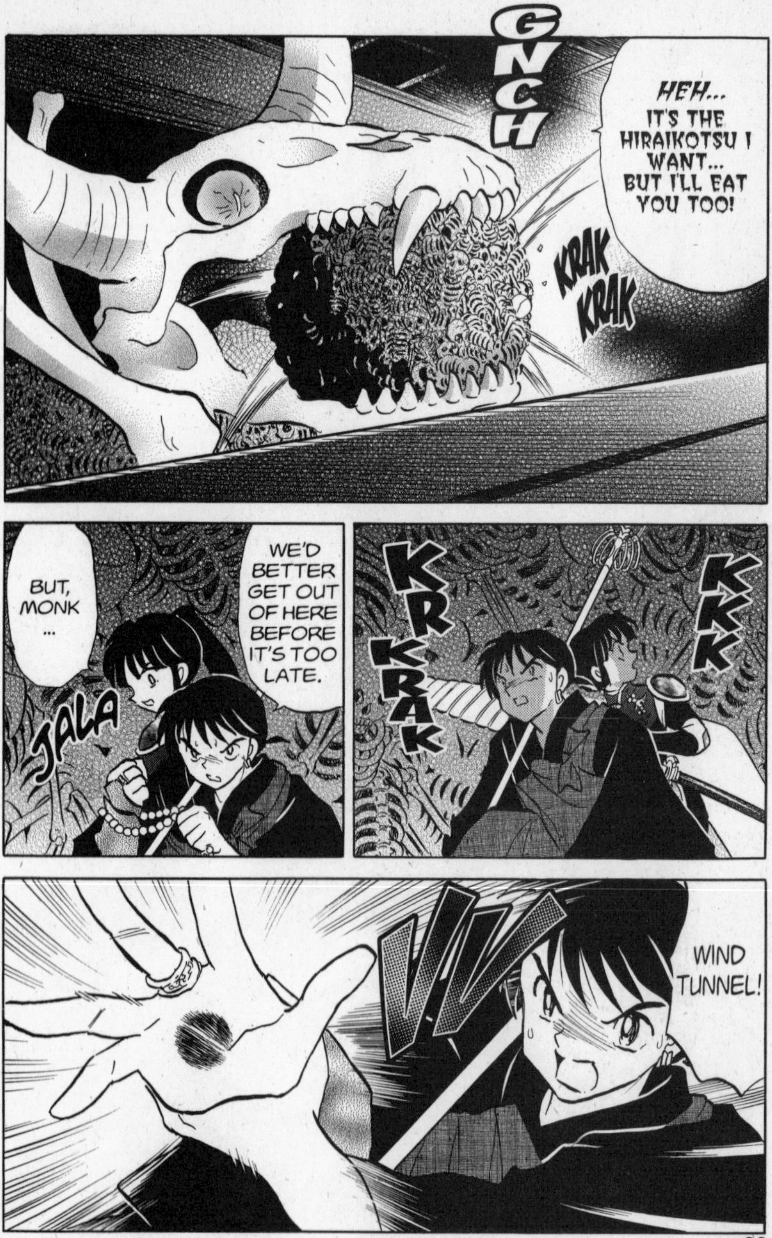

HEH... IT'S THE HIRAIKOTSU I WANT... BUT I'LL EAT YOU TOO!
GNCH
KRAK KRAK
KKK
KR KRAK
WE'D BETTER GET OUT OF HERE BEFORE IT'S TOO LATE.
BUT, MONK ...
JALA
WIND TUNNEL!

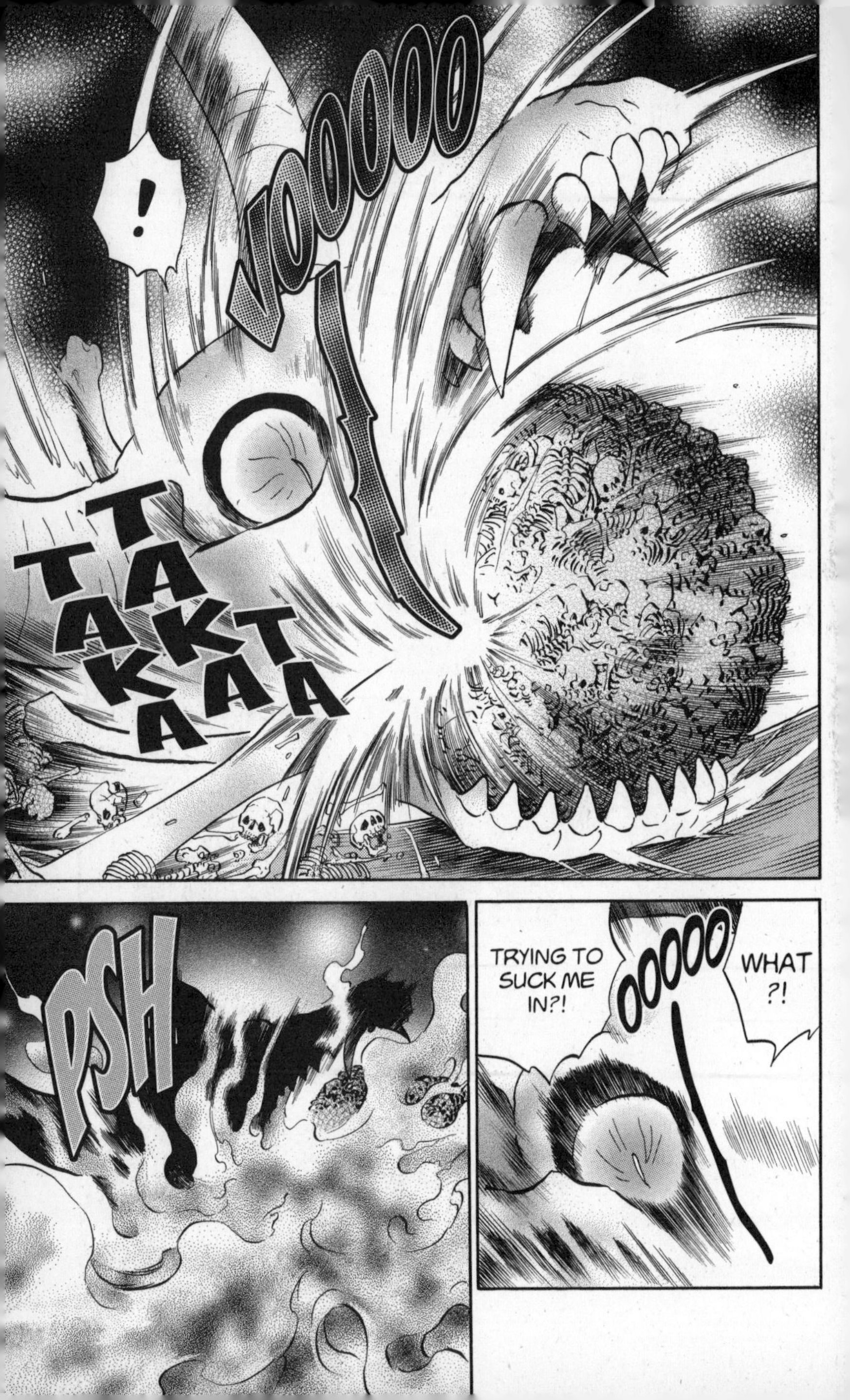
VOOOOO
!
TAKATAKATAA
WHAT ?!
OOOOO
TRYING TO SUCK ME IN?!
PSH

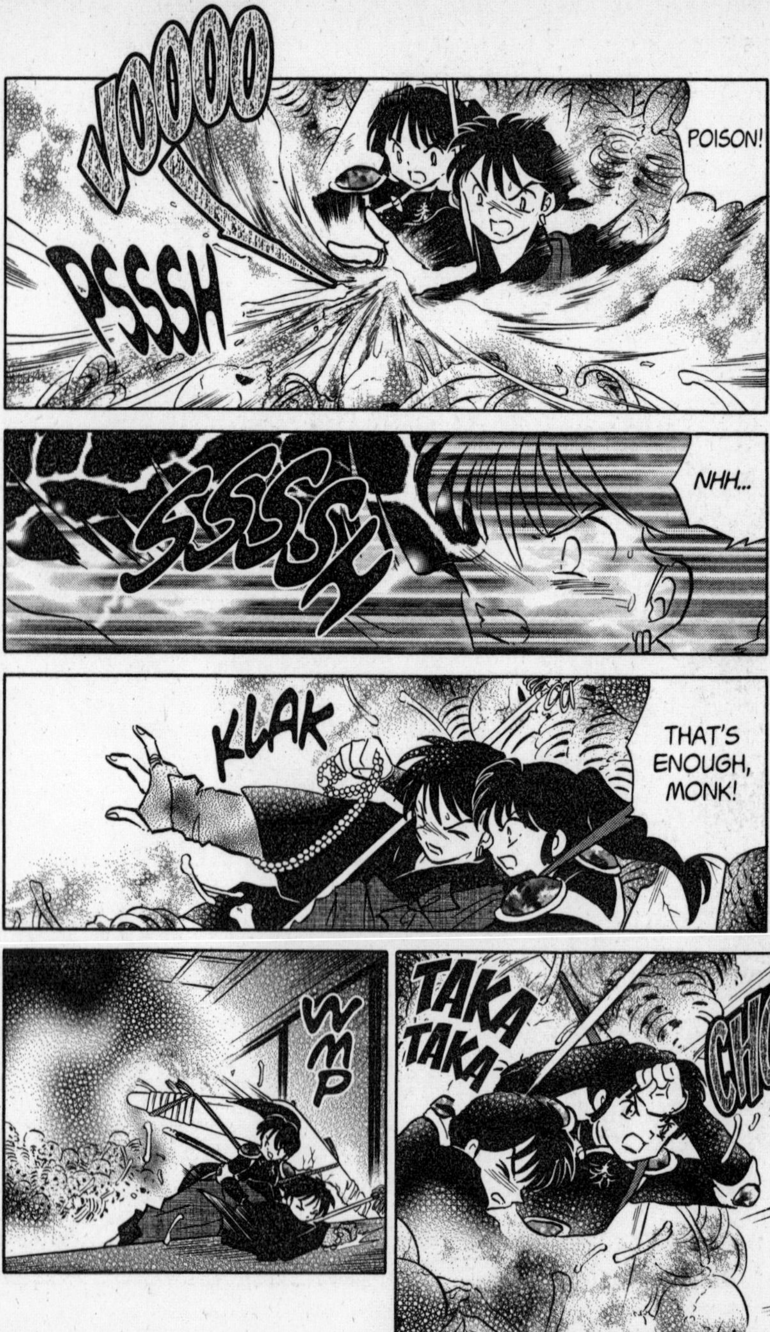
POISON!
VOOOO
PSSSH
NHH...
SSSSH
THAT'S ENOUGH, MONK!
KLAK
CHOK
TAKA TAKA
WMP

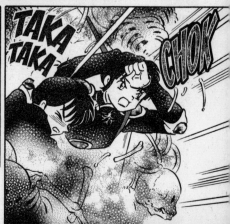

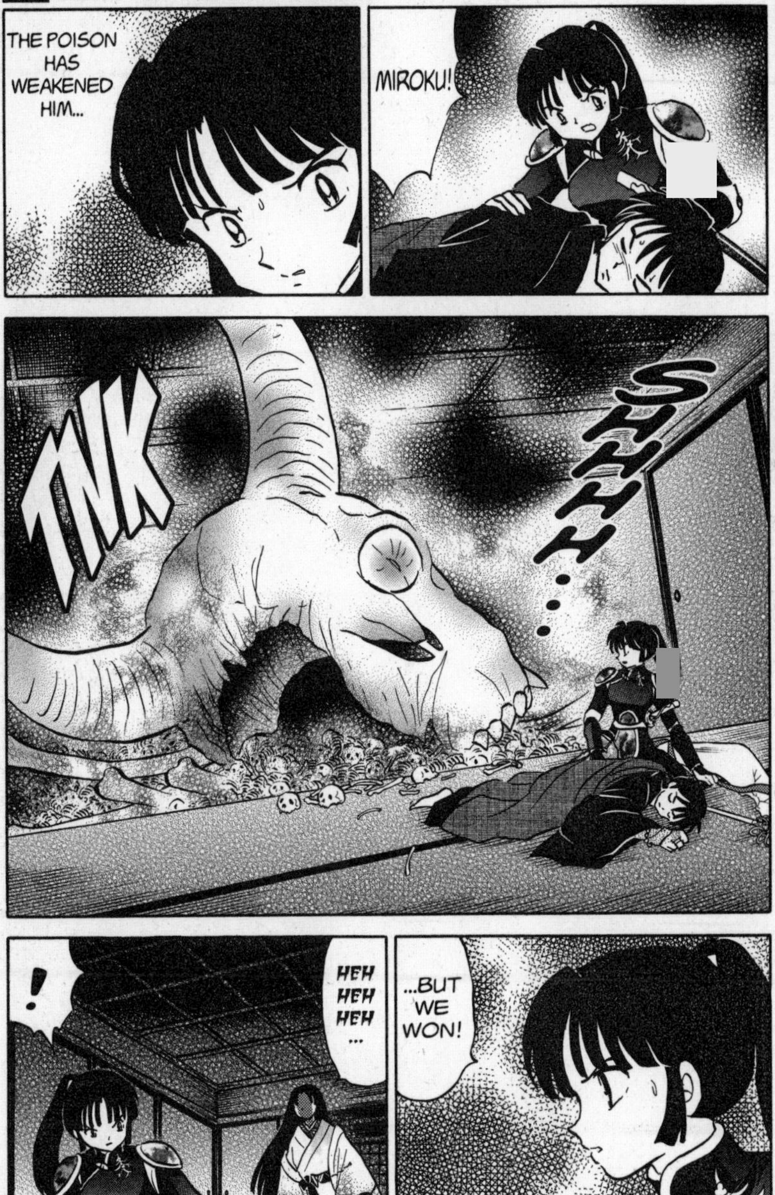
MIROKU!
THE POISON HAS WEAKENED HIM...
SHHHH...
TNK
...BUT WE WON!
HEH HEH HEH...
!

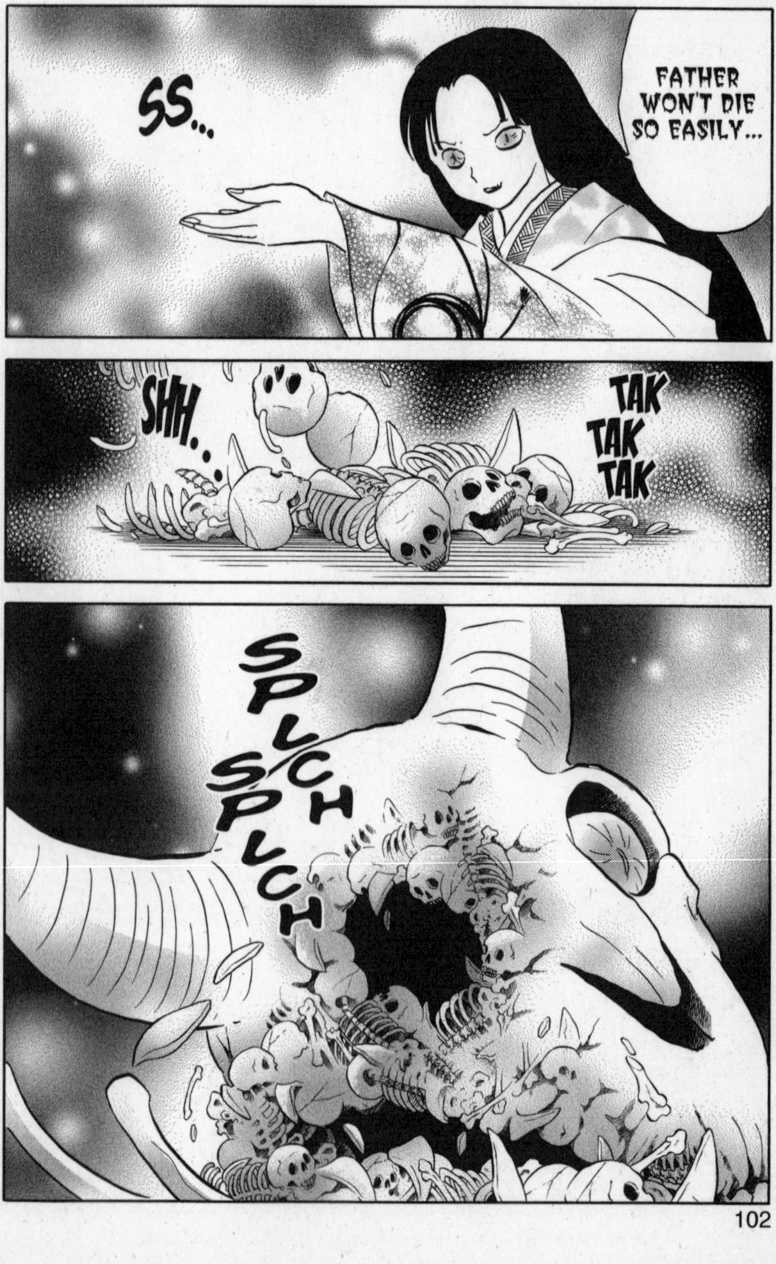
FATHER WON'T DIE SO EASILY...
SS...
TAK TAK TAK
SHH...
SPLUCH
SPLUCH

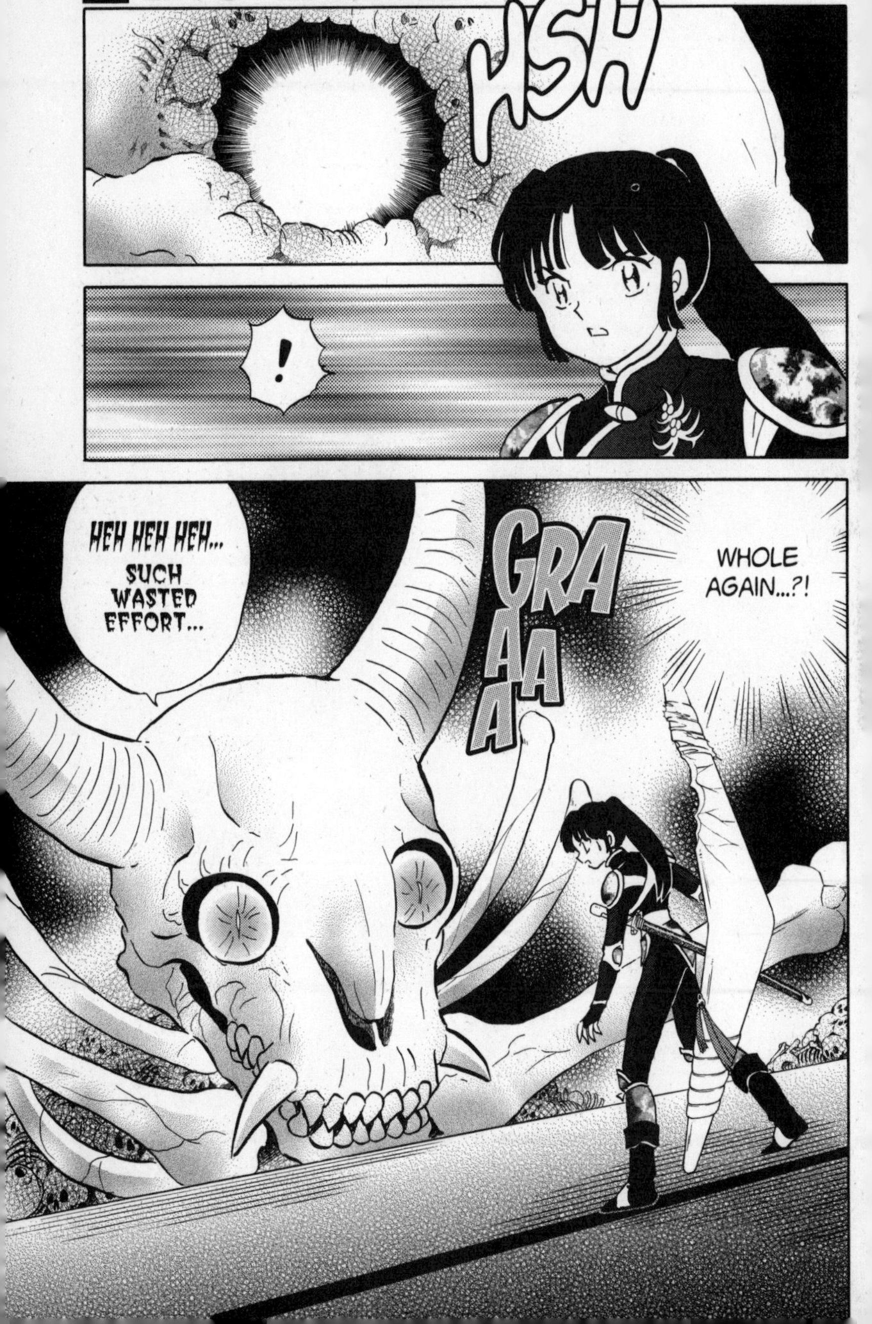
HSH
!
WHOLE AGAIN...?!
GRAAAA
HEH HEH HEH... SUCH WASTED EFFORT...

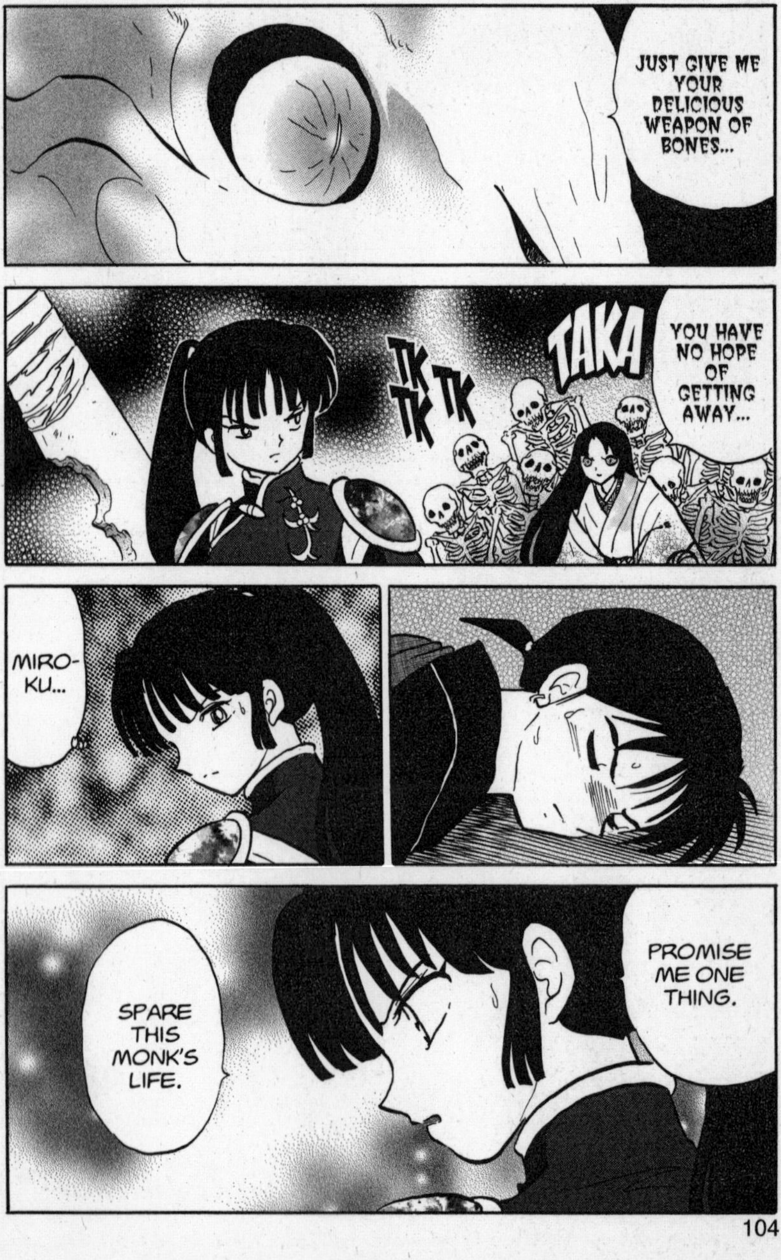
JUST GIVE ME YOUR DELICIOUS WEAPON OF BONES...
YOU HAVE NO HOPE OF GETTING AWAY...
TAKA
TK TK TK
MIRO-KU...
PROMISE ME ONE THING.
SPARE THIS MONK'S LIFE.

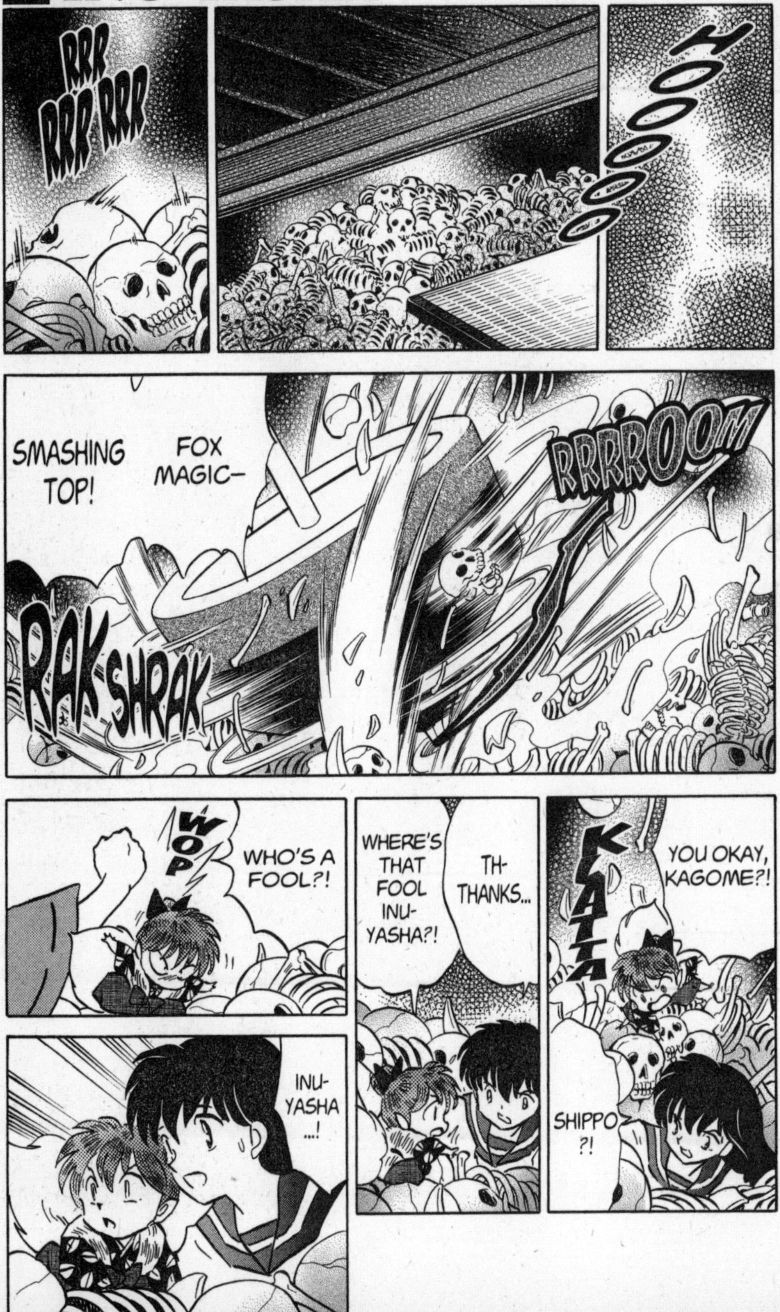
HOOOOOOO
RRR RRR RRR
RRRROOM
FOX MAGIC—
SMASHING TOP!
RAK SHRAK
YOU OKAY, KAGOME?!
KATTA
SHIPPO?!
TH-THANKS...
WHERE'S THAT FOOL INU-YASHA?!
WOP
WHO'S A FOOL?!
INU-YASHA...!

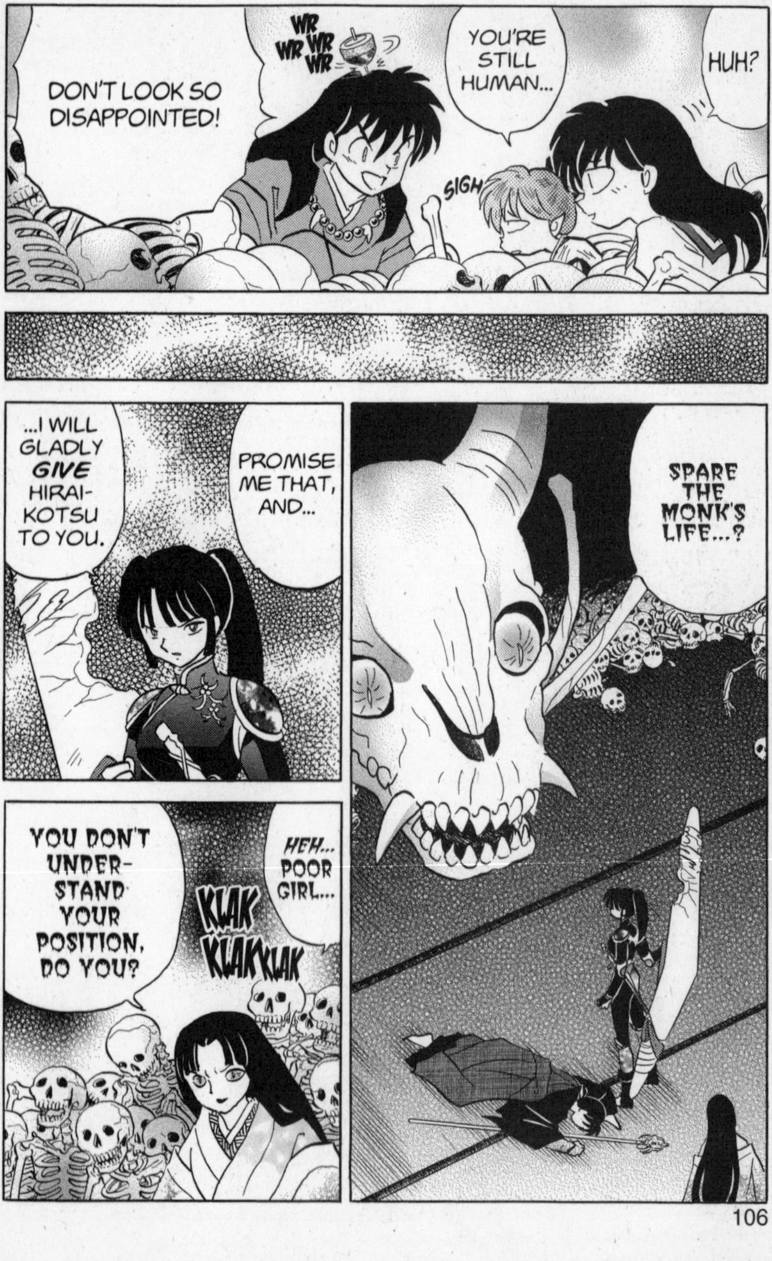
HUH?
YOU'RE STILL HUMAN...
SIGH
WR WR WR WR
DON'T LOOK SO DISAPPOINTED!
SPARE THE MONK'S LIFE...?
PROMISE ME THAT, AND...
...I WILL GLADLY *GIVE* HIRAI-KOTSU TO YOU.
HEH... POOR GIRL...
KLAK KLAK KLAK
YOU DON'T UNDER-STAND YOUR POSITION, DO YOU?

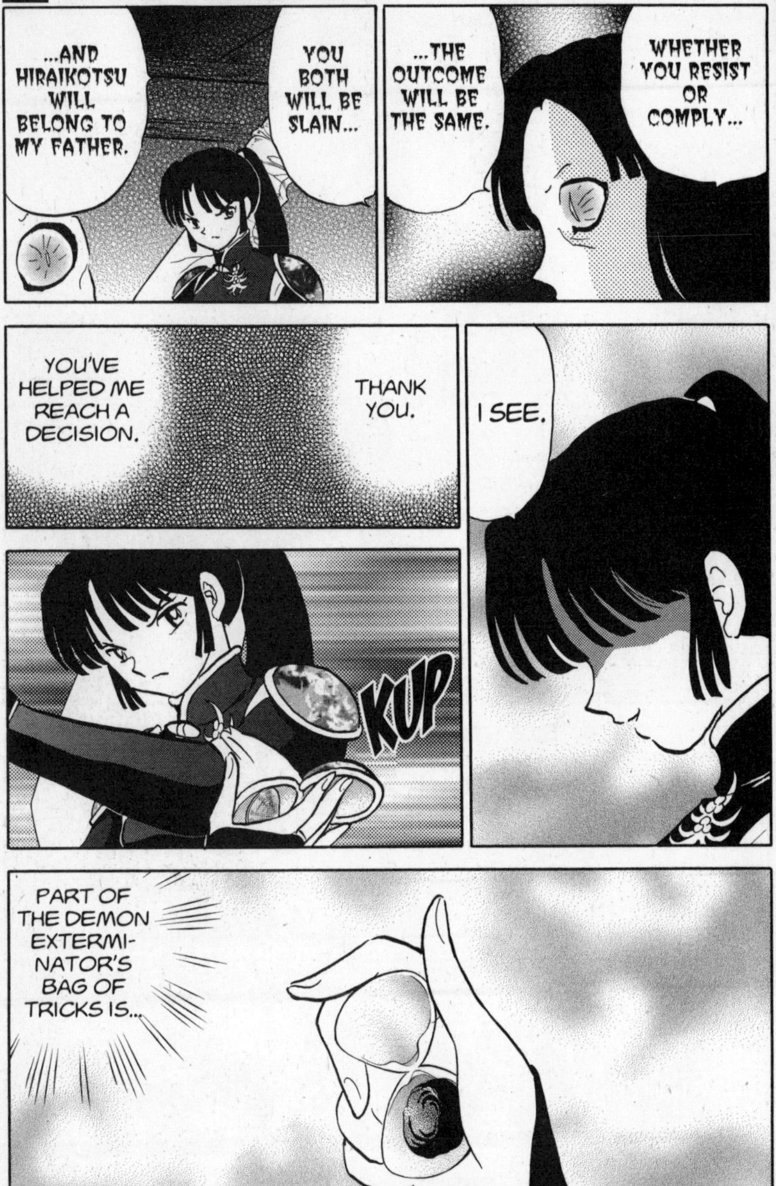
WHETHER YOU RESIST OR COMPLY...
...THE OUTCOME WILL BE THE SAME.
YOU BOTH WILL BE SLAIN...
...AND HIRAIKOTSU WILL BELONG TO MY FATHER.
I SEE.
THANK YOU.
YOU'VE HELPED ME REACH A DECISION.
KUP
PART OF THE DEMON EXTERMI-NATOR'S BAG OF TRICKS IS...

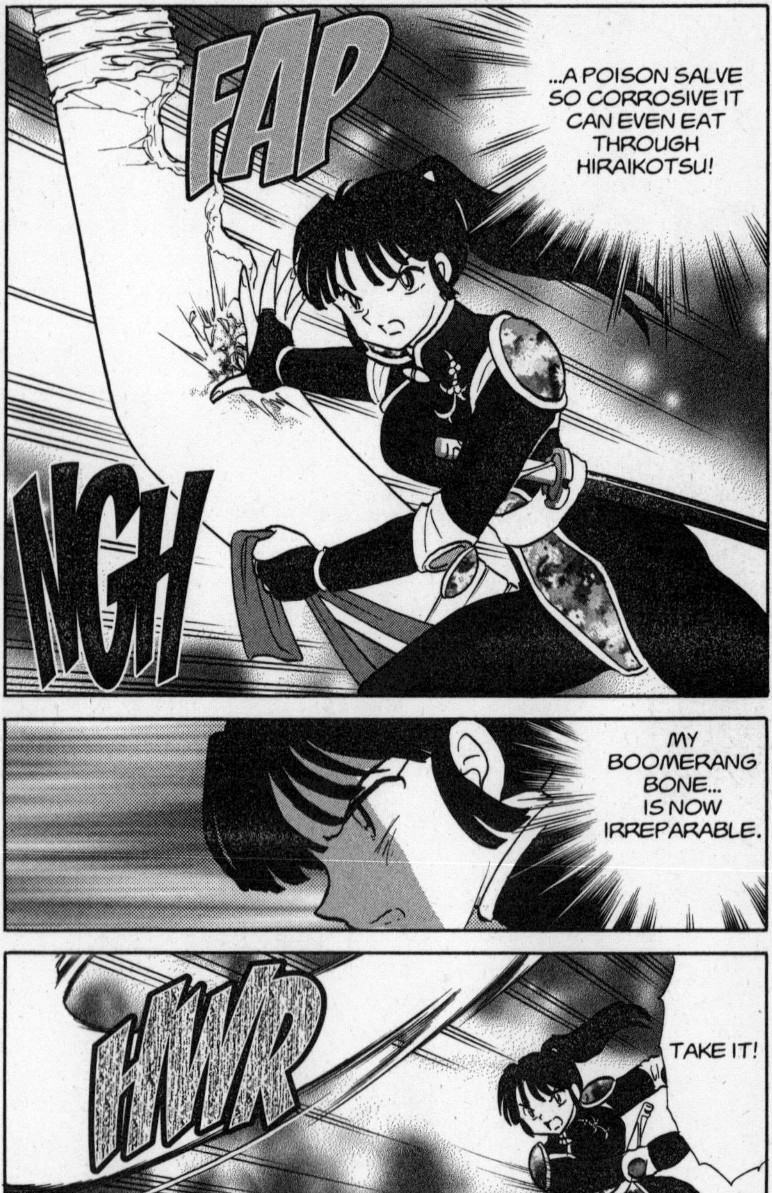
FAP
...A POISON SALVE SO CORROSIVE IT CAN EVEN EAT THROUGH HIRAIKOTSU!
NGH
MY BOOMERANG BONE... IS NOW IRREPARABLE.
HWR
TAKE IT!

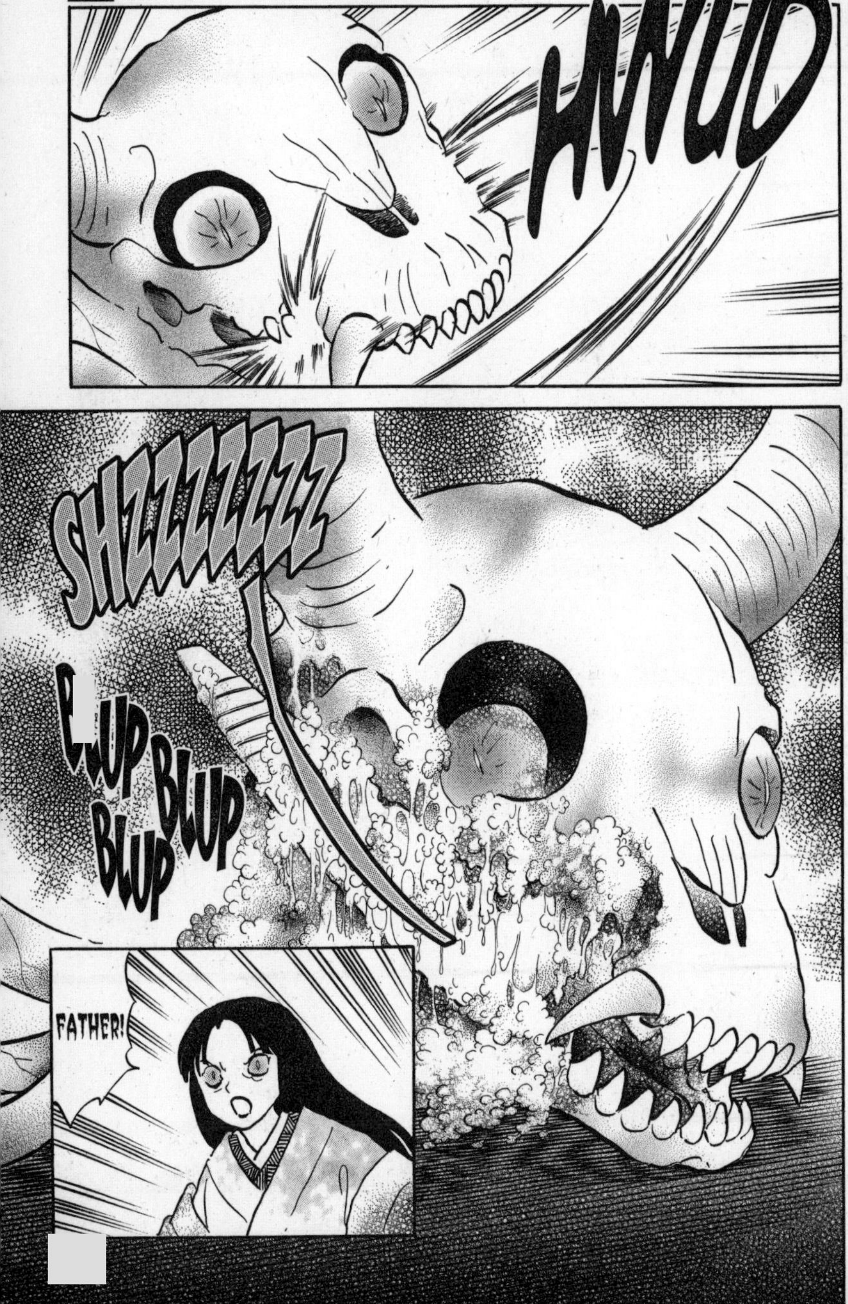
HWUD
SHZZZZZZZ
BLUP
BLUP
FATHER!

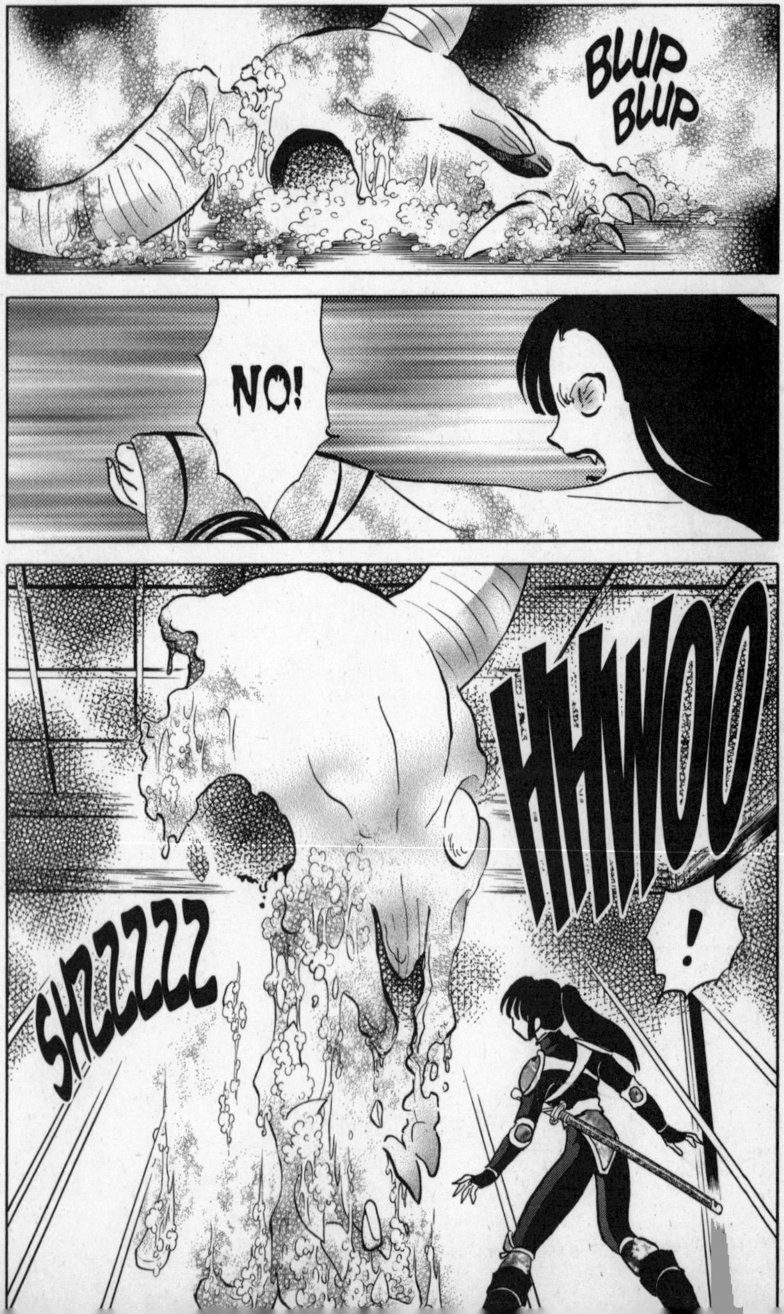
BLUP
BLUP
NO!
HHWOO
!
SHZZZZZ

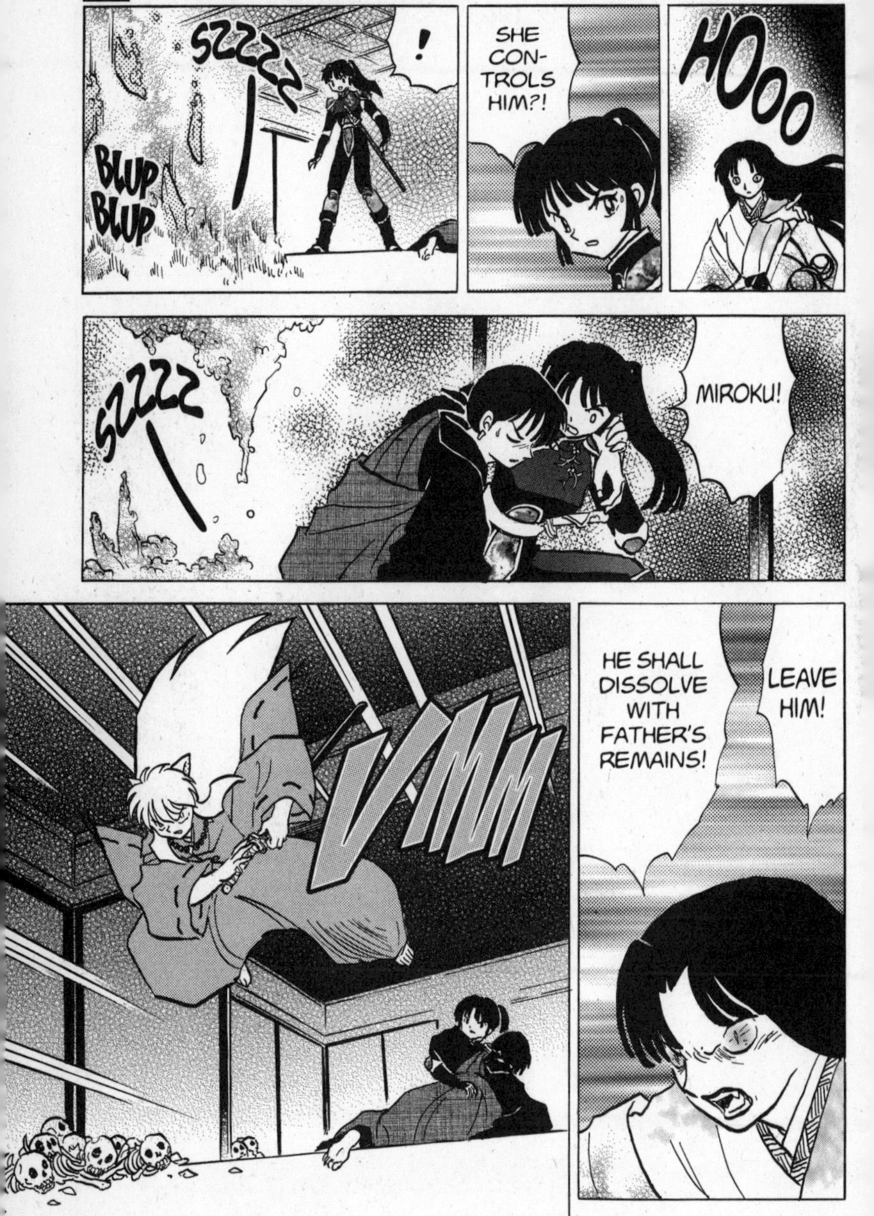
HOOO
SHE CONTROLS HIM?!
!
SZZZZ
BLUP BLUP
MIROKU!
SZZZZ
LEAVE HIM!
HE SHALL DISSOLVE WITH FATHER'S REMAINS!
VMM

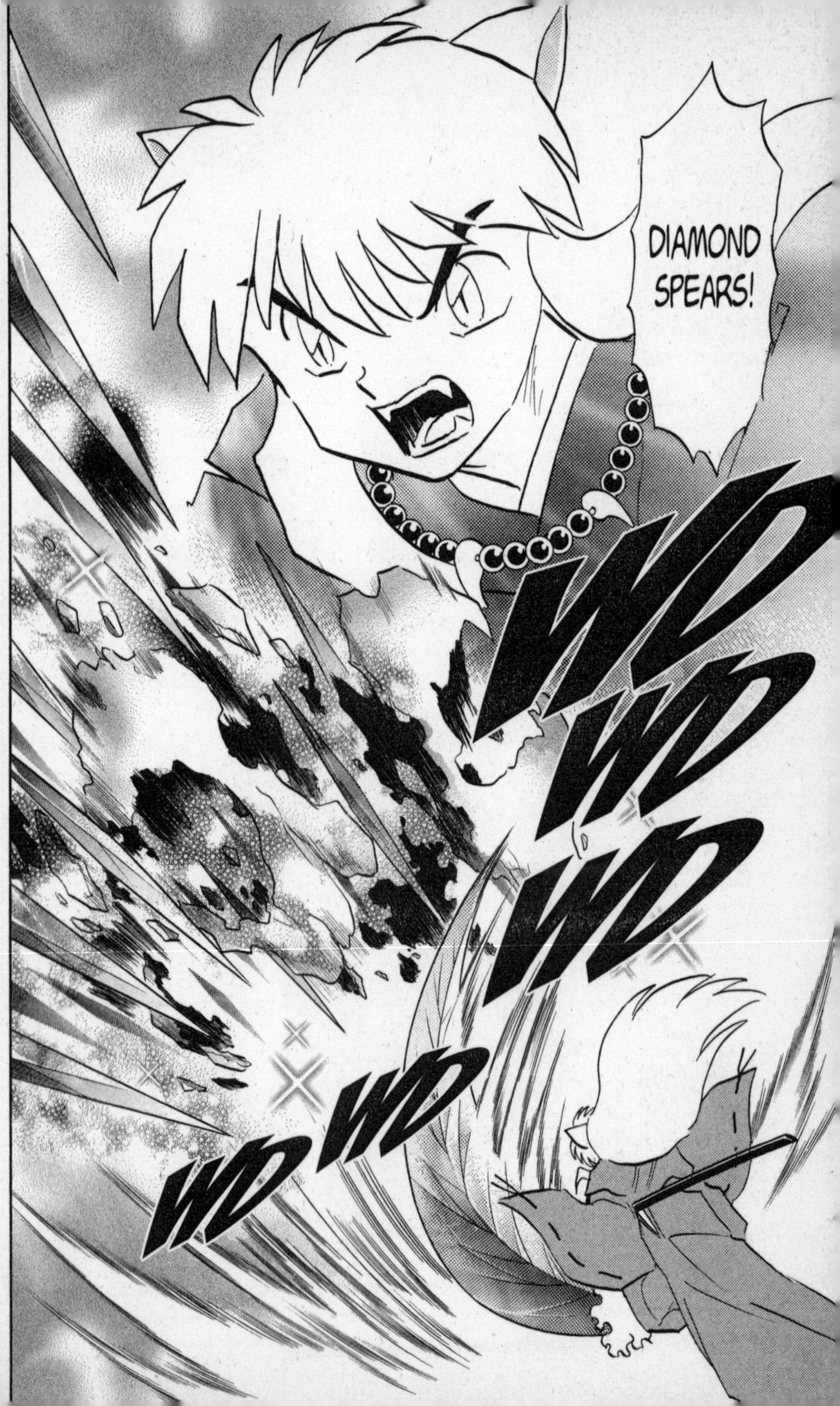
DIAMOND SPEARS!

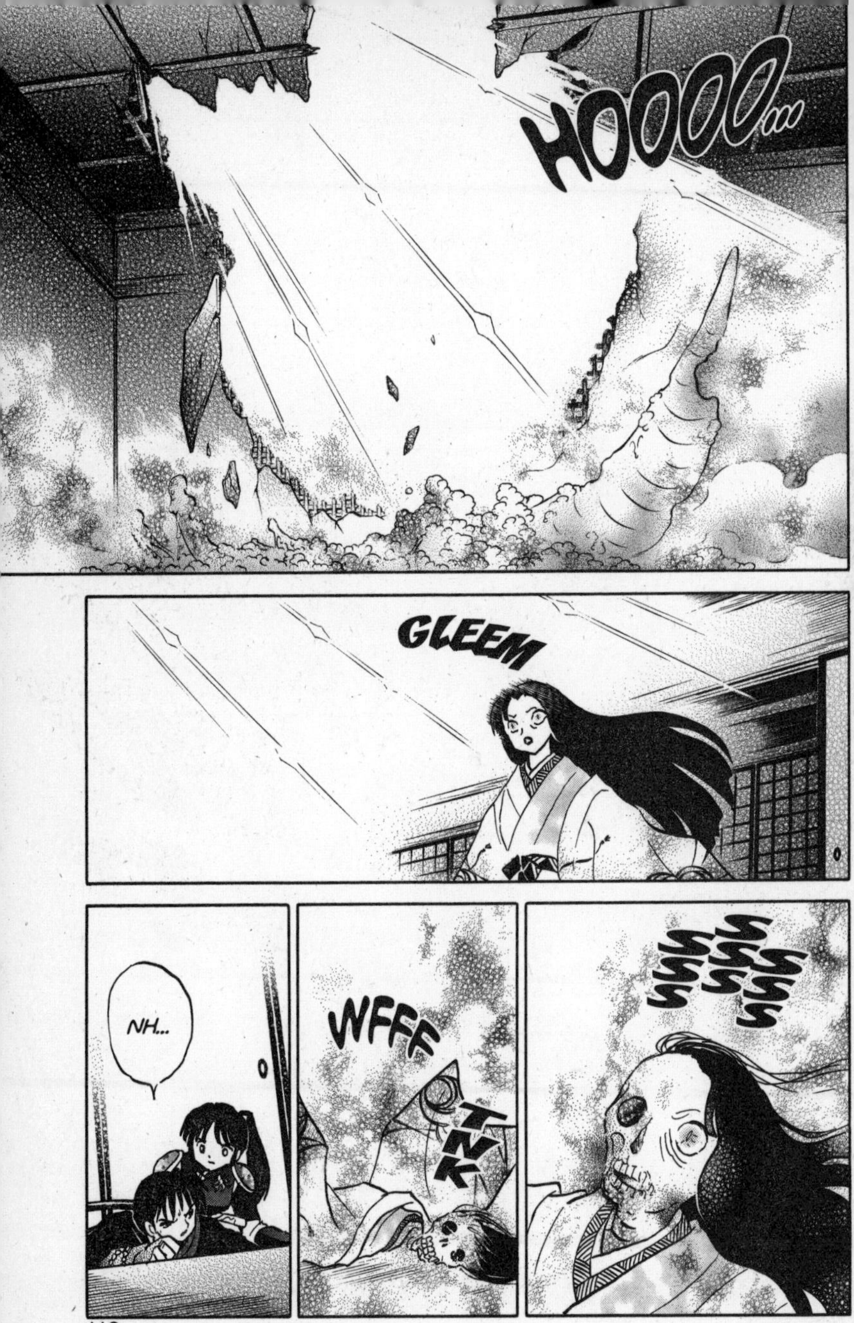
HOOOO...
GLEEM
SSSS SSSS SSSS
WFFF
TNK
NH...

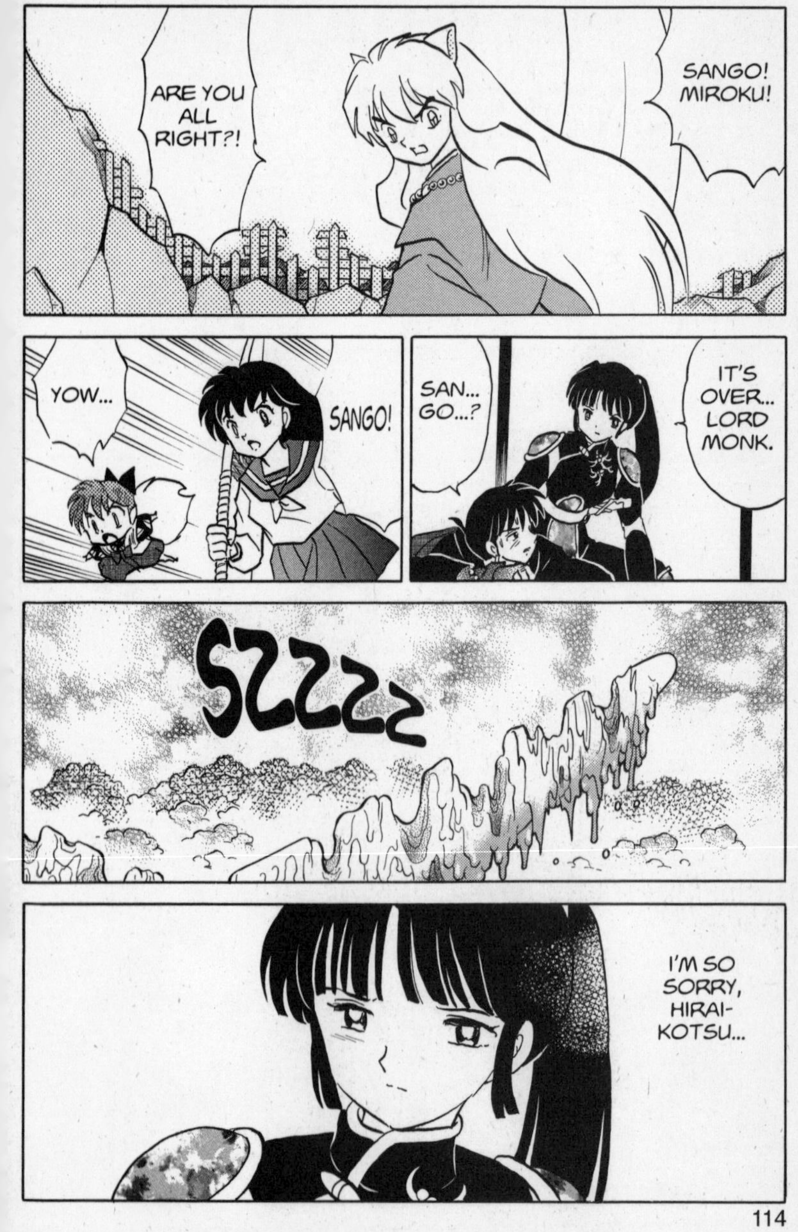
SANGO! MIROKU!
ARE YOU ALL RIGHT?!
IT'S OVER... LORD MONK.
SAN... GO...?
SANGO!
YOW...
SZZZZ
I'M SO SORRY, HIRAI-KOTSU...

SCROLL 7
MASTER OF POTIONS

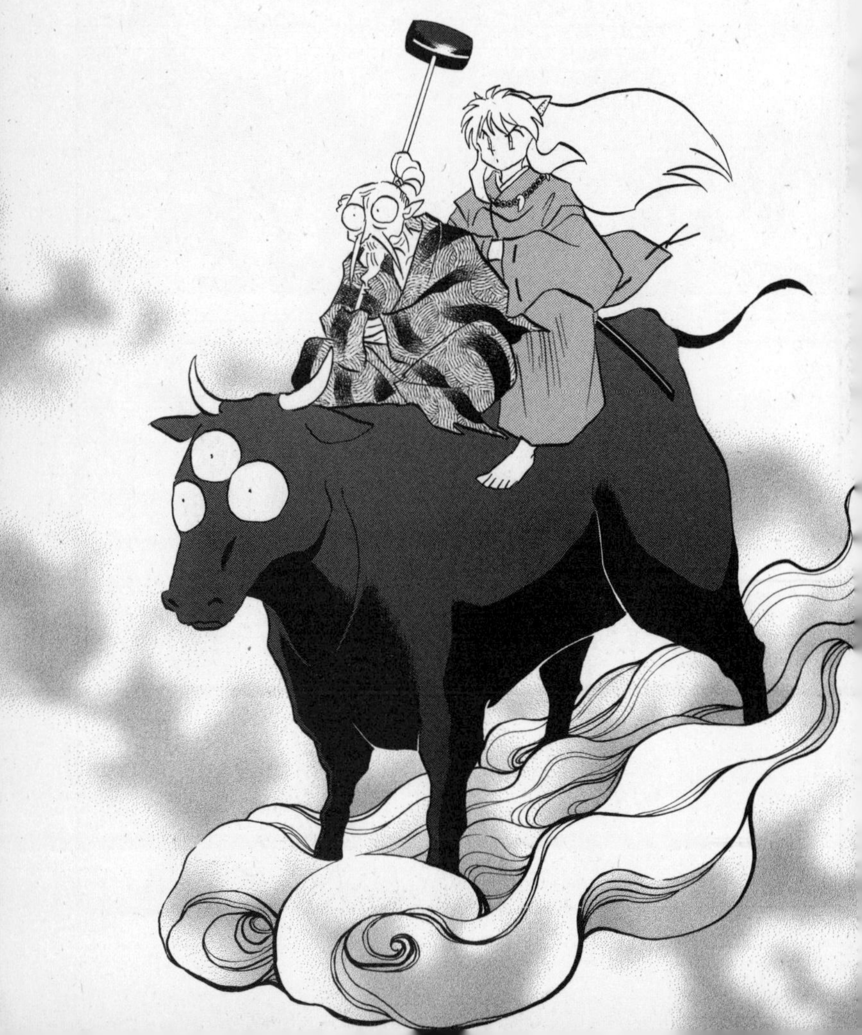

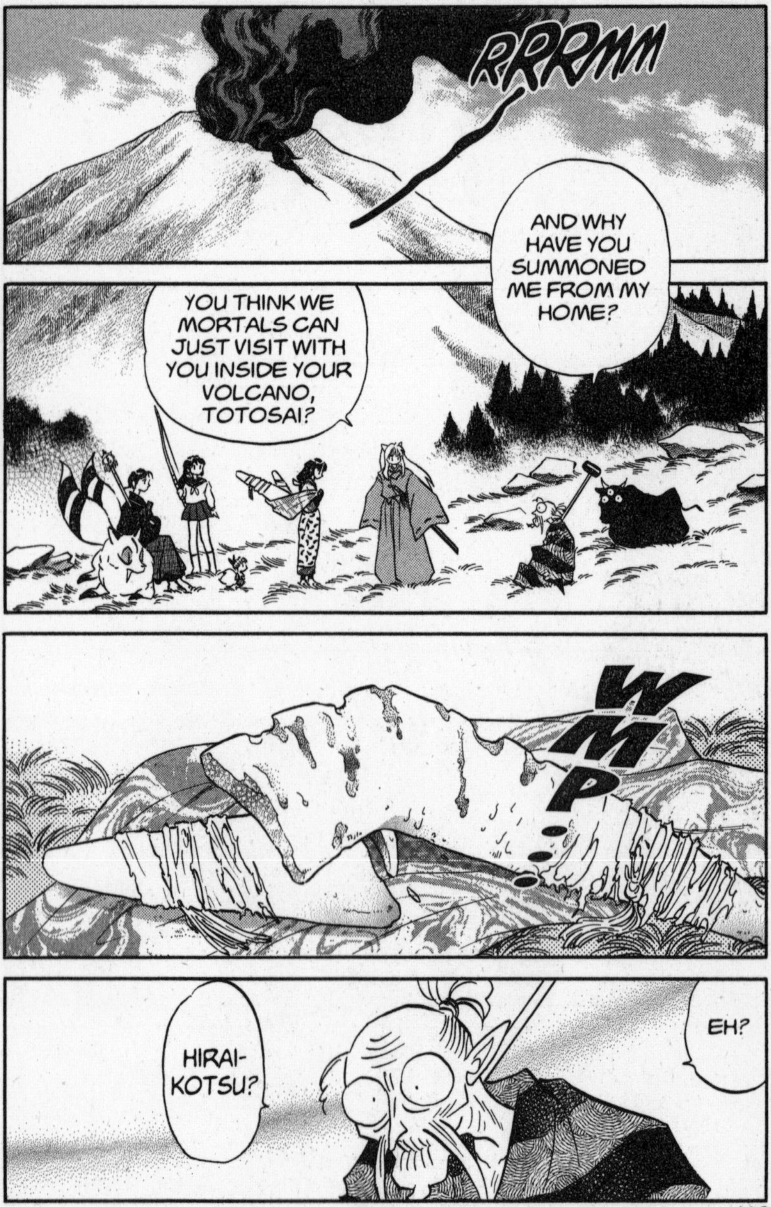
RRRMM
AND WHY HAVE YOU SUMMONED ME FROM MY HOME?
YOU THINK WE MORTALS CAN JUST VISIT WITH YOU INSIDE YOUR VOLCANO, TOTOSAI?
WMP
EH?
HIRAI-KOTSU?

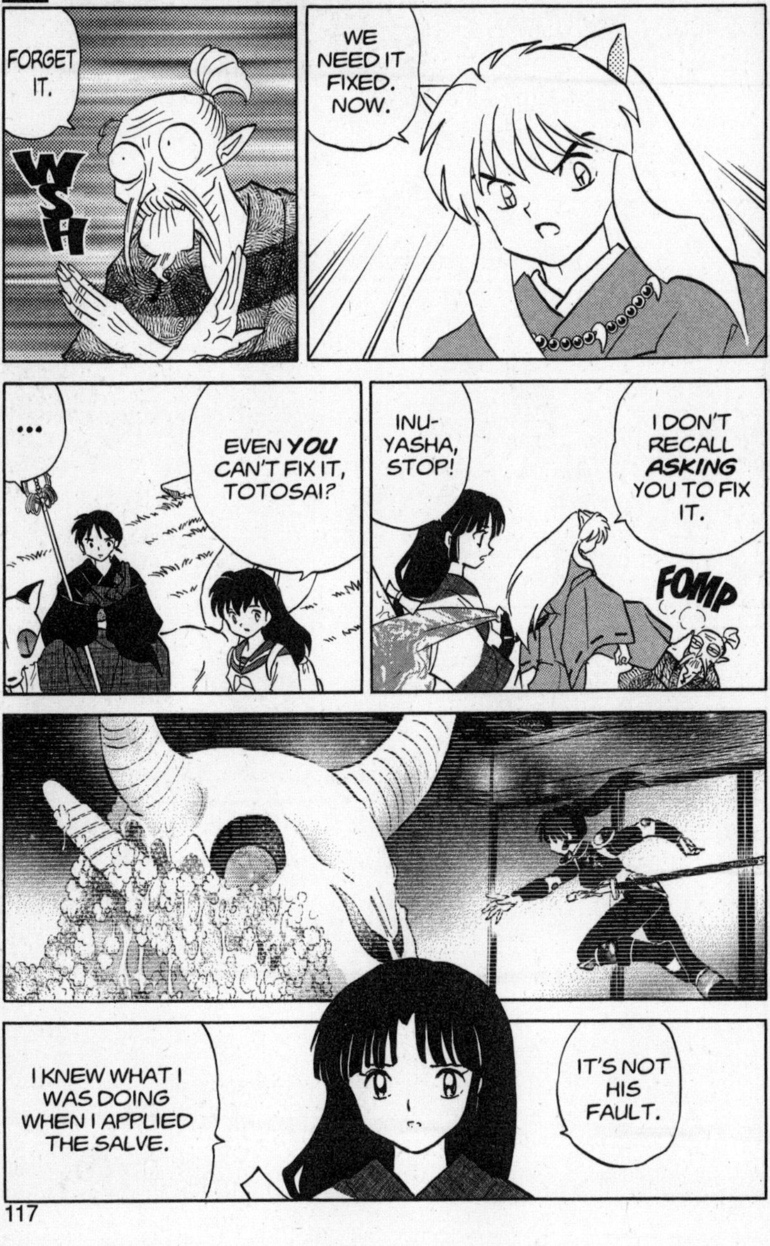
WE NEED IT FIXED. NOW.
FORGET IT.
WSH
I DON'T RECALL **ASKING** YOU TO FIX IT.
INU-YASHA, STOP!
FOMP
EVEN ***YOU*** CAN'T FIX IT, TOTOSAI?
...
IT'S NOT HIS FAULT.
I KNEW WHAT I WAS DOING WHEN I APPLIED THE SALVE.

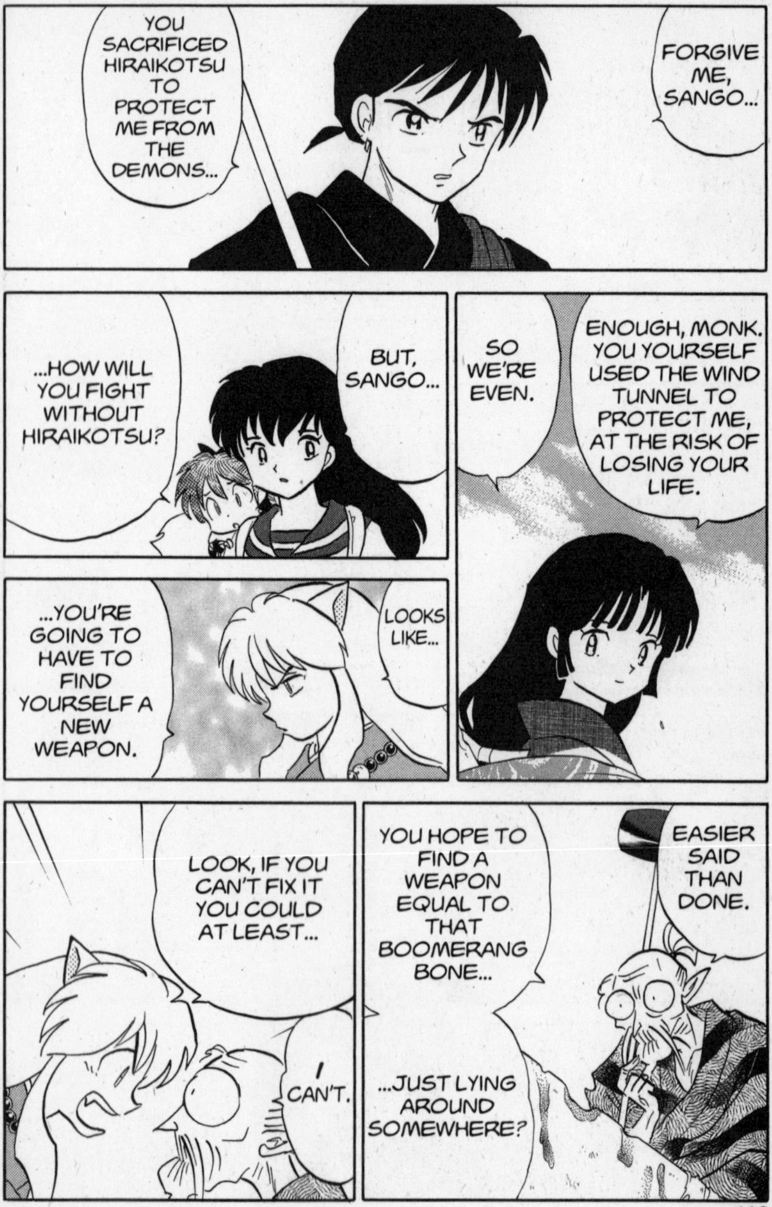
FORGIVE ME, SANGO...
YOU SACRIFICED HIRAIKOTSU TO PROTECT ME FROM THE DEMONS...
ENOUGH, MONK. YOU YOURSELF USED THE WIND TUNNEL TO PROTECT ME, AT THE RISK OF LOSING YOUR LIFE.
SO WE'RE EVEN.
BUT, SANGO...
...HOW WILL YOU FIGHT WITHOUT HIRAIKOTSU?
LOOKS LIKE...
...YOU'RE GOING TO HAVE TO FIND YOURSELF A NEW WEAPON.
EASIER SAID THAN DONE.
YOU HOPE TO FIND A WEAPON EQUAL TO THAT BOOMERANG BONE...
...JUST LYING AROUND SOMEWHERE?
LOOK, IF YOU CAN'T FIX IT YOU COULD AT LEAST...
I CAN'T.

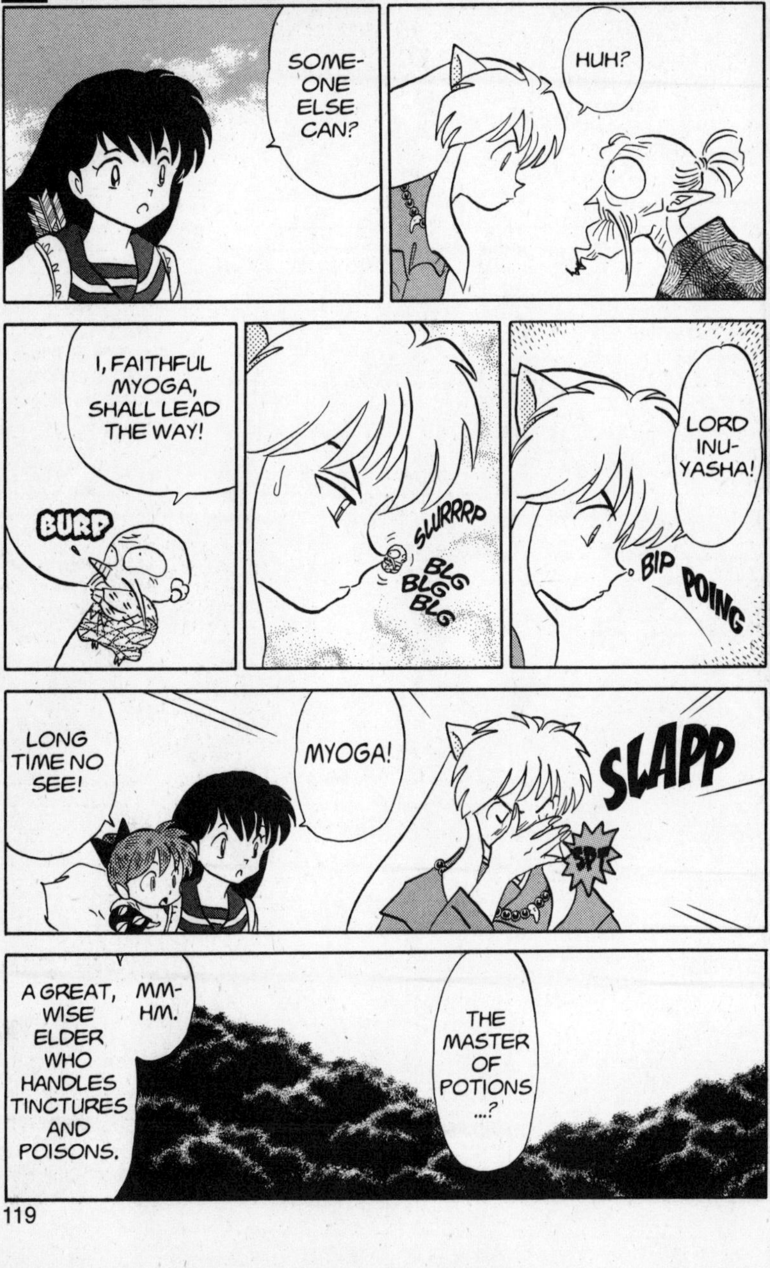
HUH?
SOME-ONE ELSE CAN?
LORD INU-YASHA!
BIP
POING
SLURRRP
BLG BLG BLG
I, FAITHFUL MYOGA, SHALL LEAD THE WAY!
BURP
SLAPP
SPT
MYOGA!
LONG TIME NO SEE!
THE MASTER OF POTIONS ...?
MM-HM.
A GREAT, WISE ELDER WHO HANDLES TINCTURES AND POISONS.

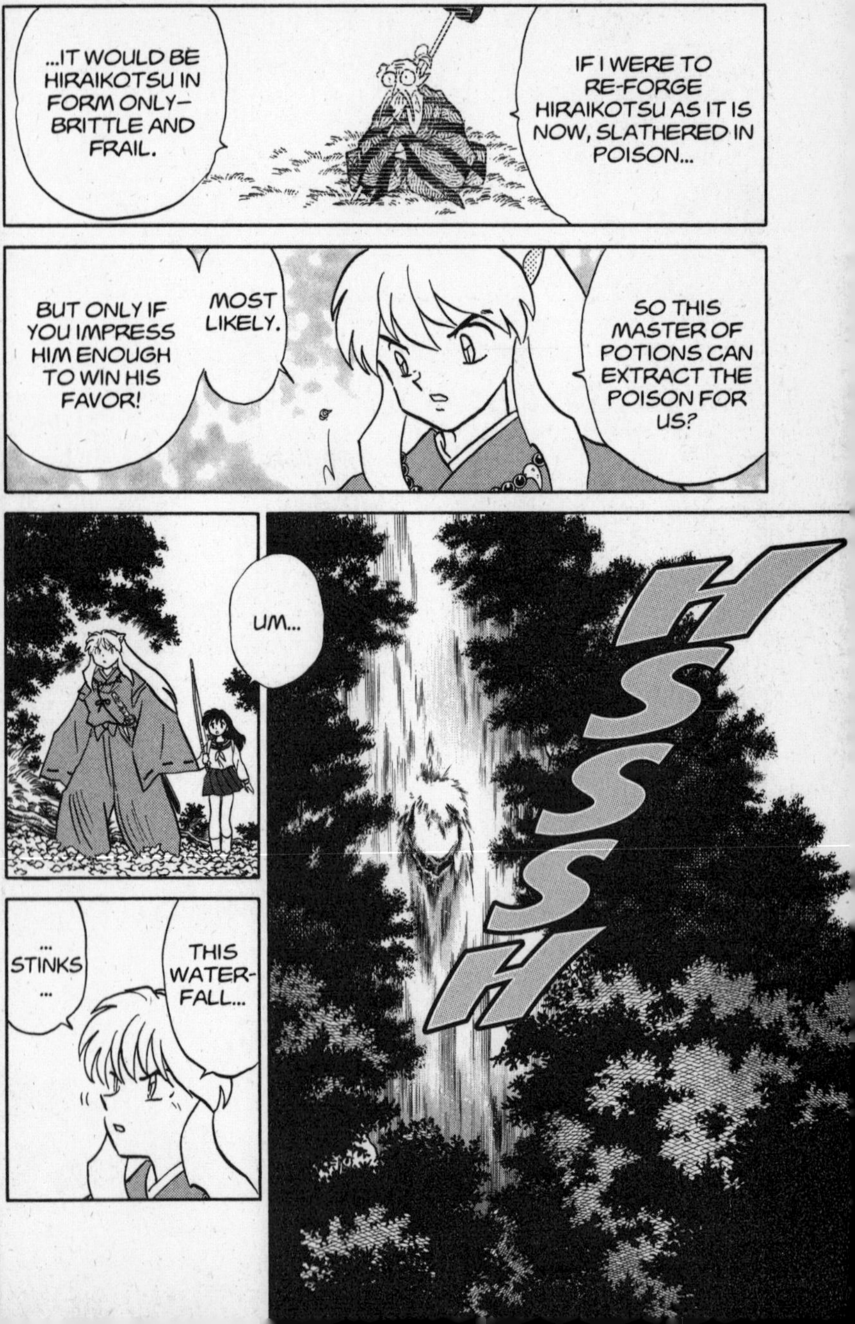
IF I WERE TO RE-FORGE HIRAIKOTSU AS IT IS NOW, SLATHERED IN POISON...
...IT WOULD BE HIRAIKOTSU IN FORM ONLY— BRITTLE AND FRAIL.
SO THIS MASTER OF POTIONS CAN EXTRACT THE POISON FOR US?
MOST LIKELY.
BUT ONLY IF YOU IMPRESS HIM ENOUGH TO WIN HIS FAVOR!
HSSSH
UM...
THIS WATER-FALL...
... STINKS ...

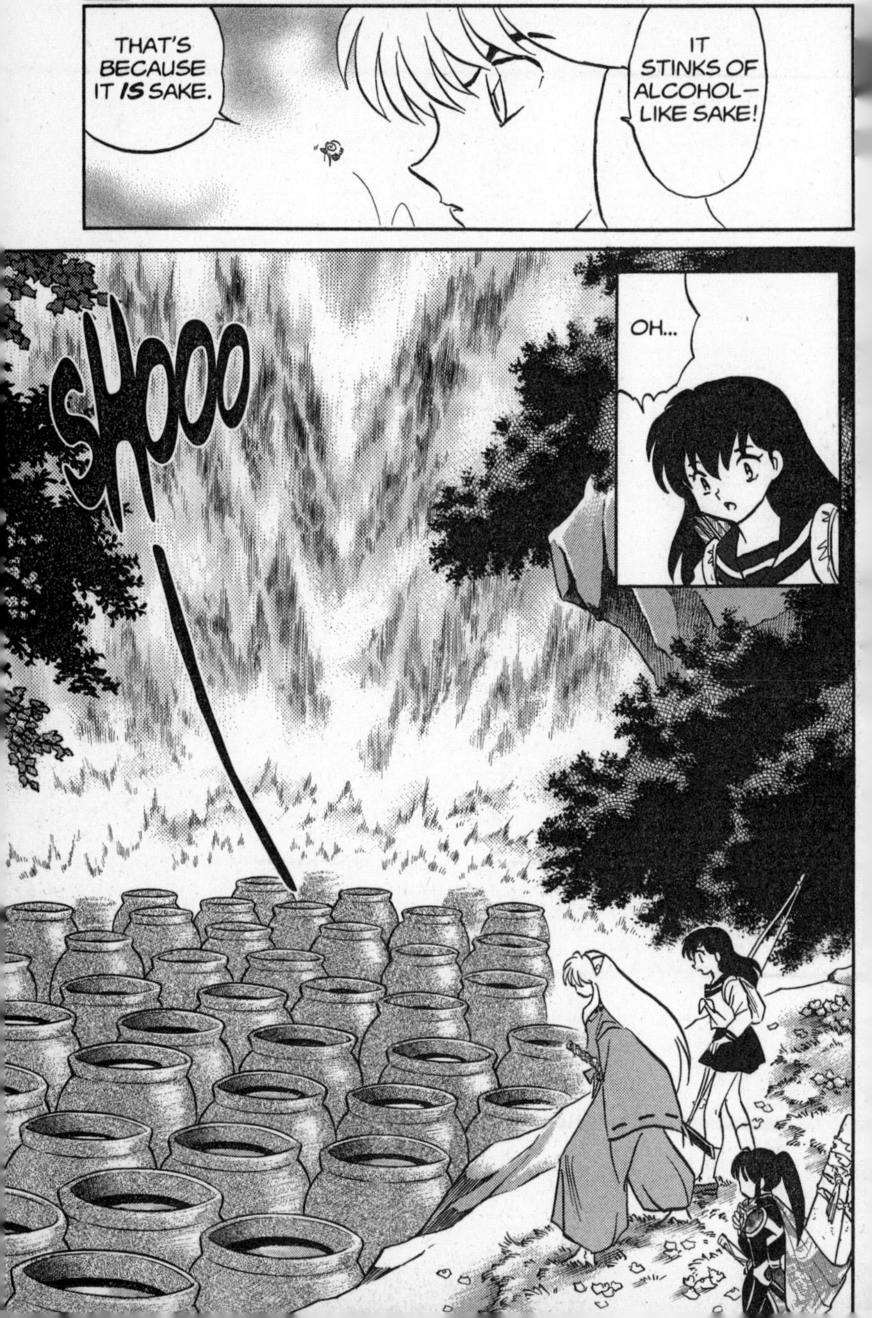
IT STINKS OF ALCOHOL— LIKE SAKE!
THAT'S BECAUSE IT *IS* SAKE.
OH...
SHOOO

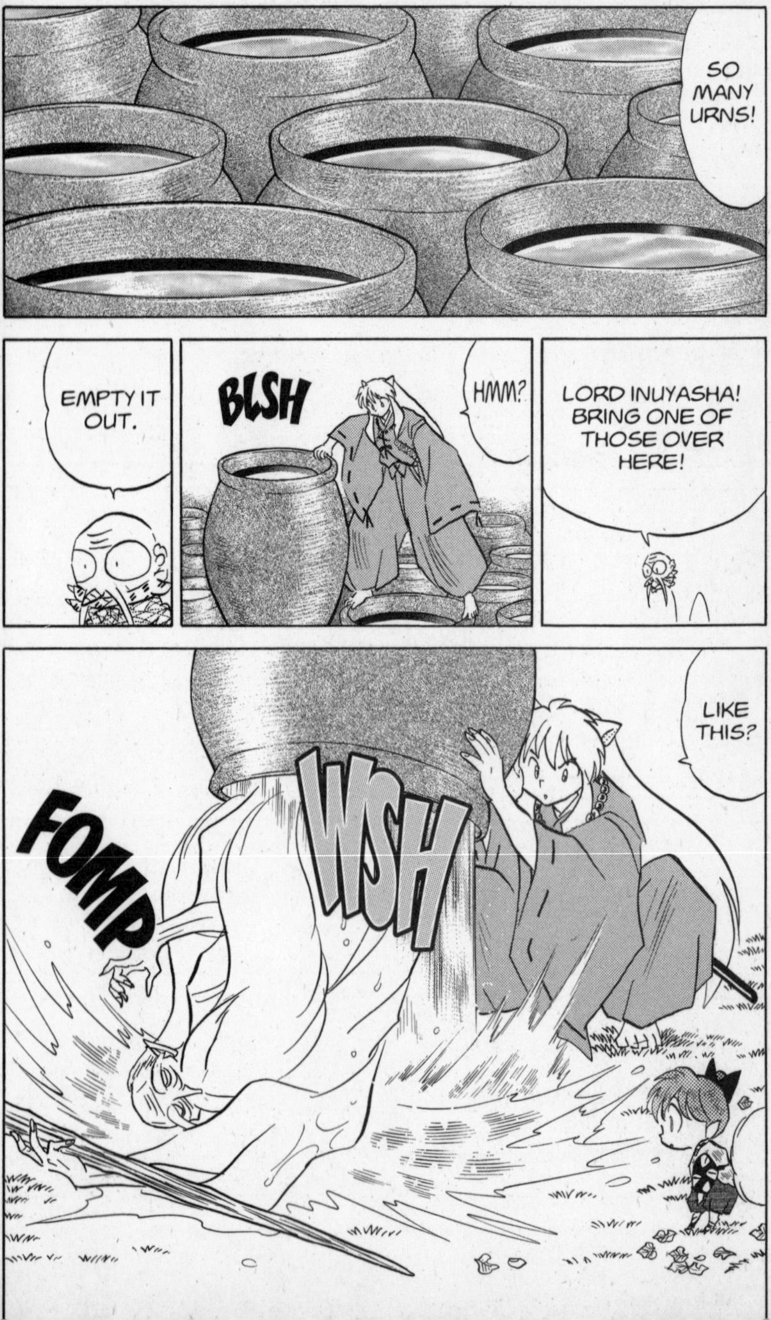
SO MANY URNS!
LORD INUYASHA! BRING ONE OF THOSE OVER HERE!
HMM?
BLSH
EMPTY IT OUT.
LIKE THIS?
WSH
FOMP

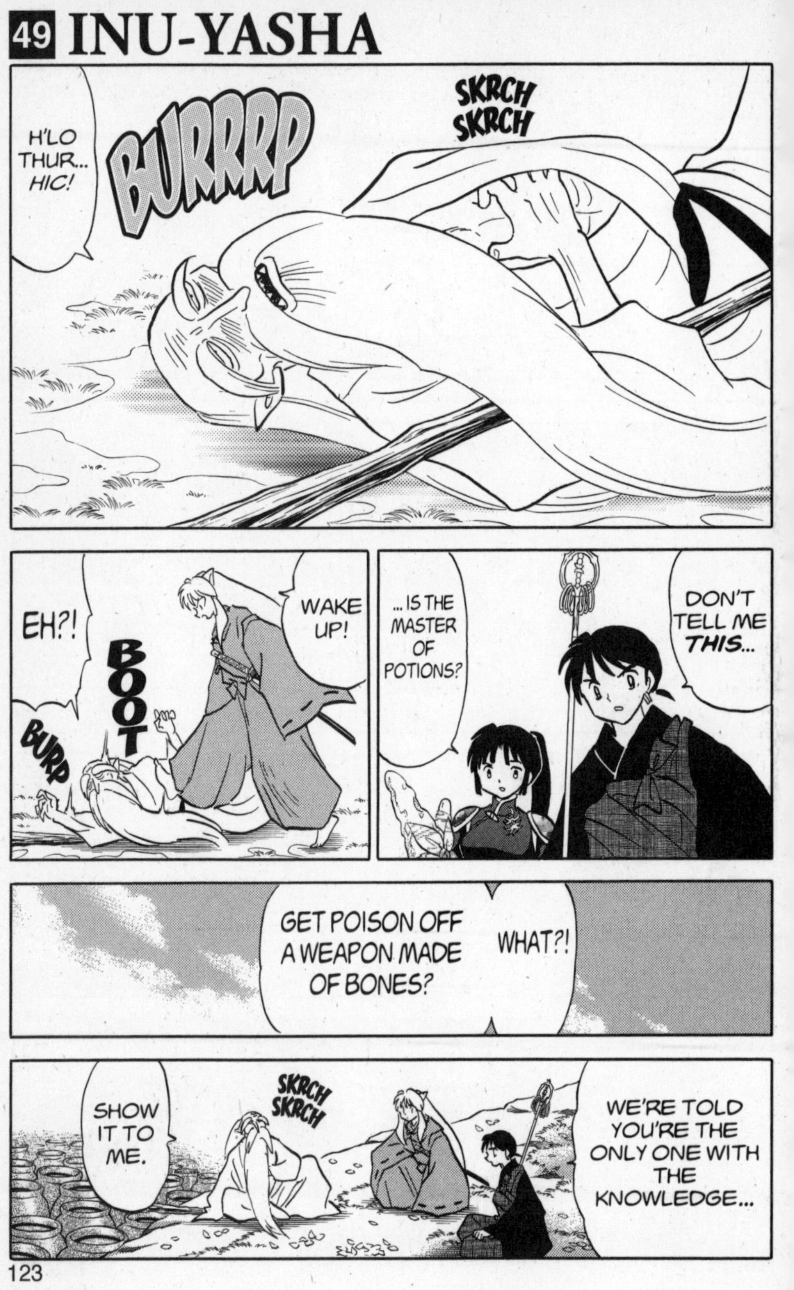
SKRCH SKRCH
BURRRP
H'LO THUR... HIC!
DON'T TELL ME THIS...
...IS THE MASTER OF POTIONS?
WAKE UP!
BOOT
EH?!
BURP
WHAT?!
GET POISON OFF A WEAPON MADE OF BONES?
WE'RE TOLD YOU'RE THE ONLY ONE WITH THE KNOWLEDGE...
SKRCH SKRCH
SHOW IT TO ME.

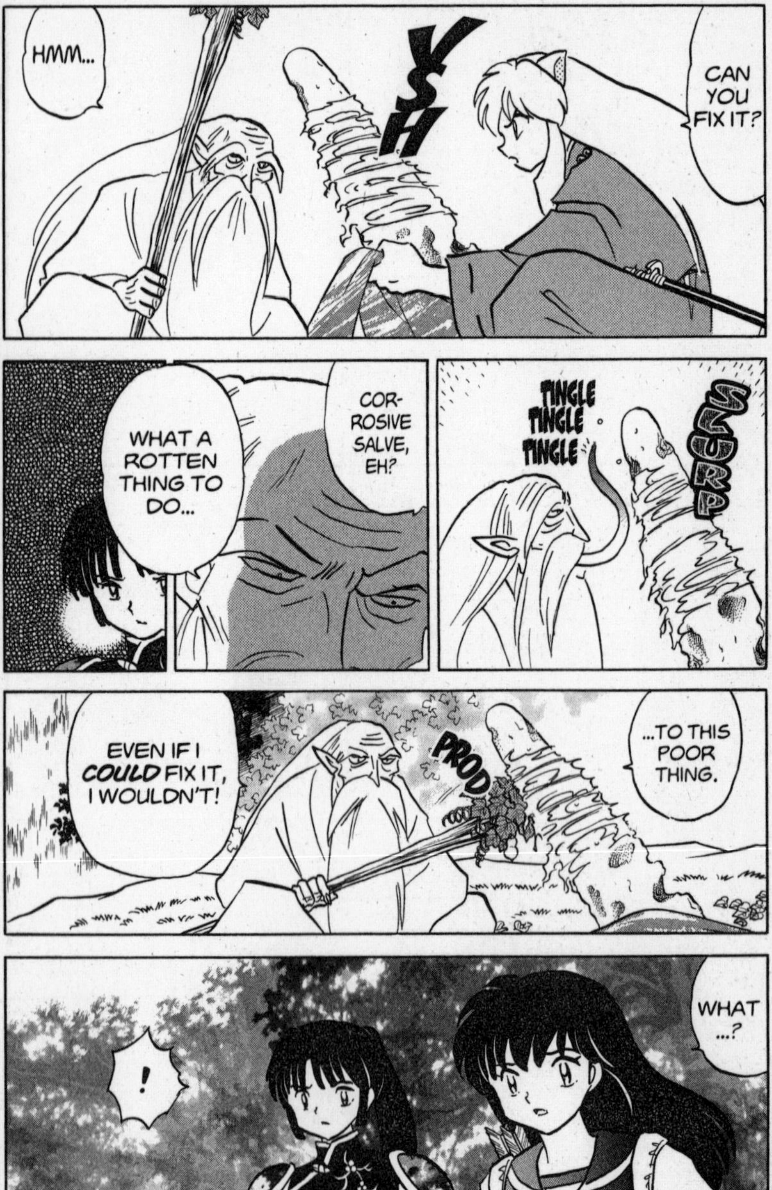
CAN YOU FIX IT?
VSH
HMM...
SLURP
TINGLE TINGLE TINGLE
COR-ROSIVE SALVE, EH?
WHAT A ROTTEN THING TO DO...
...TO THIS POOR THING.
PROD
EVEN IF I **COULD** FIX IT, I WOULDN'T!
WHAT ...?
!

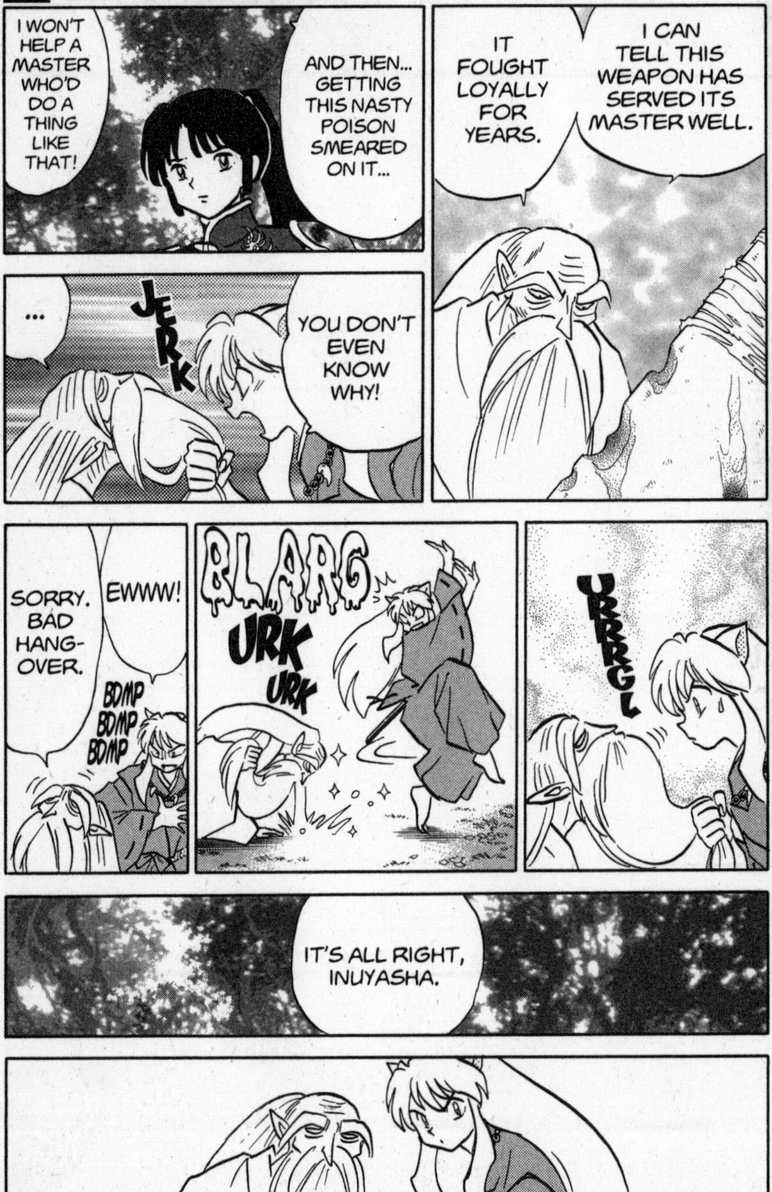
I CAN TELL THIS WEAPON HAS SERVED ITS MASTER WELL.
IT FOUGHT LOYALLY FOR YEARS.
AND THEN... GETTING THIS NASTY POISON SMEARED ON IT...
I WON'T HELP A MASTER WHO'D DO A THING LIKE THAT!
YOU DON'T EVEN KNOW WHY!
JERK
...
URRRGL
BLARG
URK
URK
EWWW!
SORRY. BAD HANG-OVER.
BDMP BDMP BDMP
IT'S ALL RIGHT, INUYASHA.

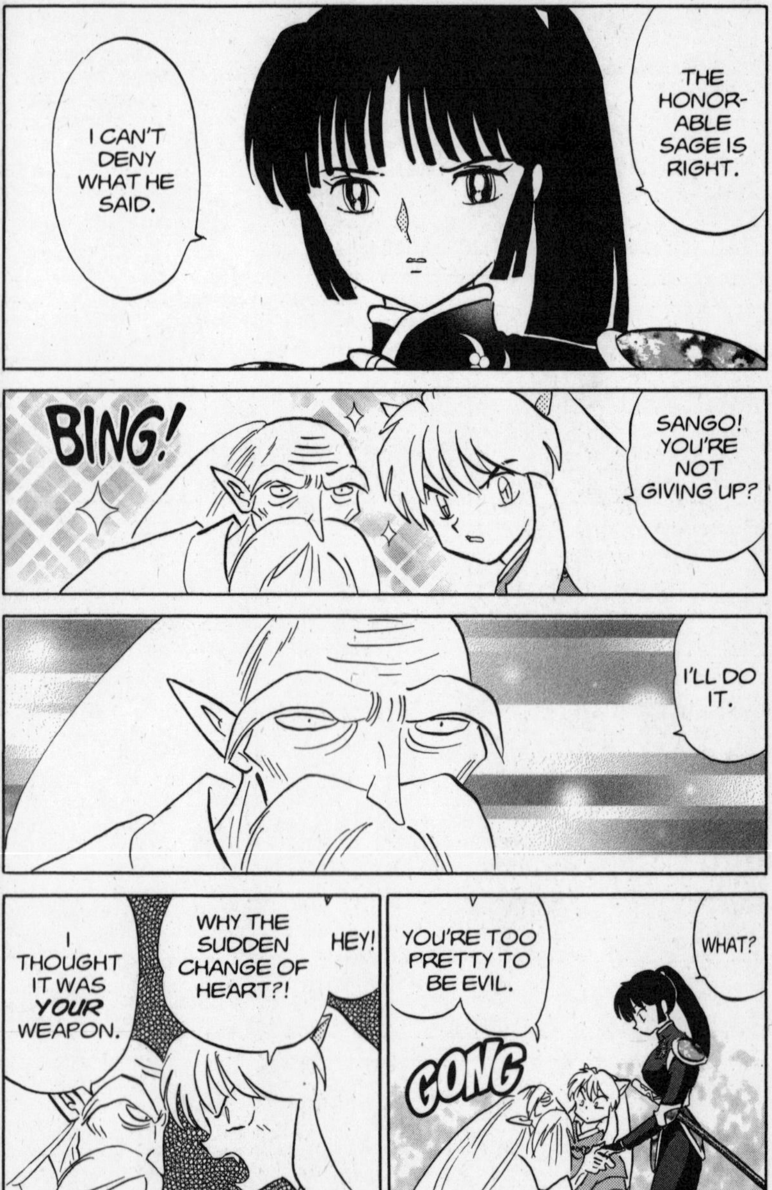
THE HONORABLE SAGE IS RIGHT.
I CAN'T DENY WHAT HE SAID.
SANGO! YOU'RE NOT GIVING UP?
BING!
I'LL DO IT.
WHAT?
YOU'RE TOO PRETTY TO BE EVIL.
GONG
HEY!
WHY THE SUDDEN CHANGE OF HEART?!
I THOUGHT IT WAS YOUR WEAPON.

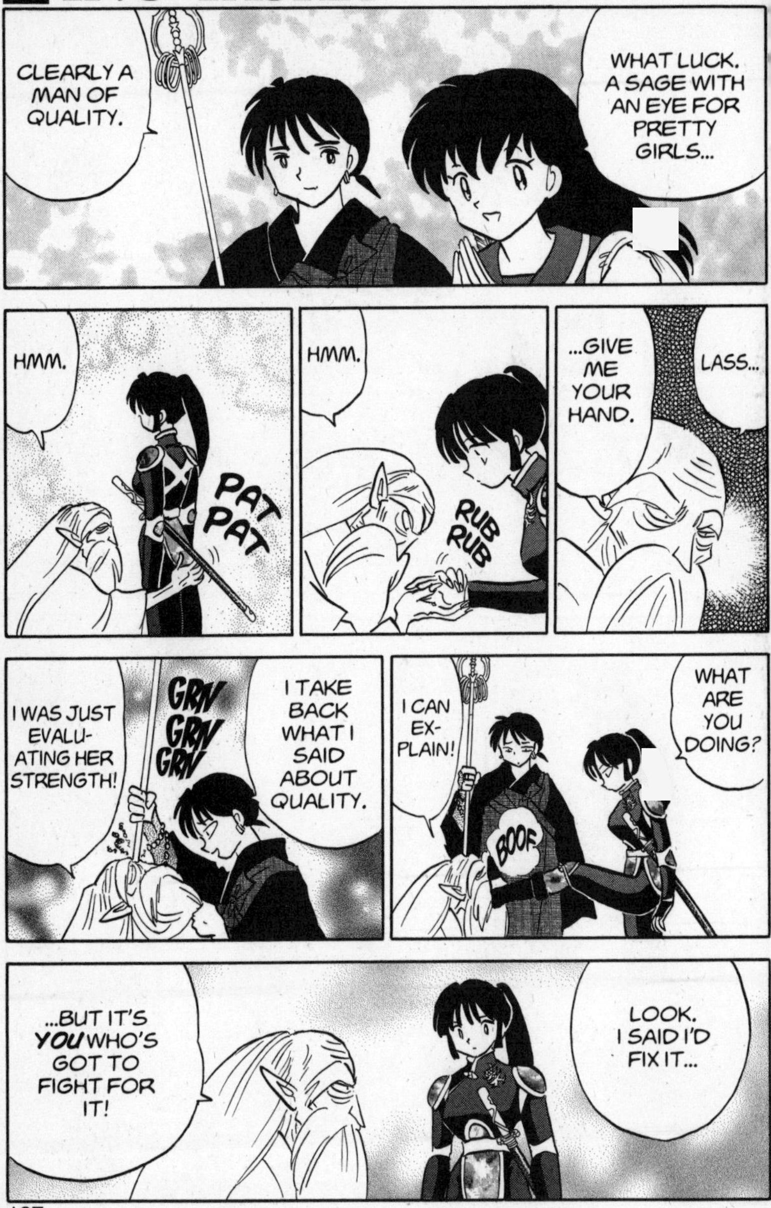
WHAT LUCK. A SAGE WITH AN EYE FOR PRETTY GIRLS...
CLEARLY A MAN OF QUALITY.
LASS...
...GIVE ME YOUR HAND.
HMM.
RUB RUB
HMM.
PAT PAT
WHAT ARE YOU DOING?
I CAN EX-PLAIN!
BOOF
I TAKE BACK WHAT I SAID ABOUT QUALITY.
GRIN GRIN GRIN
I WAS JUST EVALU-ATING HER STRENGTH!
LOOK. I SAID I'D FIX IT...
...BUT IT'S YOU WHO'S GOT TO FIGHT FOR IT!

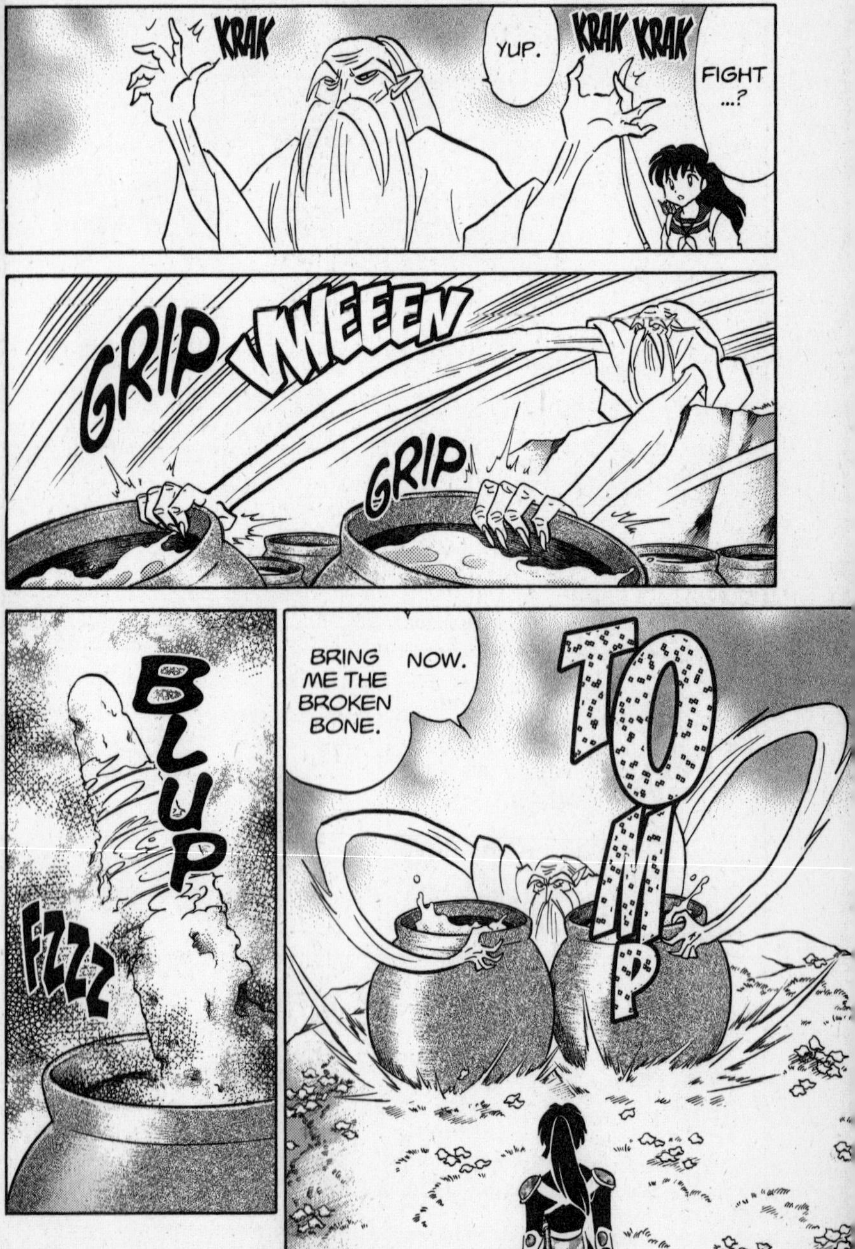
FIGHT ...?
KRAK KRAK
YUP.
KRAK
VWEEEN
GRIP
GRIP
TOMP
NOW.
BRING ME THE BROKEN BONE.
BLUP
FZZZ

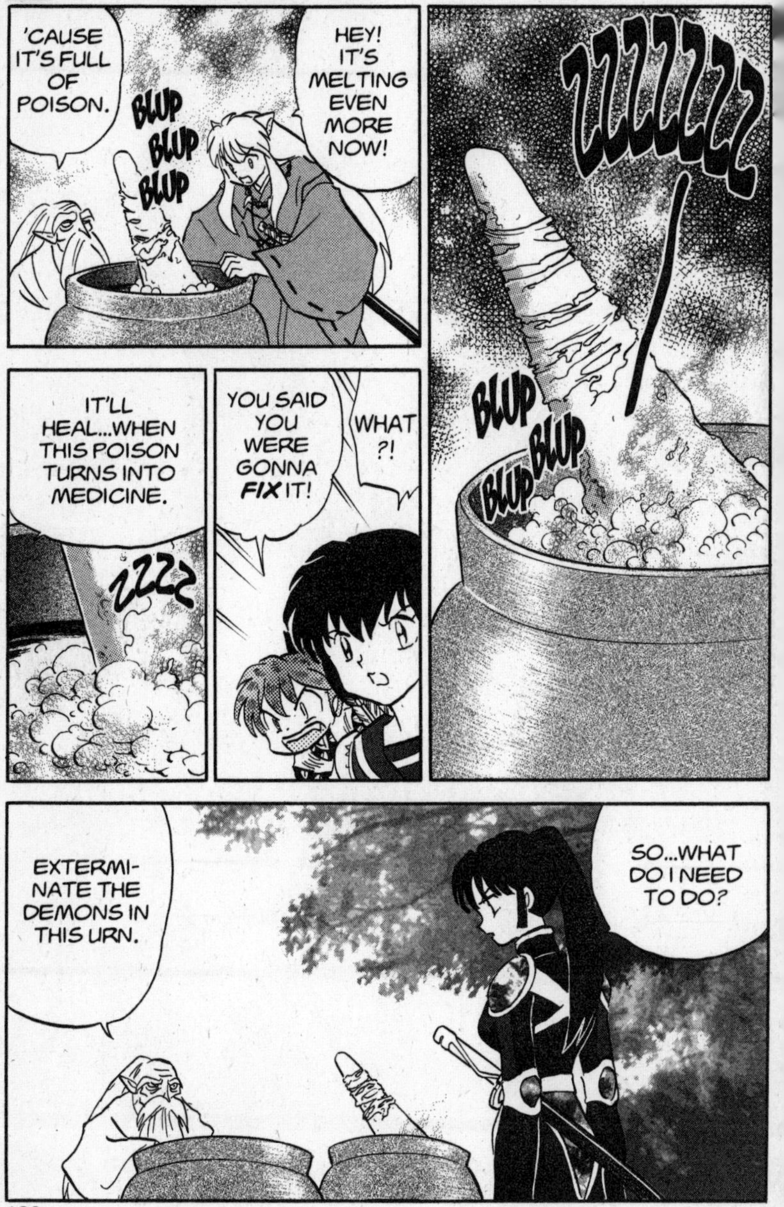
ZZZZZZZ
BLUP BLUP BLUP
HEY! IT'S MELTING EVEN MORE NOW!
'CAUSE IT'S FULL OF POISON.
BLUP BLUP BLUP
WHAT ?!
YOU SAID YOU WERE GONNA *FIX* IT!
IT'LL HEAL...WHEN THIS POISON TURNS INTO MEDICINE.
ZZZZ
SO...WHAT DO I NEED TO DO?
EXTERMI-NATE THE DEMONS IN THIS URN.

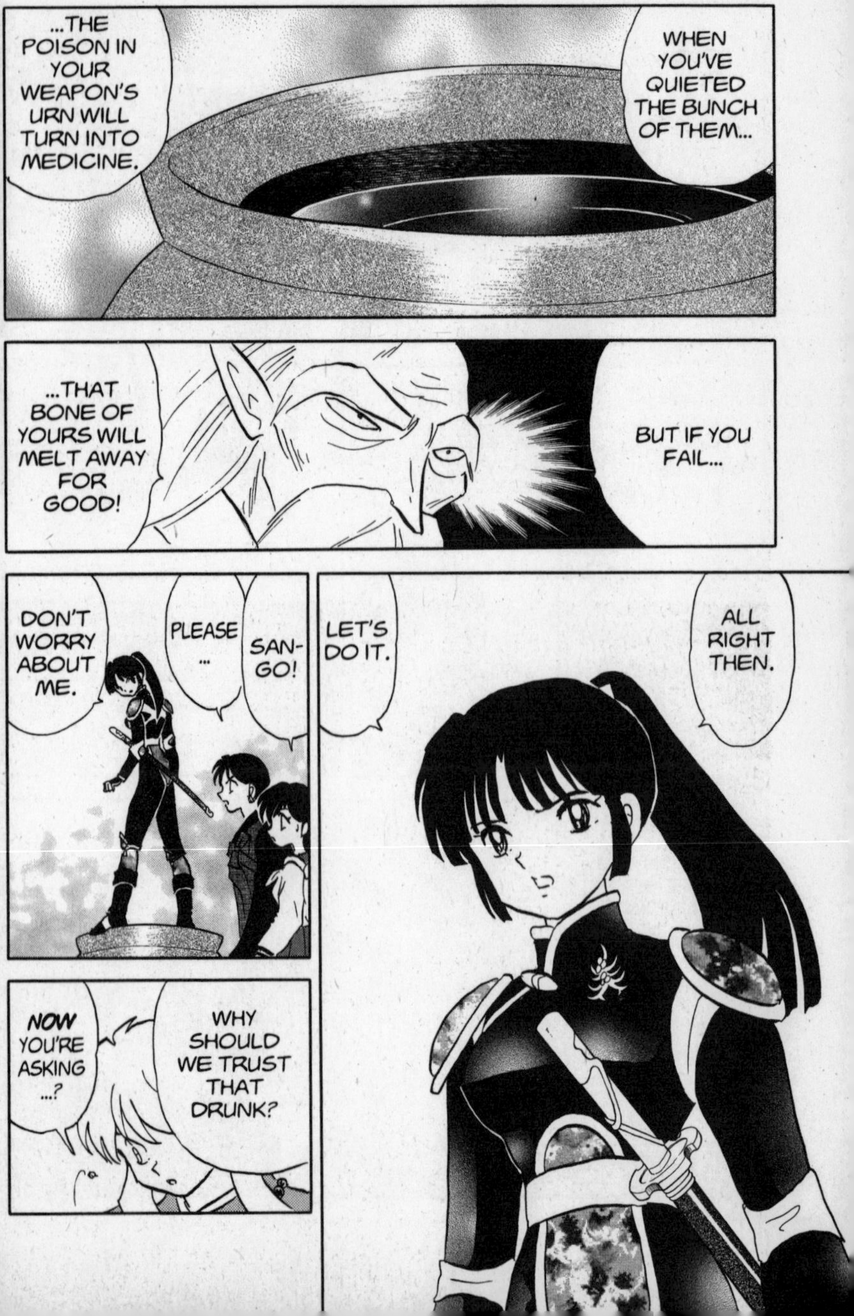
WHEN YOU'VE QUIETED THE BUNCH OF THEM...
...THE POISON IN YOUR WEAPON'S URN WILL TURN INTO MEDICINE.
BUT IF YOU FAIL...
...THAT BONE OF YOURS WILL MELT AWAY FOR GOOD!
ALL RIGHT THEN.
LET'S DO IT.
SAN-GO!
PLEASE...
DON'T WORRY ABOUT ME.
WHY SHOULD WE TRUST THAT DRUNK?
NOW YOU'RE ASKING...?

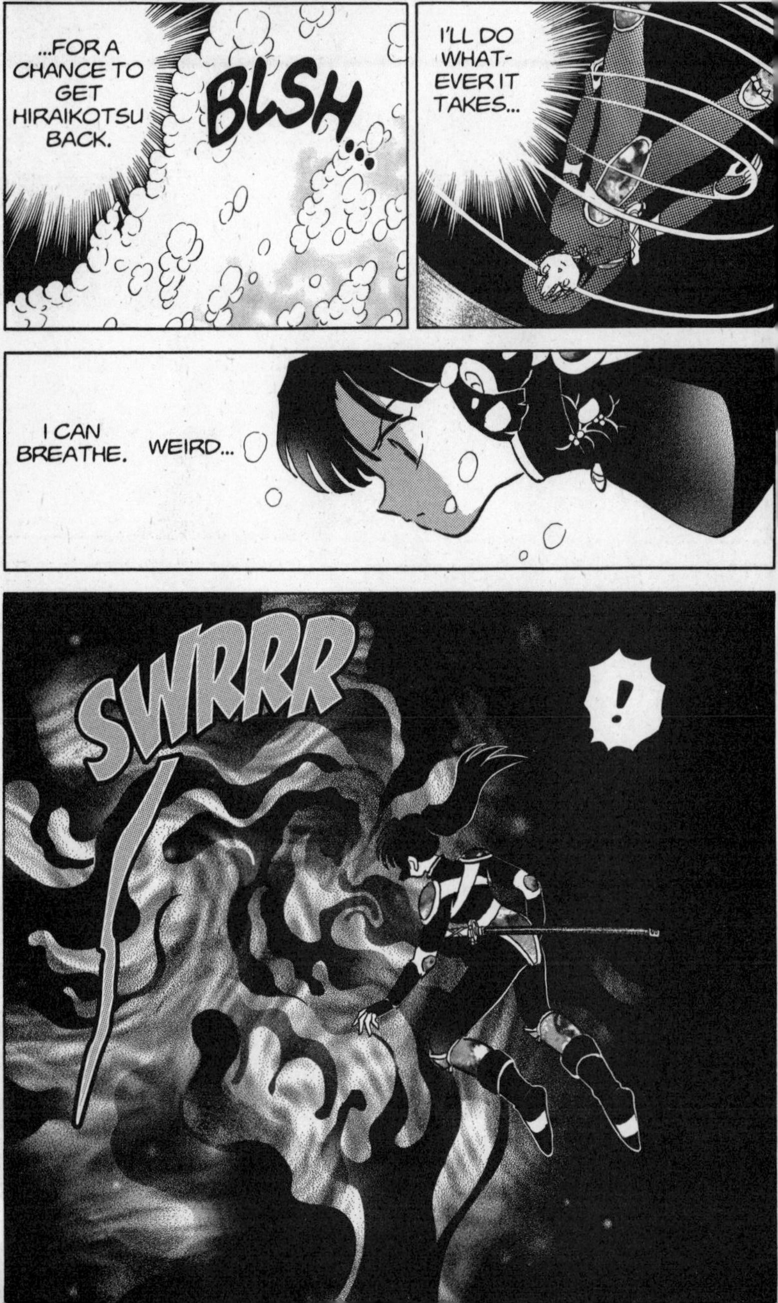
I'LL DO WHAT-EVER IT TAKES...
...FOR A CHANCE TO GET HIRAIKOTSU BACK.
BLSH...
WEIRD...
I CAN BREATHE.
!
SWRRR

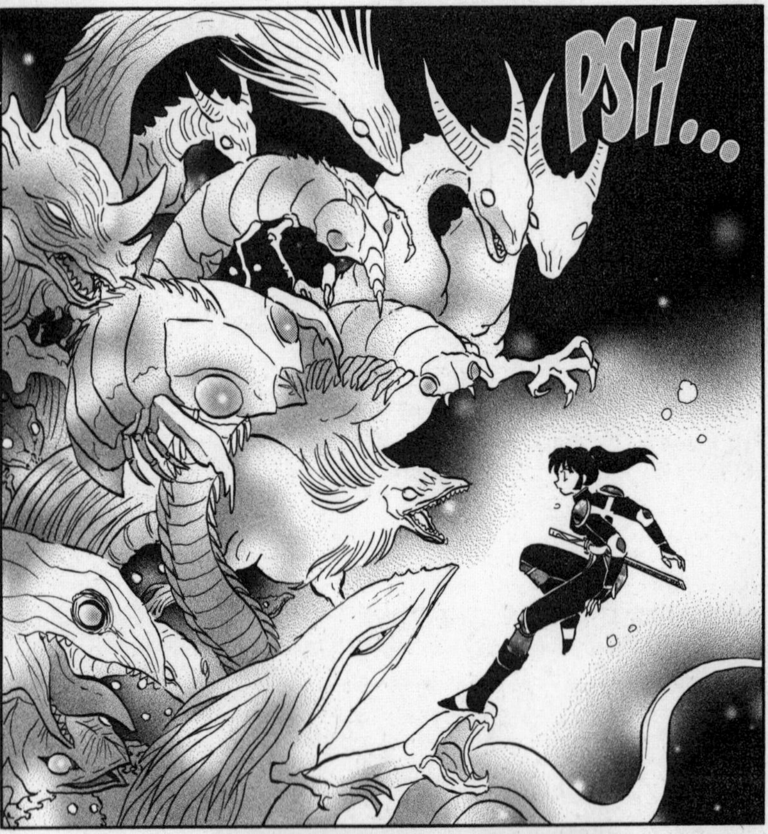
PSH...

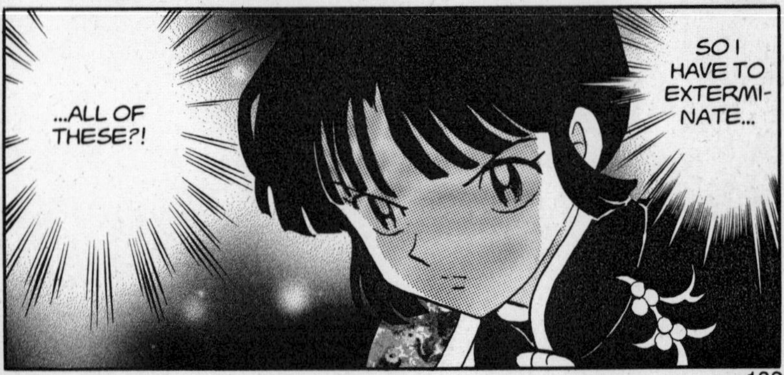
SO I HAVE TO EXTERMI-NATE...
...ALL OF THESE?!

SCROLL 8

INSIDE THE URN

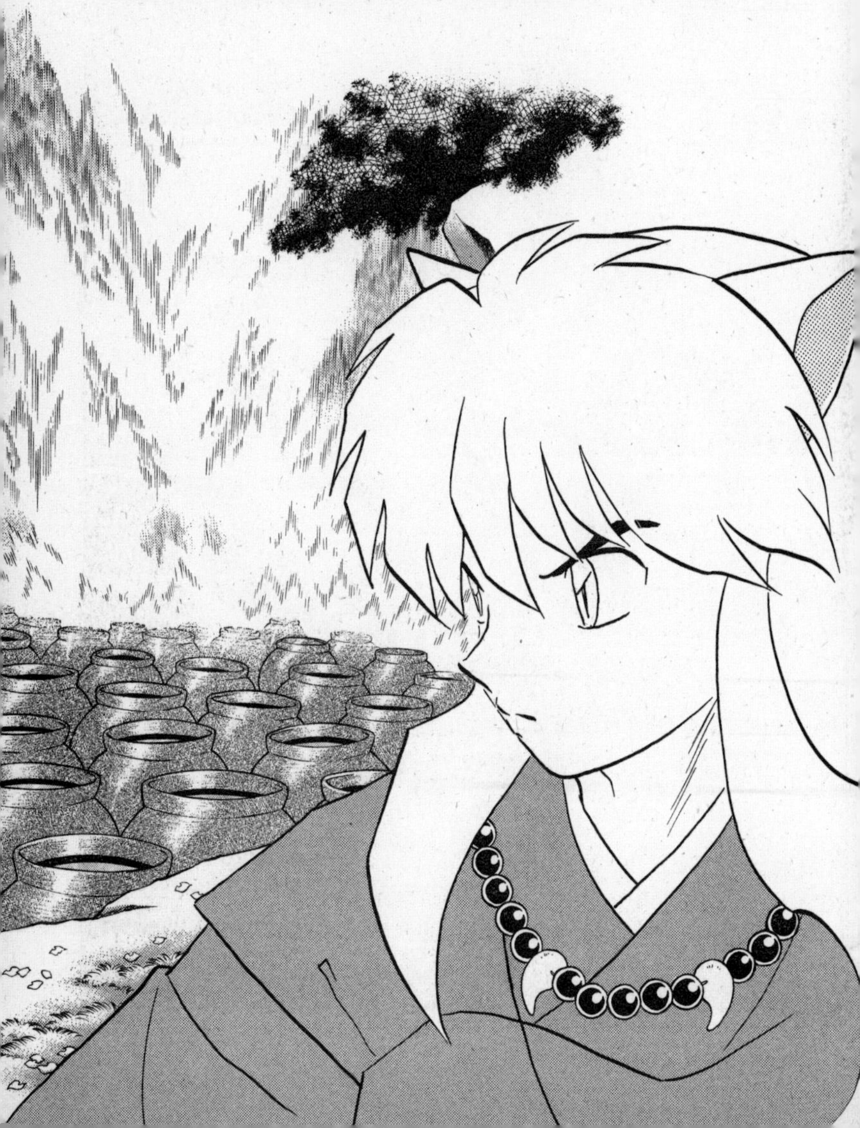

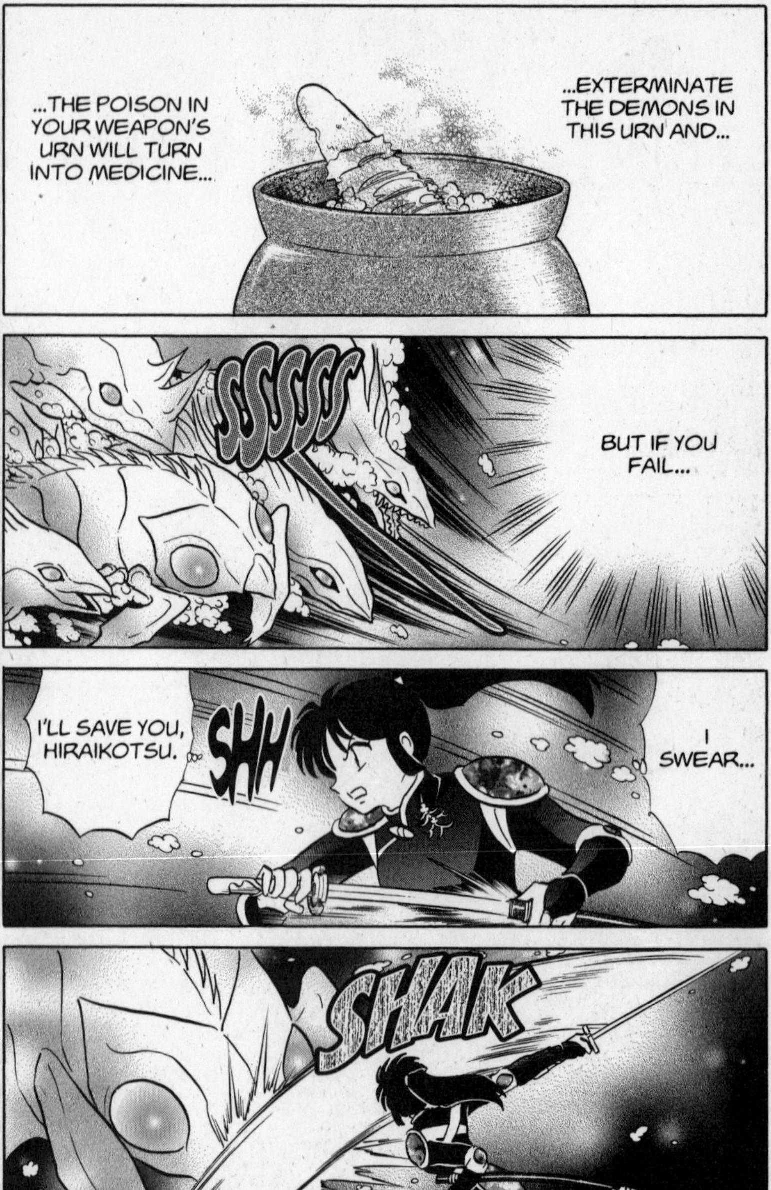
...EXTERMINATE THE DEMONS IN THIS URN AND...
...THE POISON IN YOUR WEAPON'S URN WILL TURN INTO MEDICINE...
BUT IF YOU FAIL...
SSSSS
I SWEAR...
SHH
I'LL SAVE YOU, HIRAIKOTSU.
SHAK

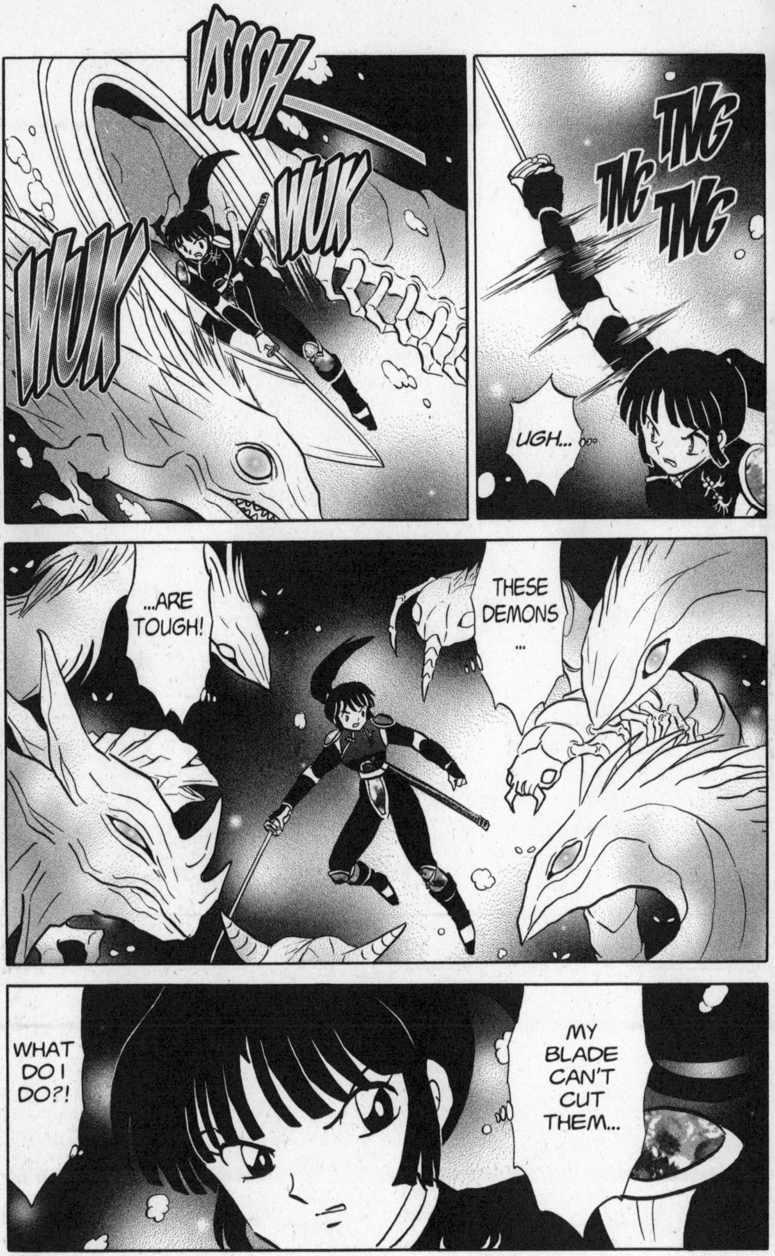
TNG TNG
TNG TNG
UGH...
VSSSH
WUK
WUK
THESE DEMONS...
...ARE TOUGH!
MY BLADE CAN'T CUT THEM...
WHAT DO I DO?!

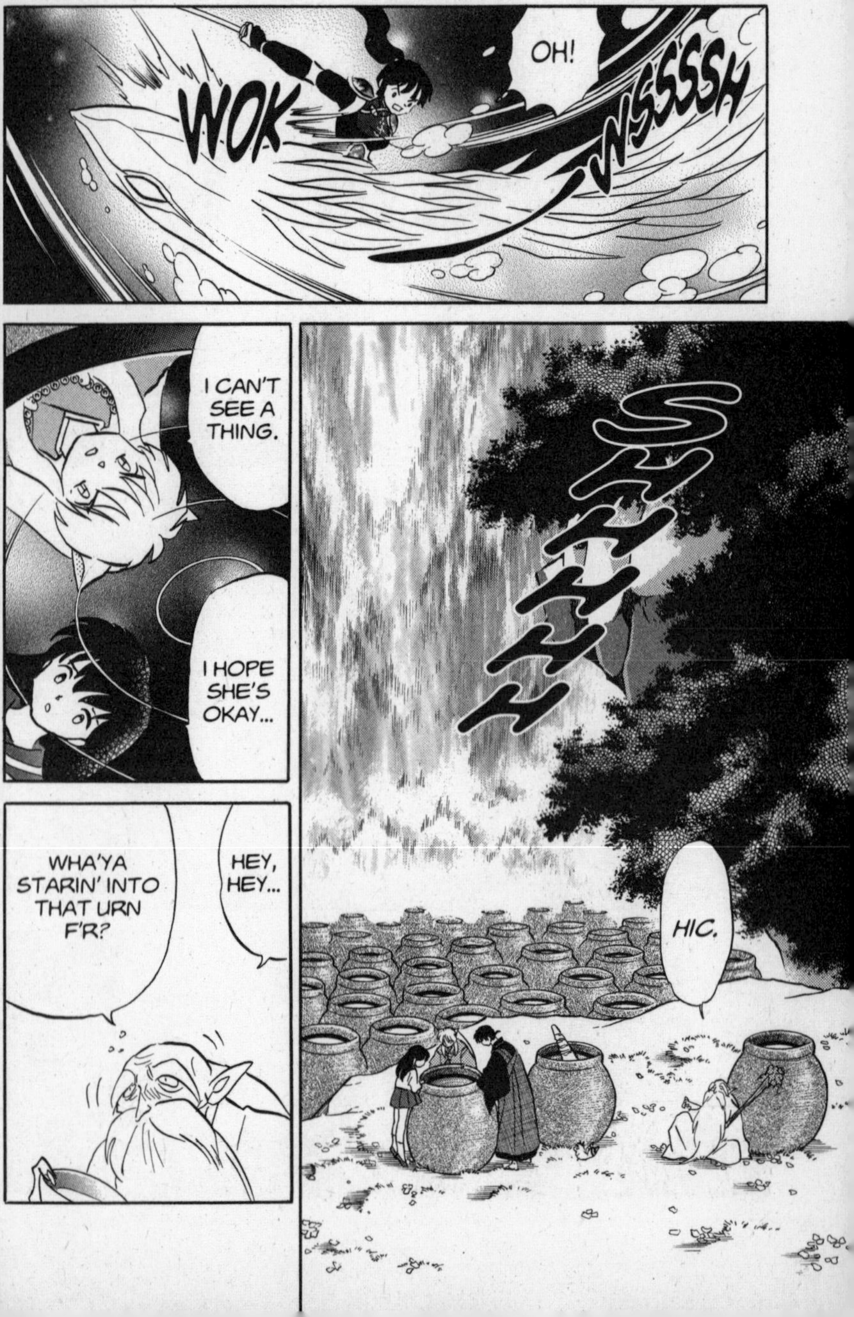
OH!
WSSSSH
WOK
SHHHHHH
HIC.
I CAN'T SEE A THING.
I HOPE SHE'S OKAY...
HEY, HEY...
WHA'YA STARIN' INTO THAT URN F'R?

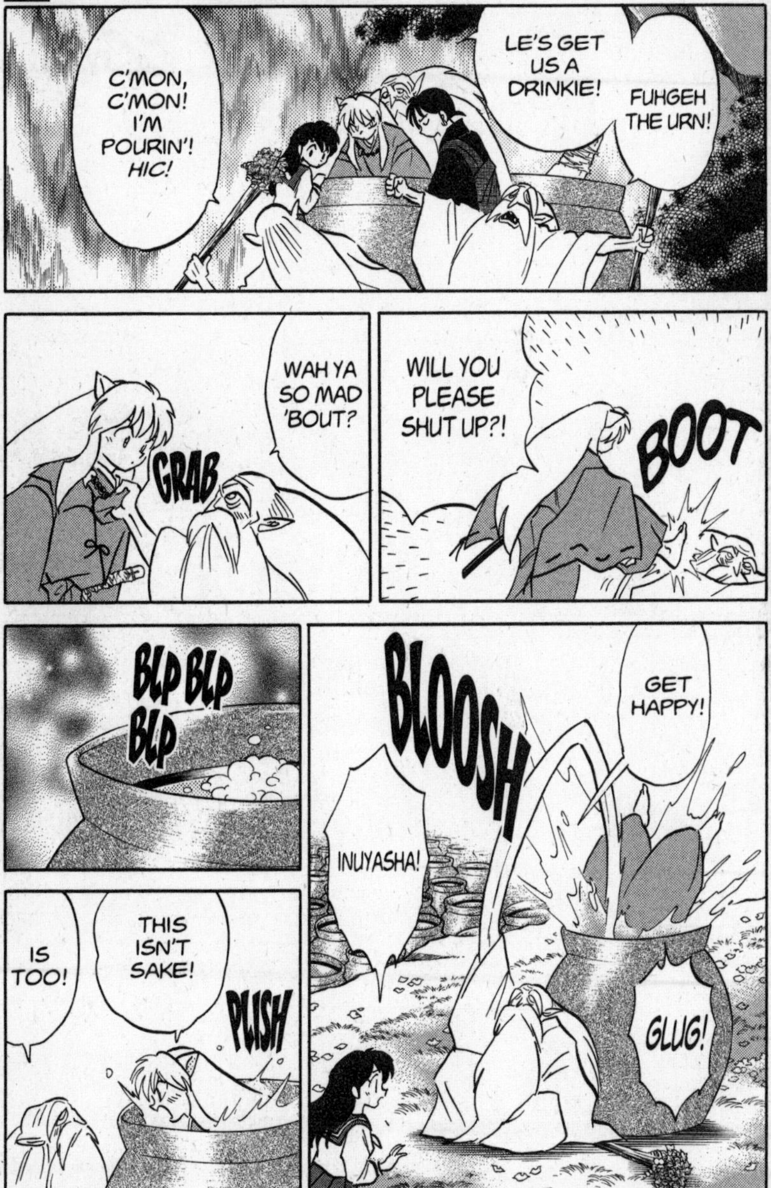
FUHGEH THE URN!
LE'S GET US A DRINKIE!
C'MON, C'MON! I'M POURIN'! HIC!
WILL YOU PLEASE SHUT UP?!
BOOT
WAH YA SO MAD 'BOUT?
GRAB
GET HAPPY!
BLOOSH
INUYASHA!
GLUG!
BLP BLP BLP
THIS ISN'T SAKE!
IS TOO!
PLISH

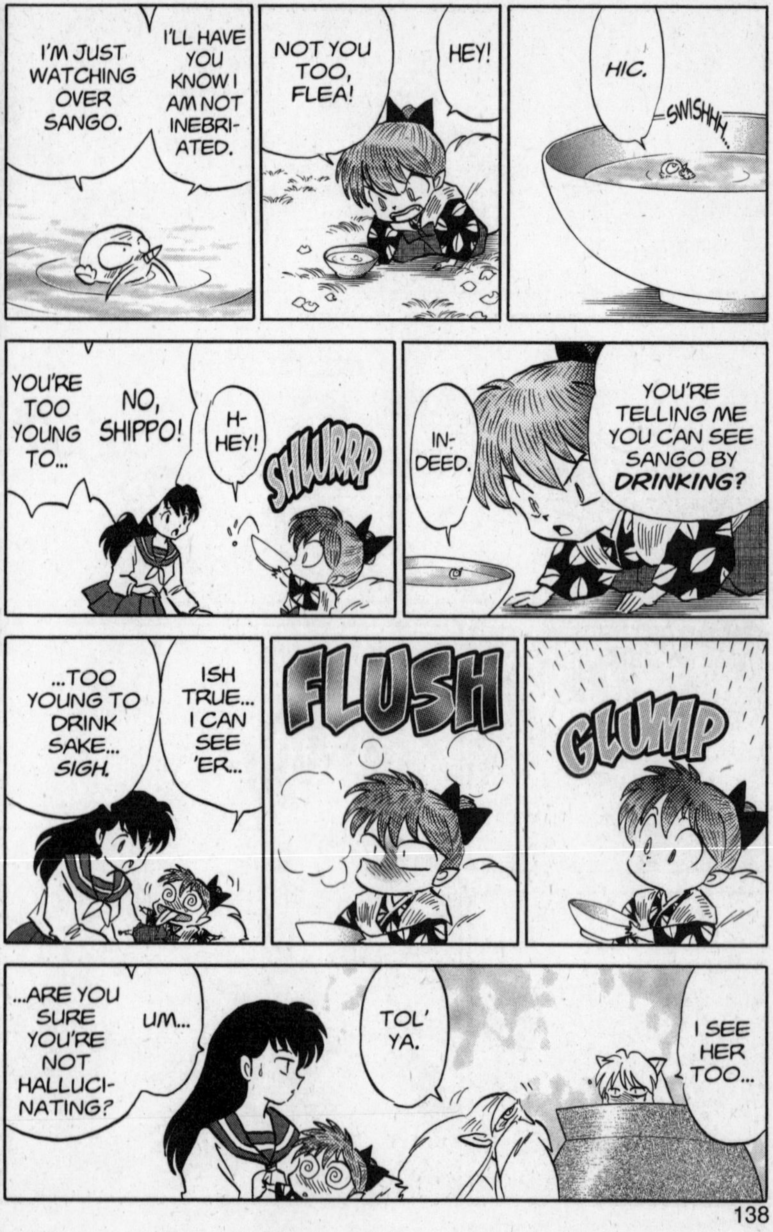
HIC.
SWISHHH...
HEY!
NOT YOU TOO, FLEA!
I'LL HAVE YOU KNOW I AM NOT INEBRIATED.
I'M JUST WATCHING OVER SANGO.
YOU'RE TELLING ME YOU CAN SEE SANGO BY **DRINKING?**
IN-DEED.
SHLURRP
H-HEY!
NO, SHIPPO!
YOU'RE TOO YOUNG TO...
GLUMP
FLUSH
ISH TRUE... I CAN SEE 'ER...
...TOO YOUNG TO DRINK SAKE... *SIGH.*
I SEE HER TOO...
TOL' YA.
UM...
...ARE YOU SURE YOU'RE NOT HALLUCINATING?

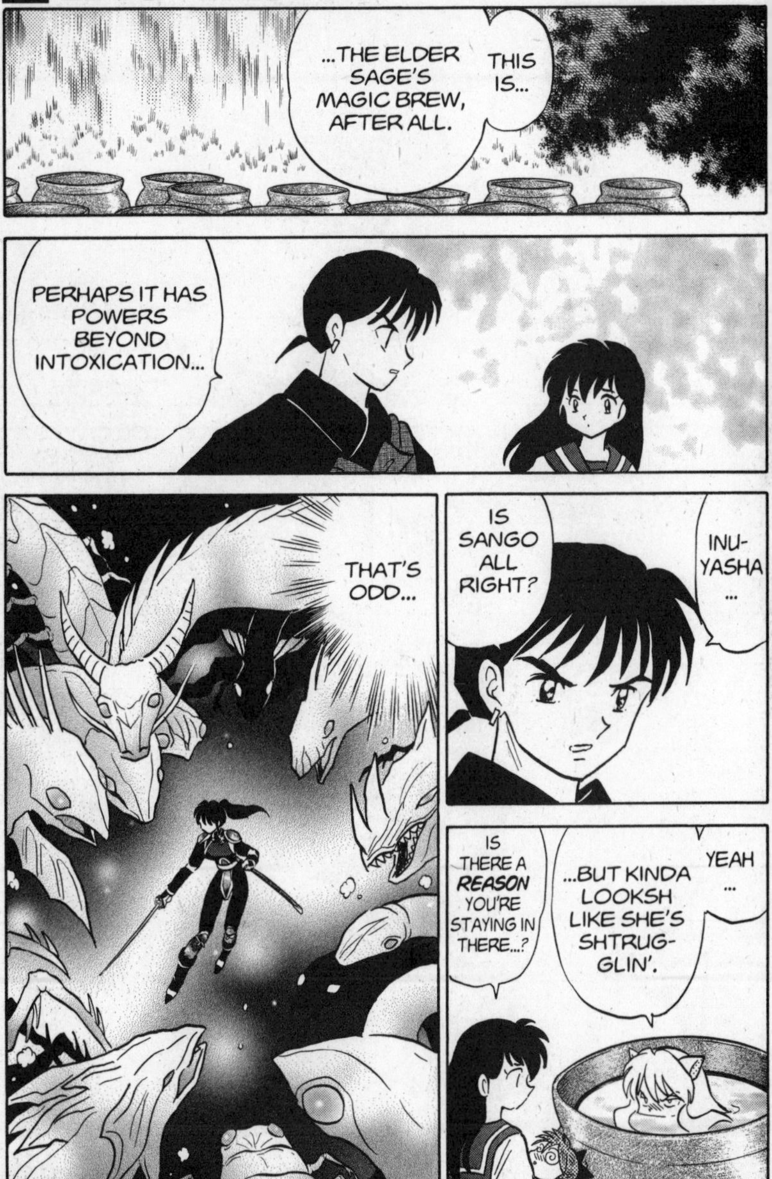
THIS IS...
...THE ELDER SAGE'S MAGIC BREW, AFTER ALL.
PERHAPS IT HAS POWERS BEYOND INTOXICATION...
INU-YASHA...
IS SANGO ALL RIGHT?
YEAH...
...BUT KINDA LOOKSH LIKE SHE'S SHTRUG-GLIN'.
IS THERE A *REASON* YOU'RE STAYING IN THERE...?
THAT'S ODD...

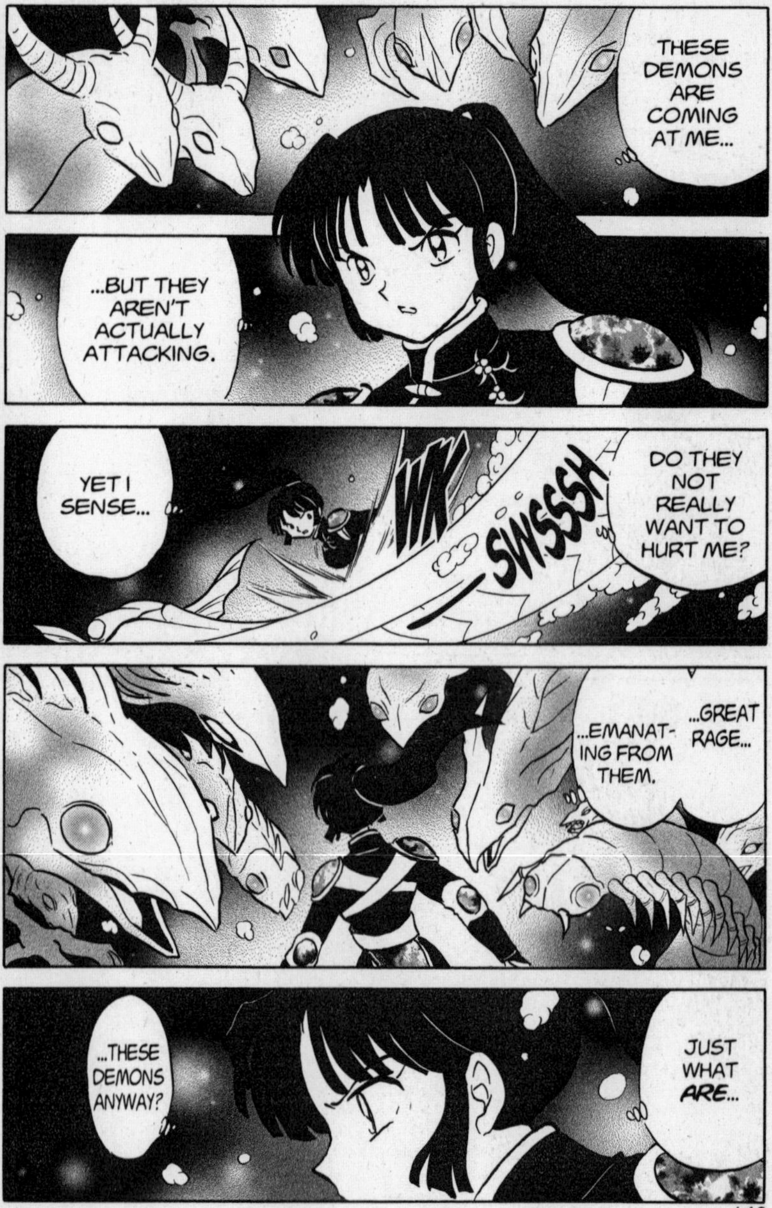
THESE DEMONS ARE COMING AT ME...
...BUT THEY AREN'T ACTUALLY ATTACKING.
DO THEY NOT REALLY WANT TO HURT ME?
SWSSSH
YET I SENSE...
...GREAT RAGE...
...EMANAT-ING FROM THEM.
JUST WHAT **ARE**...
...THESE DEMONS ANYWAY?

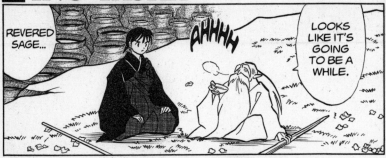

LOOKS LIKE IT'S GOING TO BE A WHILE.
AHHHH
REVERED SAGE...
HOW MUCH LONGER BEFORE HIRAIKOTSU MELTS AWAY COMPLETELY?
BLUP BLUP BLUP
HOW MUCH LONGER?
OH, IT MIGHT BE TOO LATE AL-READY.
...
HMM?
VWR
PLAN-NING TO DIVE IN AND HELP HER?
IT'S HOPE-LESS.
YOU CAN'T REACH SANGO WHERE SHE IS.

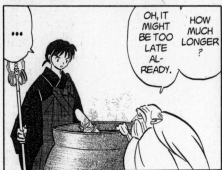

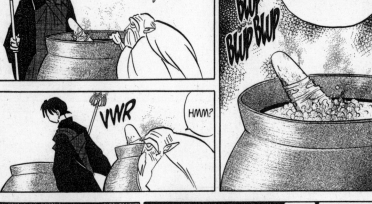

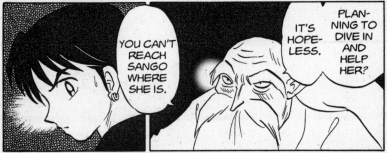

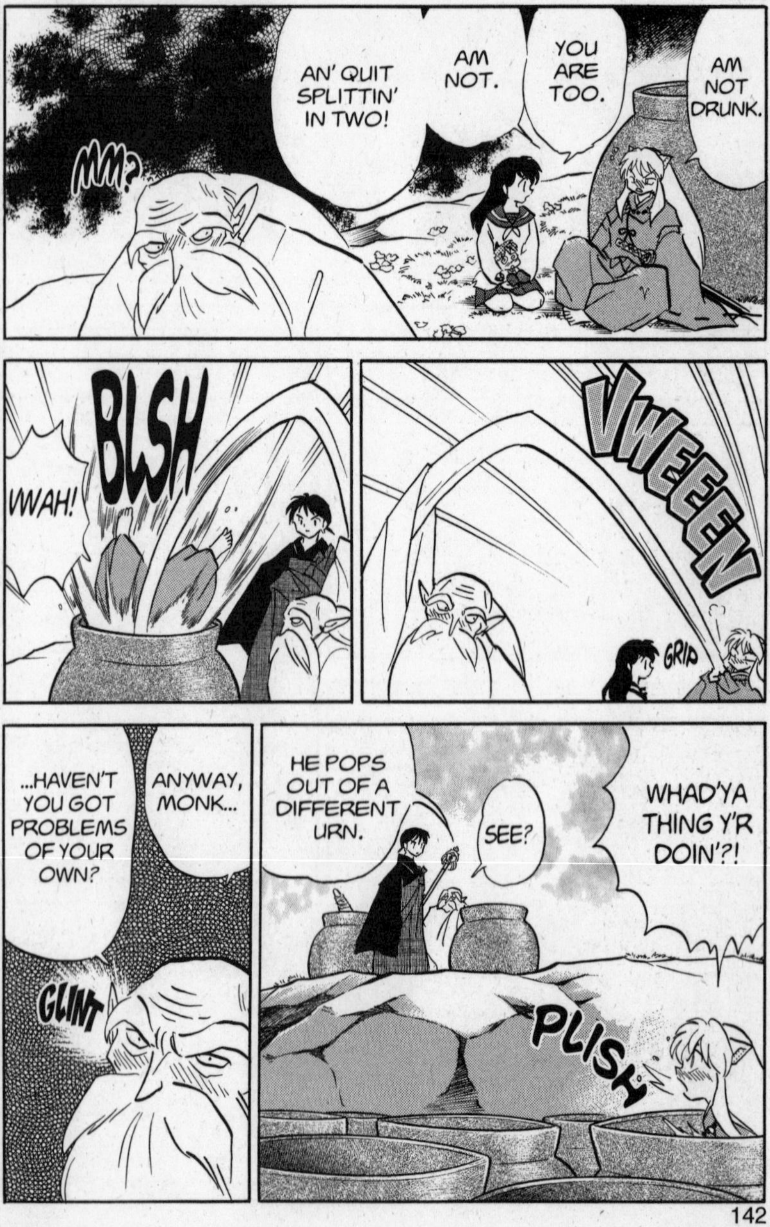
AM NOT DRUNK.
YOU ARE TOO.
AM NOT.
AN' QUIT SPLITTIN' IN TWO!
MM?
VWEEEN
GRIP
BLSH
VWAH!
WHAD'YA THING Y'R DOIN'?!
SEE?
HE POPS OUT OF A DIFFERENT URN.
PLISH
ANYWAY, MONK...
...HAVEN'T YOU GOT PROBLEMS OF YOUR OWN?
GLINT

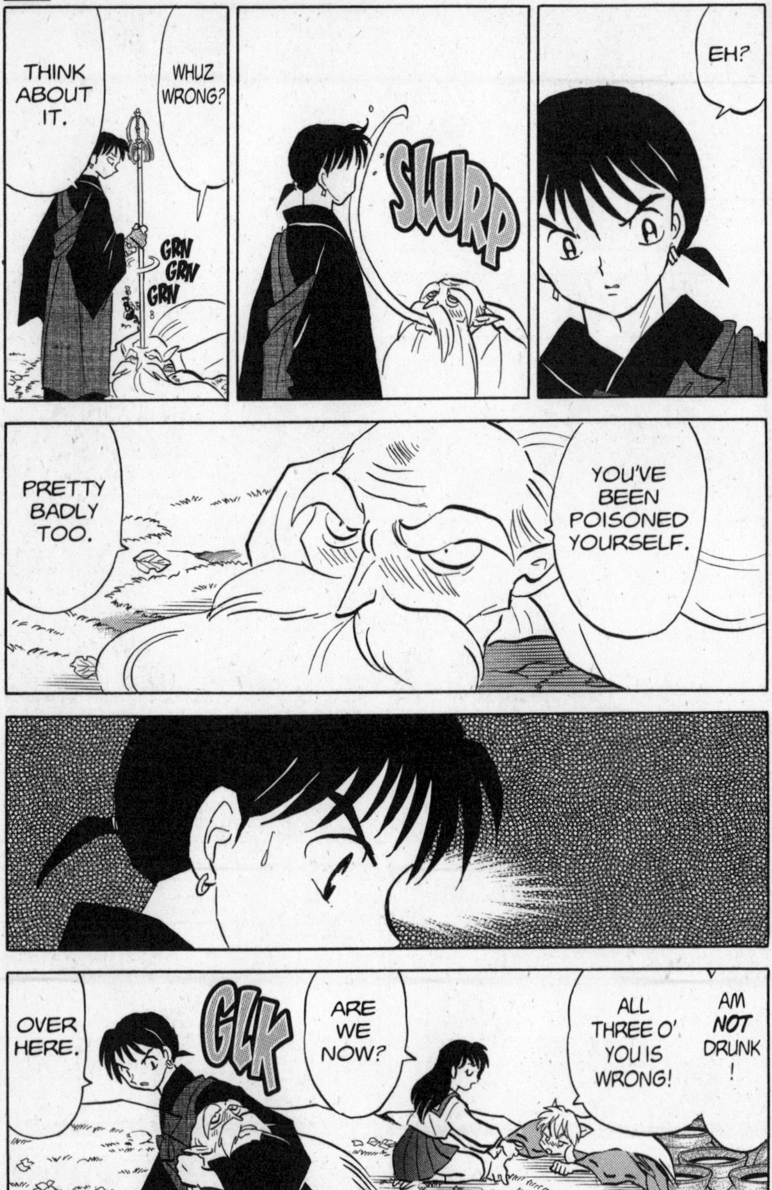
EH?
SLURP
WHUZ WRONG?
THINK ABOUT IT.
GRN GRN GRN
YOU'VE BEEN POISONED YOURSELF.
PRETTY BADLY TOO.
AM NOT DRUNK!
ALL THREE O' YOU IS WRONG!
ARE WE NOW?
GLK
OVER HERE.

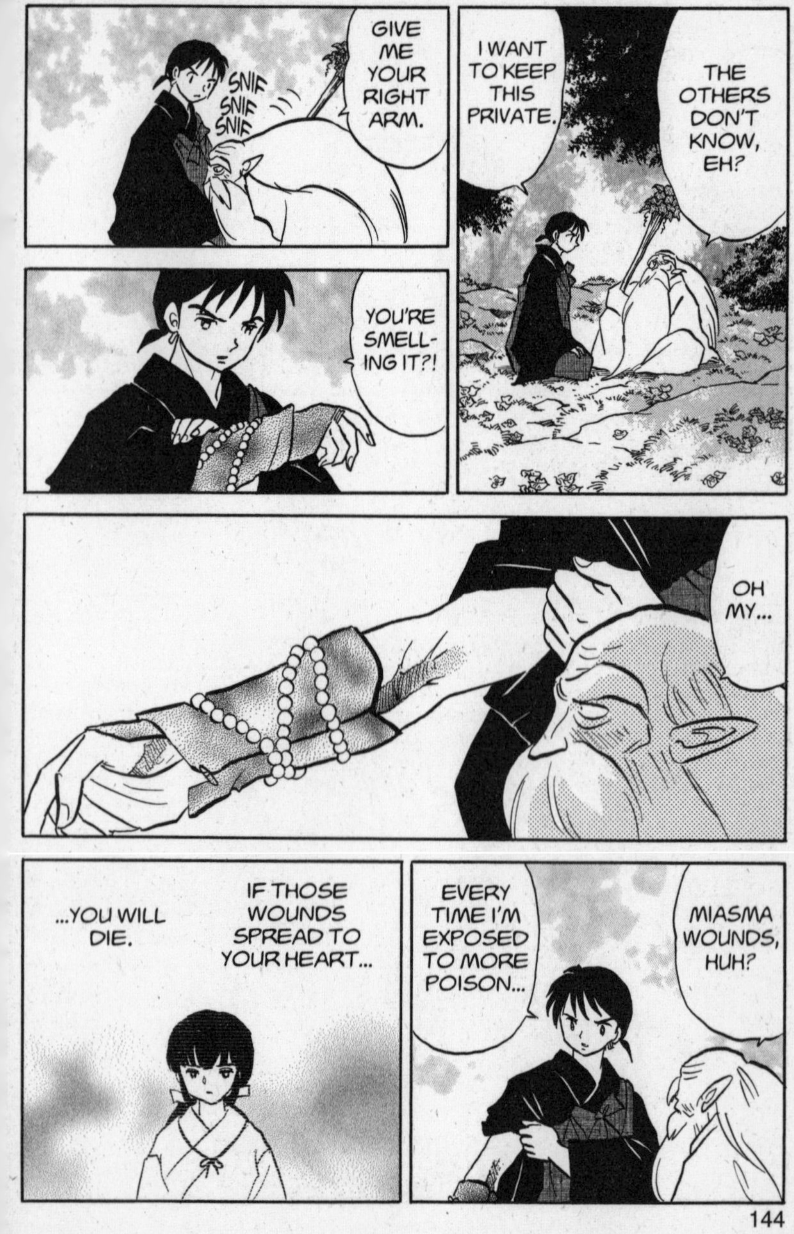
THE OTHERS DON'T KNOW, EH?
I WANT TO KEEP THIS PRIVATE.
GIVE ME YOUR RIGHT ARM.
SNIF SNIF SNIF
YOU'RE SMELLING IT?!
OH MY...
MIASMA WOUNDS, HUH?
EVERY TIME I'M EXPOSED TO MORE POISON...
IF THOSE WOUNDS SPREAD TO YOUR HEART...
...YOU WILL DIE.

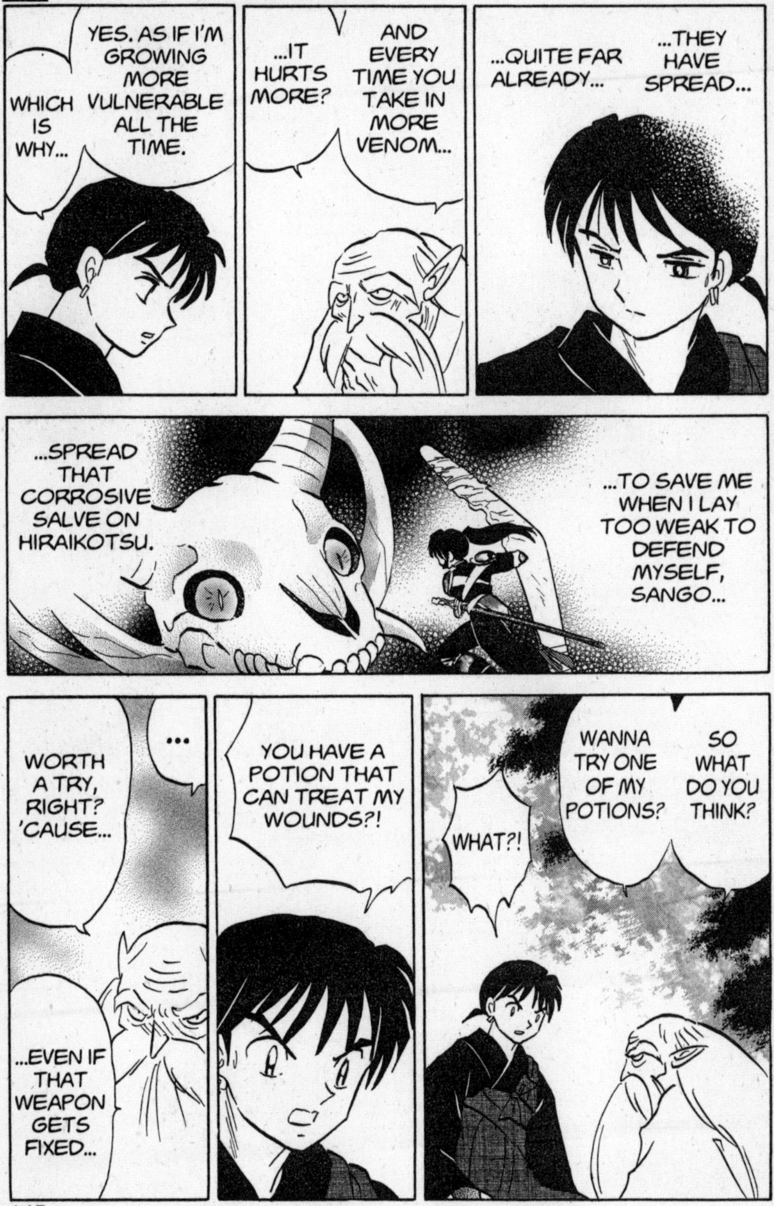
...THEY HAVE SPREAD...
...QUITE FAR ALREADY...
AND EVERY TIME YOU TAKE IN MORE VENOM...
...IT HURTS MORE?
YES. AS IF I'M GROWING MORE VULNERABLE ALL THE TIME.
WHICH IS WHY...
...TO SAVE ME WHEN I LAY TOO WEAK TO DEFEND MYSELF, SANGO...
...SPREAD THAT CORROSIVE SALVE ON HIRAIKOTSU.
SO WHAT DO YOU THINK?
WANNA TRY ONE OF MY POTIONS?
WHAT?!
YOU HAVE A POTION THAT CAN TREAT MY WOUNDS?!
...
WORTH A TRY, RIGHT? 'CAUSE...
...EVEN IF THAT WEAPON GETS FIXED...

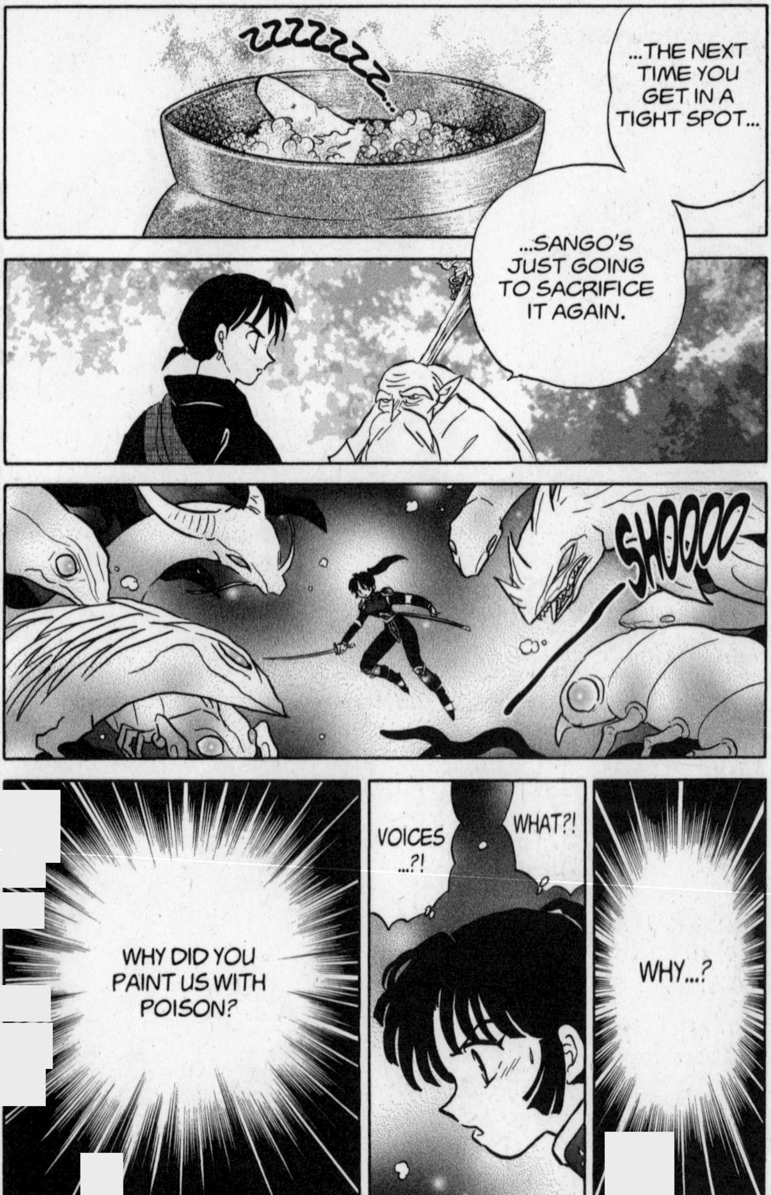
ZZZZZZZZ...
...THE NEXT TIME YOU GET IN A TIGHT SPOT...
...SANGO'S JUST GOING TO SACRIFICE IT AGAIN.
SHOOOO
WHY...?
WHAT?!
VOICES ...?!
WHY DID YOU PAINT US WITH POISON?

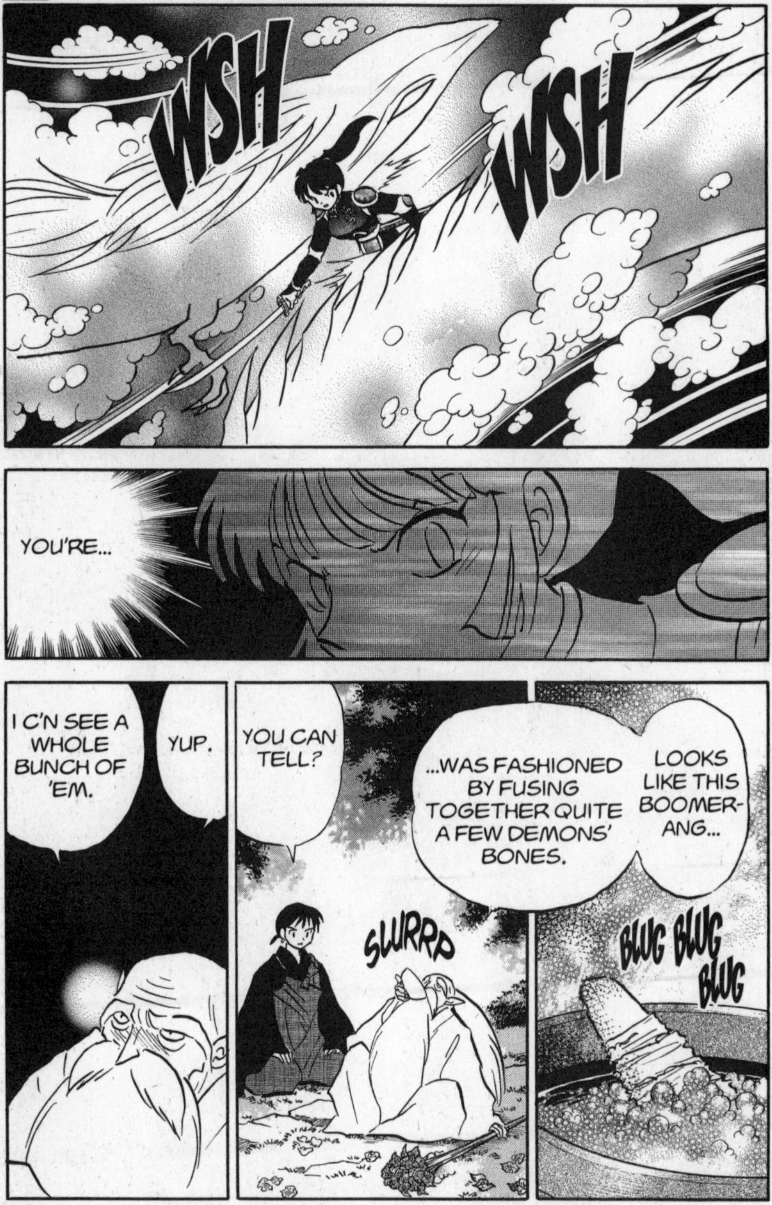
WSH
WSH
YOU'RE...
LOOKS LIKE THIS BOOMER-ANG...
...WAS FASHIONED BY FUSING TOGETHER QUITE A FEW DEMONS' BONES.
BLUG BLUG BLUG BLUG
YOU CAN TELL?
SLURRP
YUP.
I C'N SEE A WHOLE BUNCH OF 'EM.

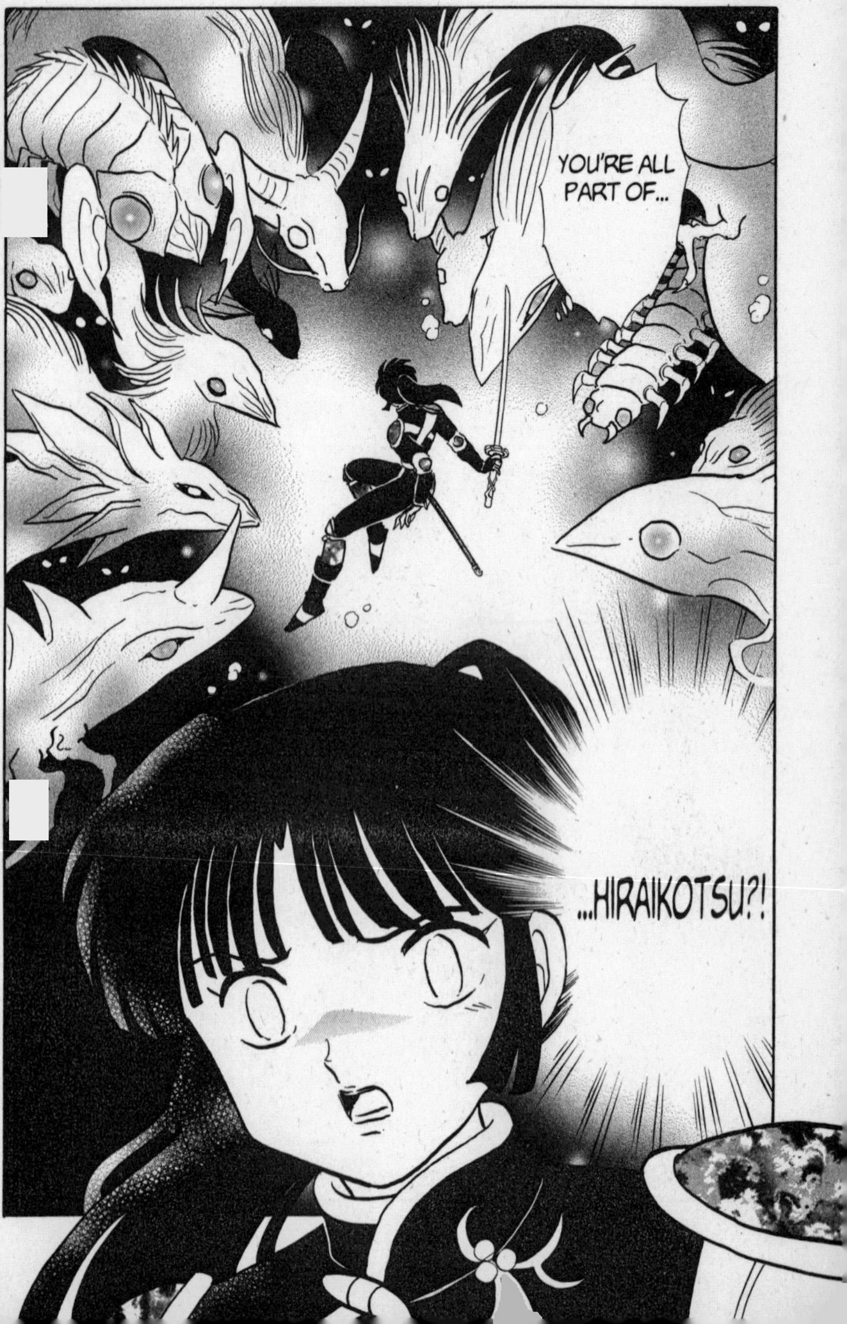
YOU'RE ALL PART OF...
...HIRAIKOTSU?!

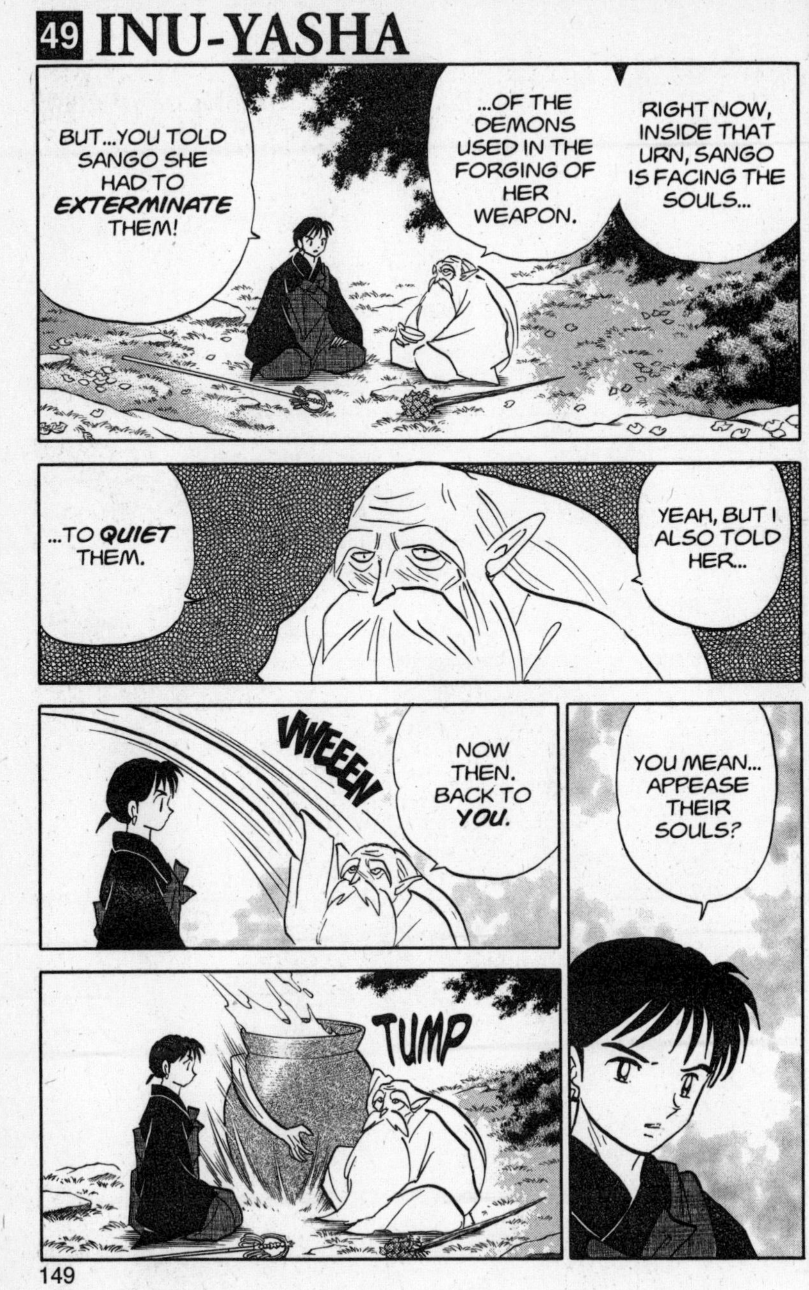
RIGHT NOW, INSIDE THAT URN, SANGO IS FACING THE SOULS...
...OF THE DEMONS USED IN THE FORGING OF HER WEAPON.
BUT...YOU TOLD SANGO SHE HAD TO ***EXTERMINATE*** THEM!
YEAH, BUT I ALSO TOLD HER...
...TO ***QUIET*** THEM.
YOU MEAN... APPEASE THEIR SOULS?
NOW THEN. BACK TO ***YOU***.
VWEEEN
TUMP

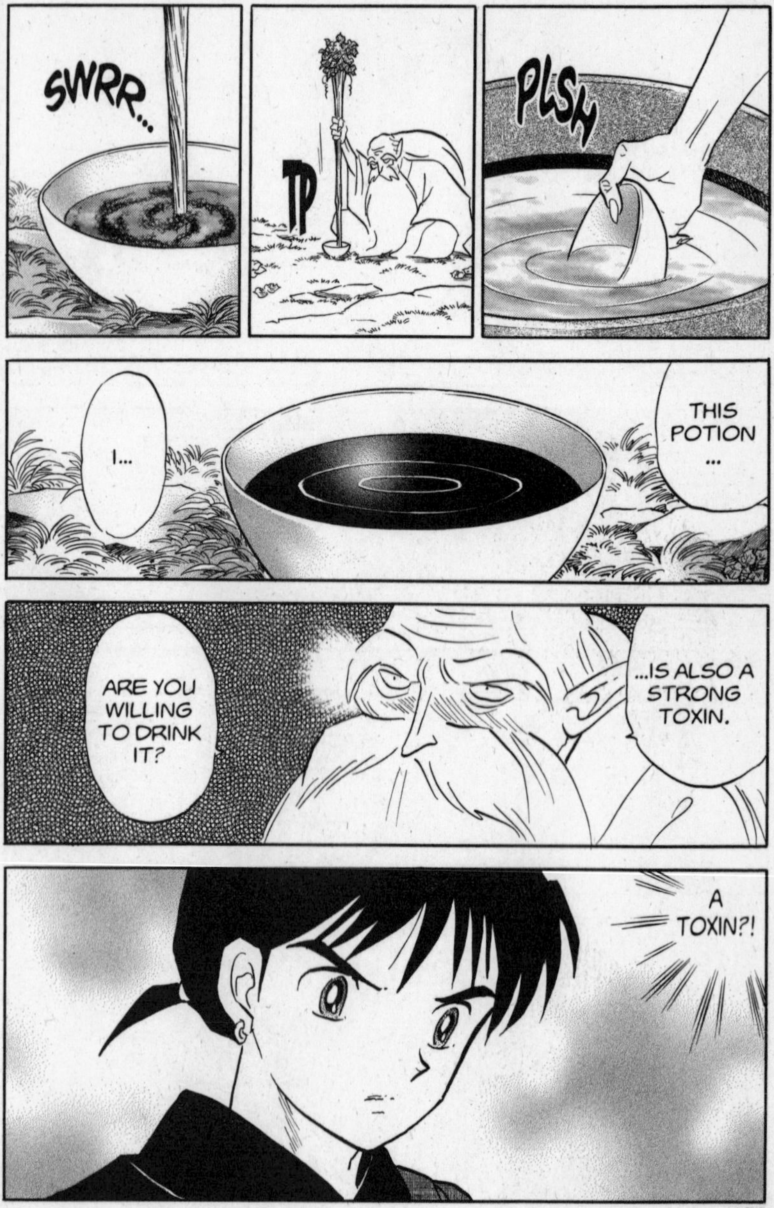
PLSH
TP
SWRR...
THIS POTION ...
I...
...IS ALSO A STRONG TOXIN.
ARE YOU WILLING TO DRINK IT?
A TOXIN?!

SCROLL 9

WAY OF LIFE

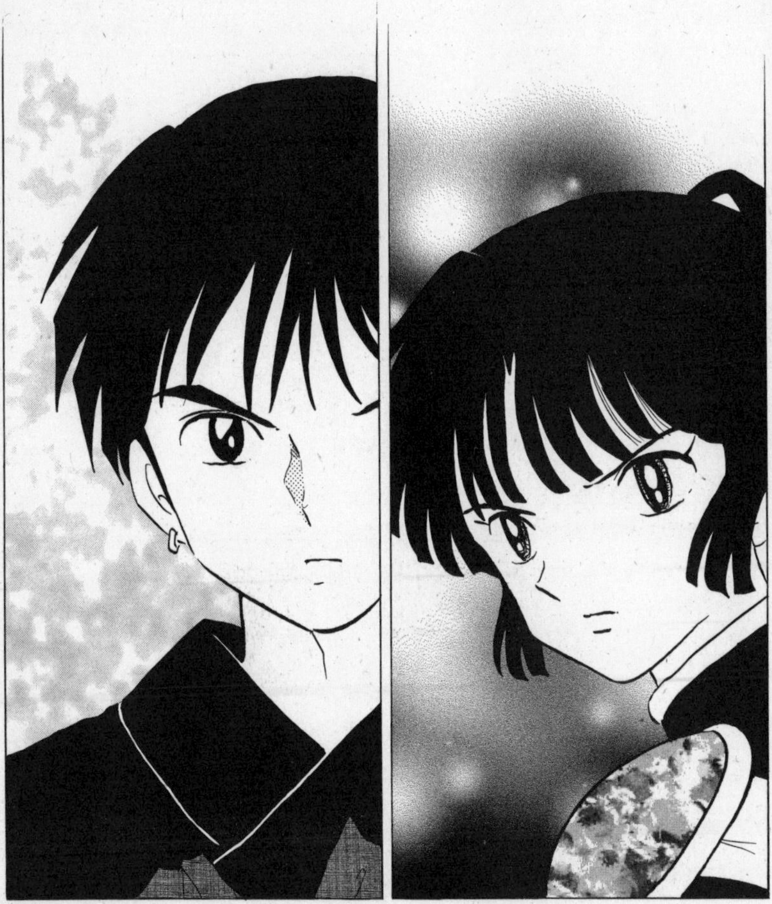

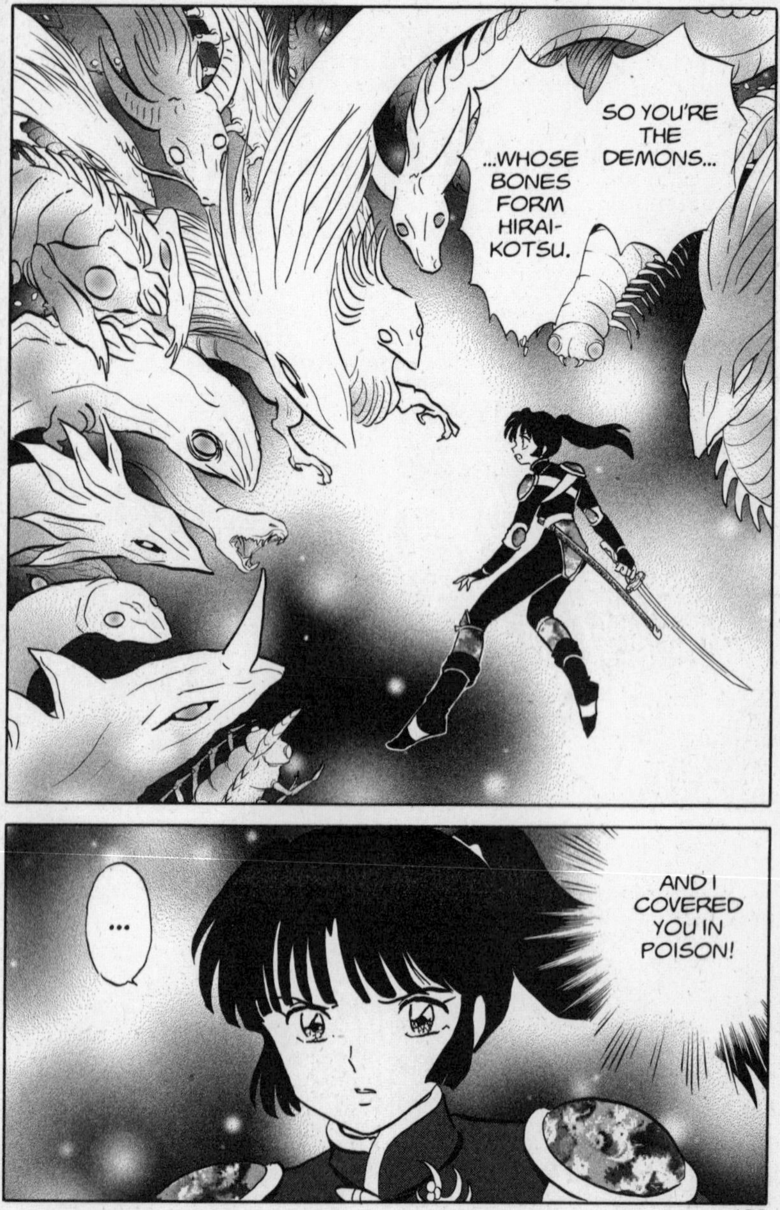
SO YOU'RE THE DEMONS...
...WHOSE BONES FORM HIRAI-KOTSU.
AND I COVERED YOU IN POISON!
...

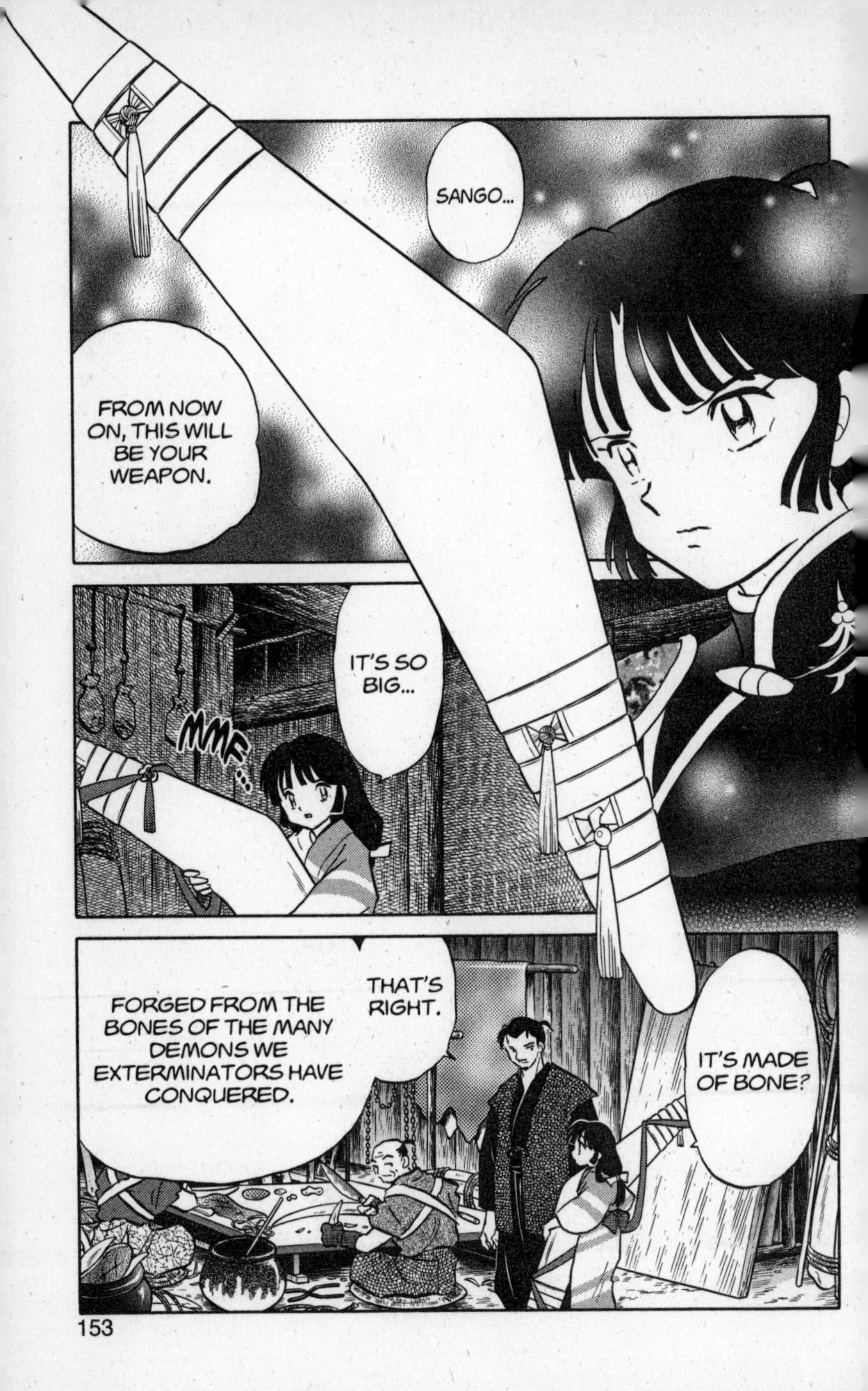
SANGO...
FROM NOW ON, THIS WILL BE YOUR WEAPON.
IT'S SO BIG...
MMF...
IT'S MADE OF BONE?
THAT'S RIGHT.
FORGED FROM THE BONES OF THE MANY DEMONS WE EXTERMINATORS HAVE CONQUERED.

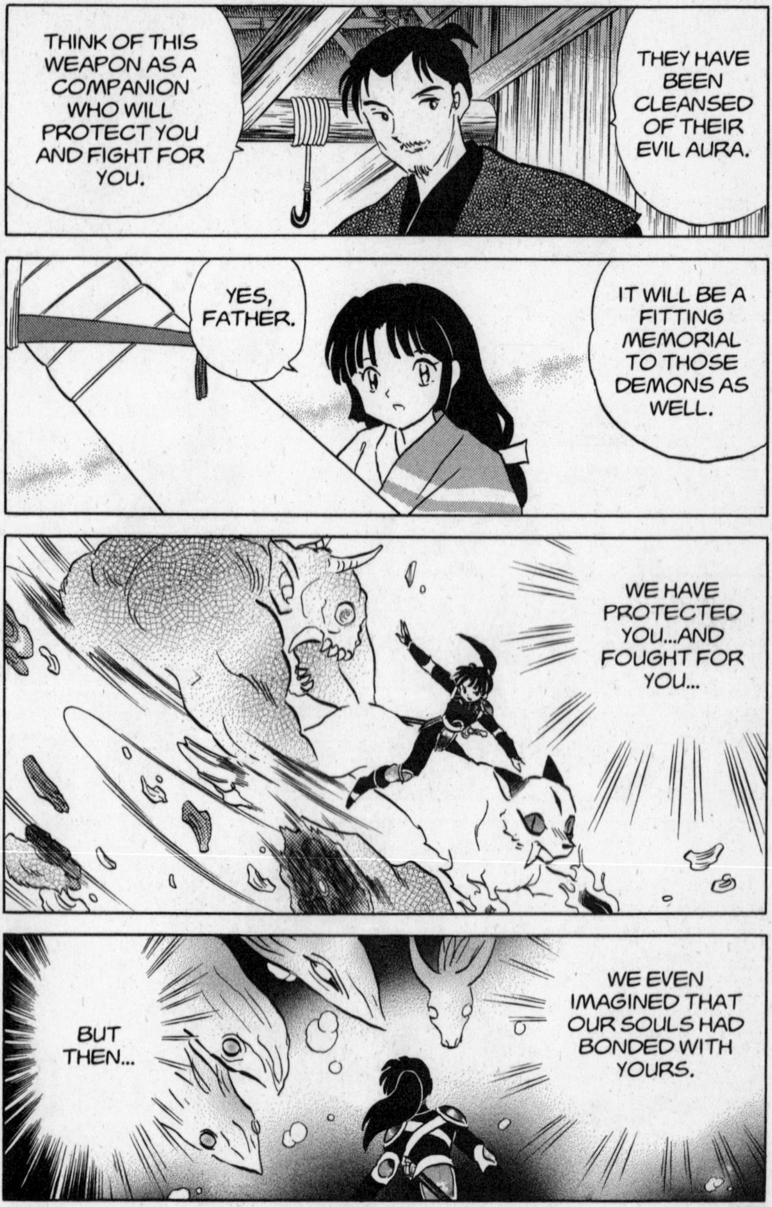
THEY HAVE BEEN CLEANSED OF THEIR EVIL AURA.
THINK OF THIS WEAPON AS A COMPANION WHO WILL PROTECT YOU AND FIGHT FOR YOU.
IT WILL BE A FITTING MEMORIAL TO THOSE DEMONS AS WELL.
YES, FATHER.
WE HAVE PROTECTED YOU...AND FOUGHT FOR YOU...
WE EVEN IMAGINED THAT OUR SOULS HAD BONDED WITH YOURS.
BUT THEN...

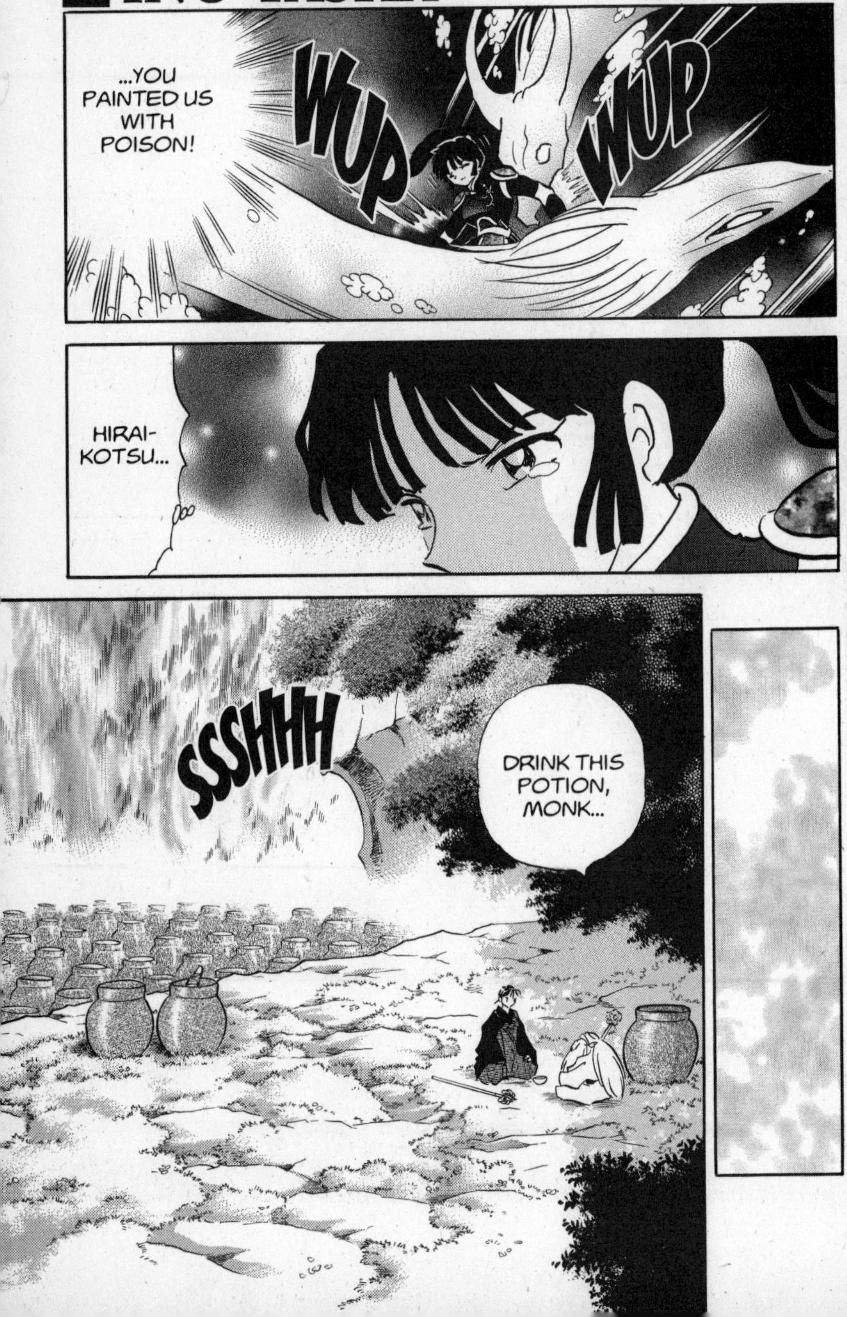
WUP WUP
...YOU PAINTED US WITH POISON!
HIRAI-KOTSU...
DRINK THIS POTION, MONK...
SSSHHH

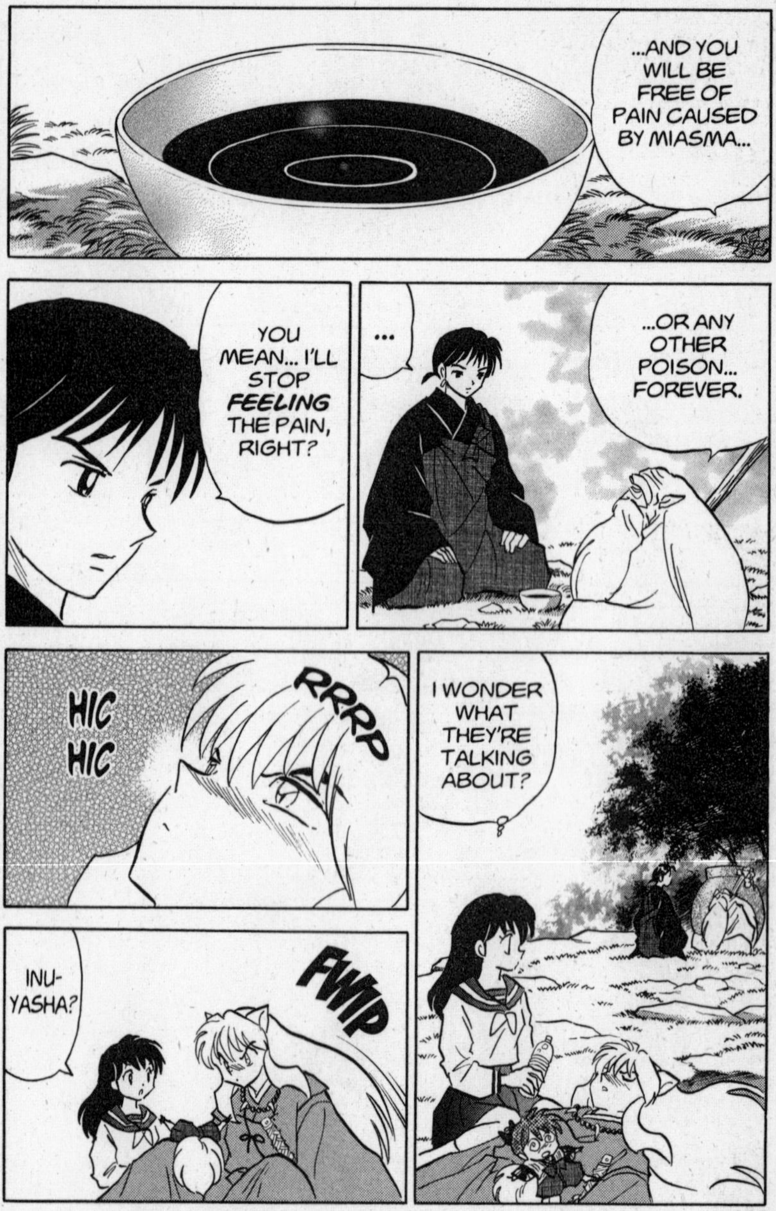
...AND YOU WILL BE FREE OF PAIN CAUSED BY MIASMA...
...OR ANY OTHER POISON... FOREVER.
...
YOU MEAN... I'LL STOP *FEELING* THE PAIN, RIGHT?
I WONDER WHAT THEY'RE TALKING ABOUT?
RRRP
HIC HIC
FWIP
INU-YASHA?

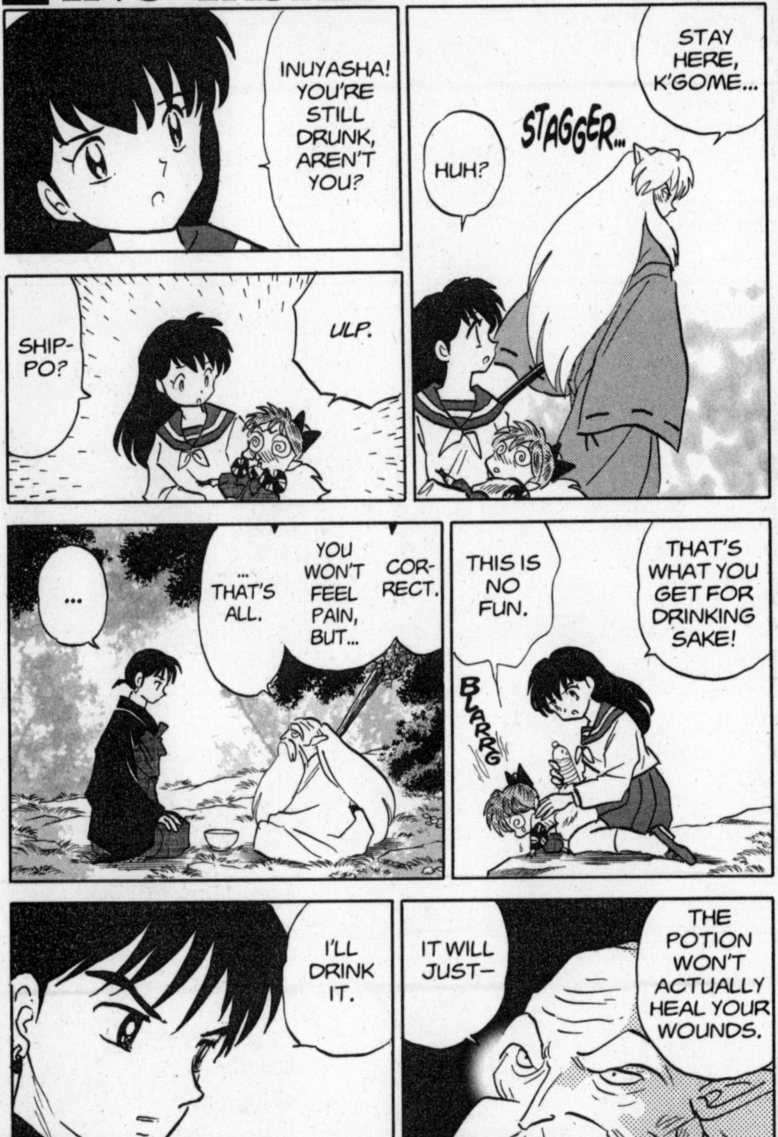
STAY HERE, K'GOME...
STAGGER...
HUH?
INUYASHA! YOU'RE STILL DRUNK, AREN'T YOU?
ULP.
SHIP-PO?
THAT'S WHAT YOU GET FOR DRINKING SAKE!
THIS IS NO FUN.
BLARRG
CORRECT.
YOU WON'T FEEL PAIN, BUT...
... THAT'S ALL.
...
THE POTION WON'T ACTUALLY HEAL YOUR WOUNDS.
IT WILL JUST—
I'LL DRINK IT.

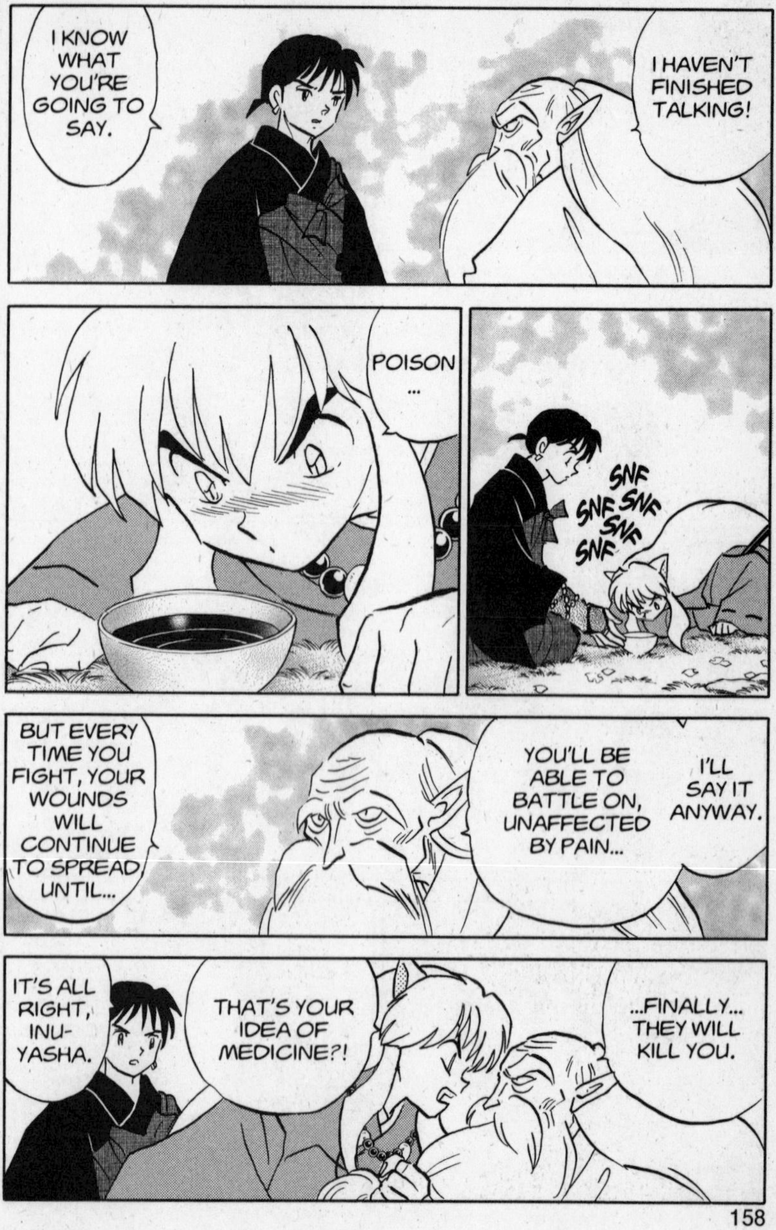
I HAVEN'T FINISHED TALKING!
I KNOW WHAT YOU'RE GOING TO SAY.
SNF SNF SNF SNF SNF
POISON ...
I'LL SAY IT ANYWAY.
YOU'LL BE ABLE TO BATTLE ON, UNAFFECTED BY PAIN...
BUT EVERY TIME YOU FIGHT, YOUR WOUNDS WILL CONTINUE TO SPREAD UNTIL...
...FINALLY... THEY WILL KILL YOU.
THAT'S YOUR IDEA OF MEDICINE?!
IT'S ALL RIGHT, INU-YASHA.

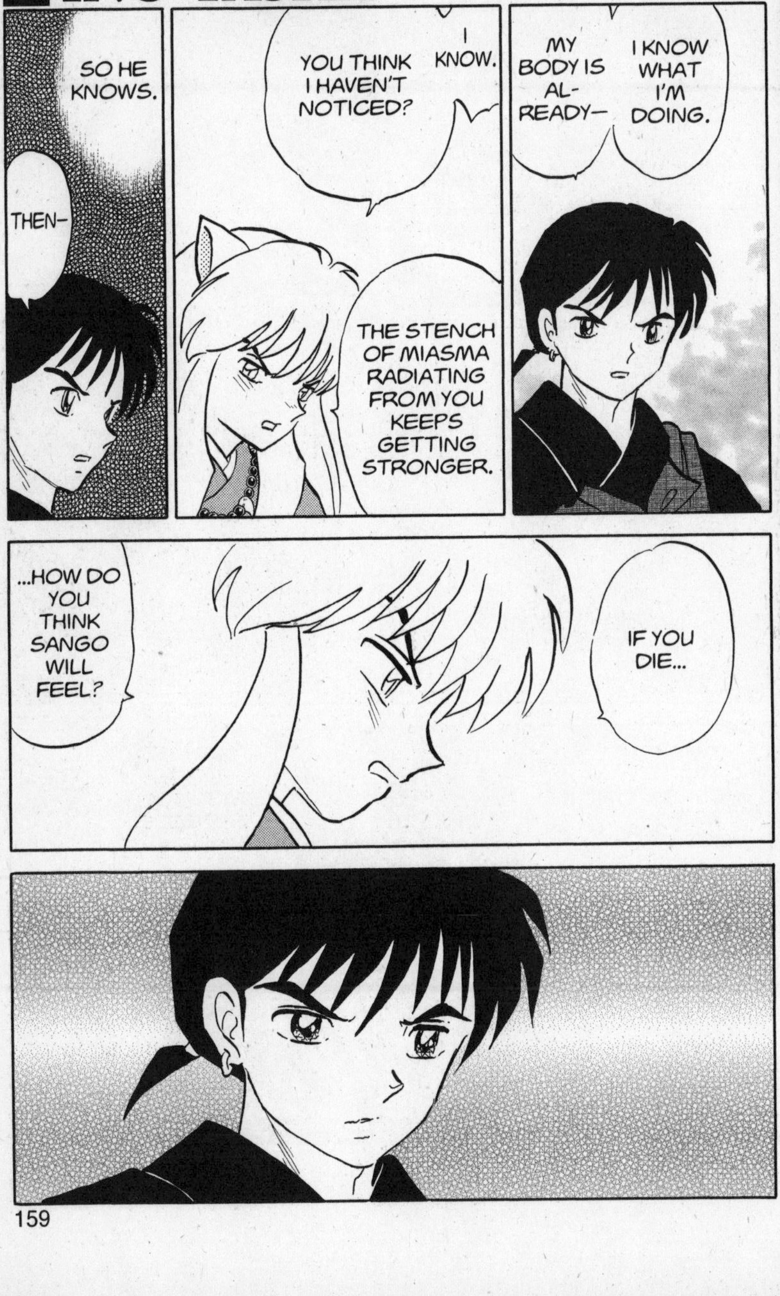
I KNOW WHAT I'M DOING.
MY BODY IS AL-READY—
I KNOW.
YOU THINK I HAVEN'T NOTICED?
THE STENCH OF MIASMA RADIATING FROM YOU KEEPS GETTING STRONGER.
SO HE KNOWS.
THEN—
IF YOU DIE...
...HOW DO YOU THINK SANGO WILL FEEL?

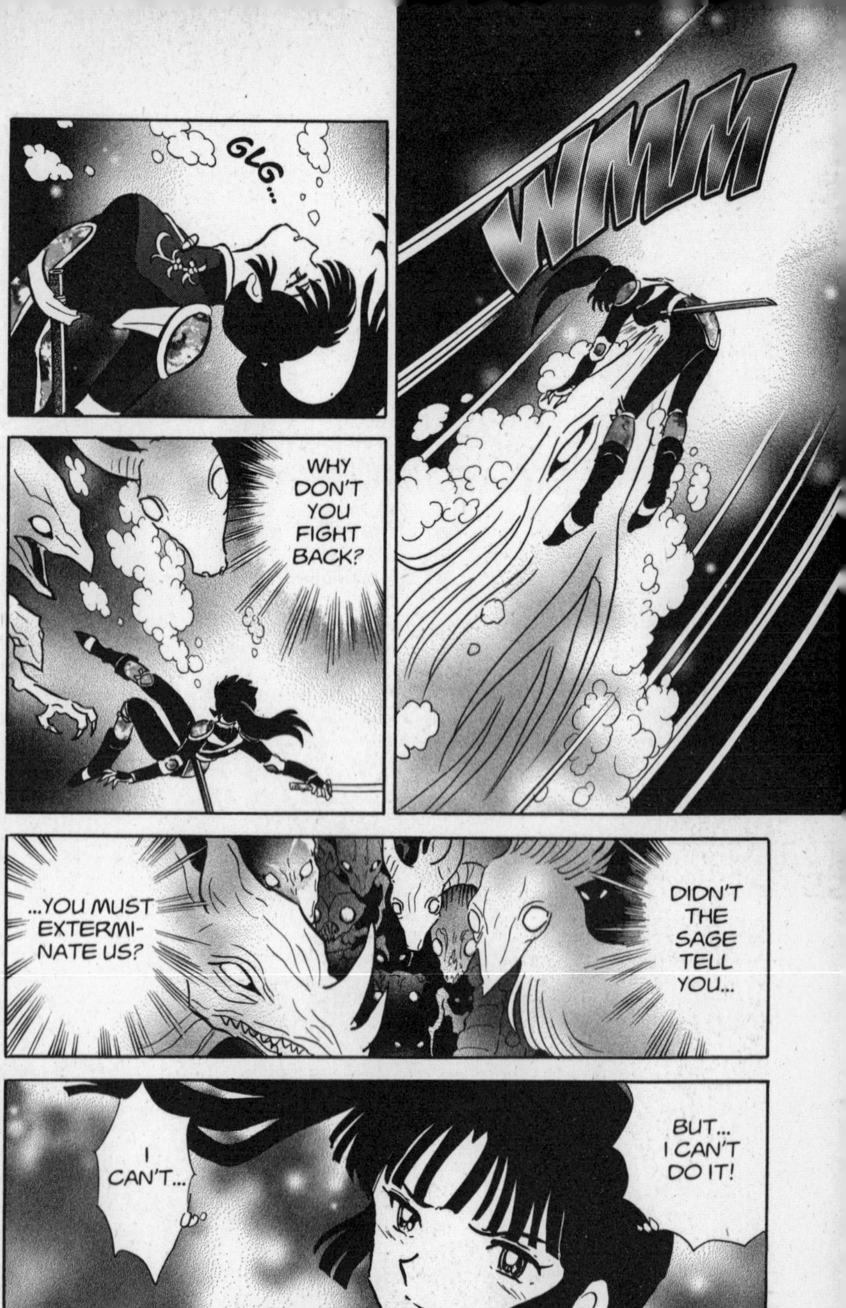
WMMM
GLG...
WHY DON'T YOU FIGHT BACK?
DIDN'T THE SAGE TELL YOU...
...YOU MUST EXTERMI-NATE US?
BUT... I CAN'T DO IT!
I CAN'T...

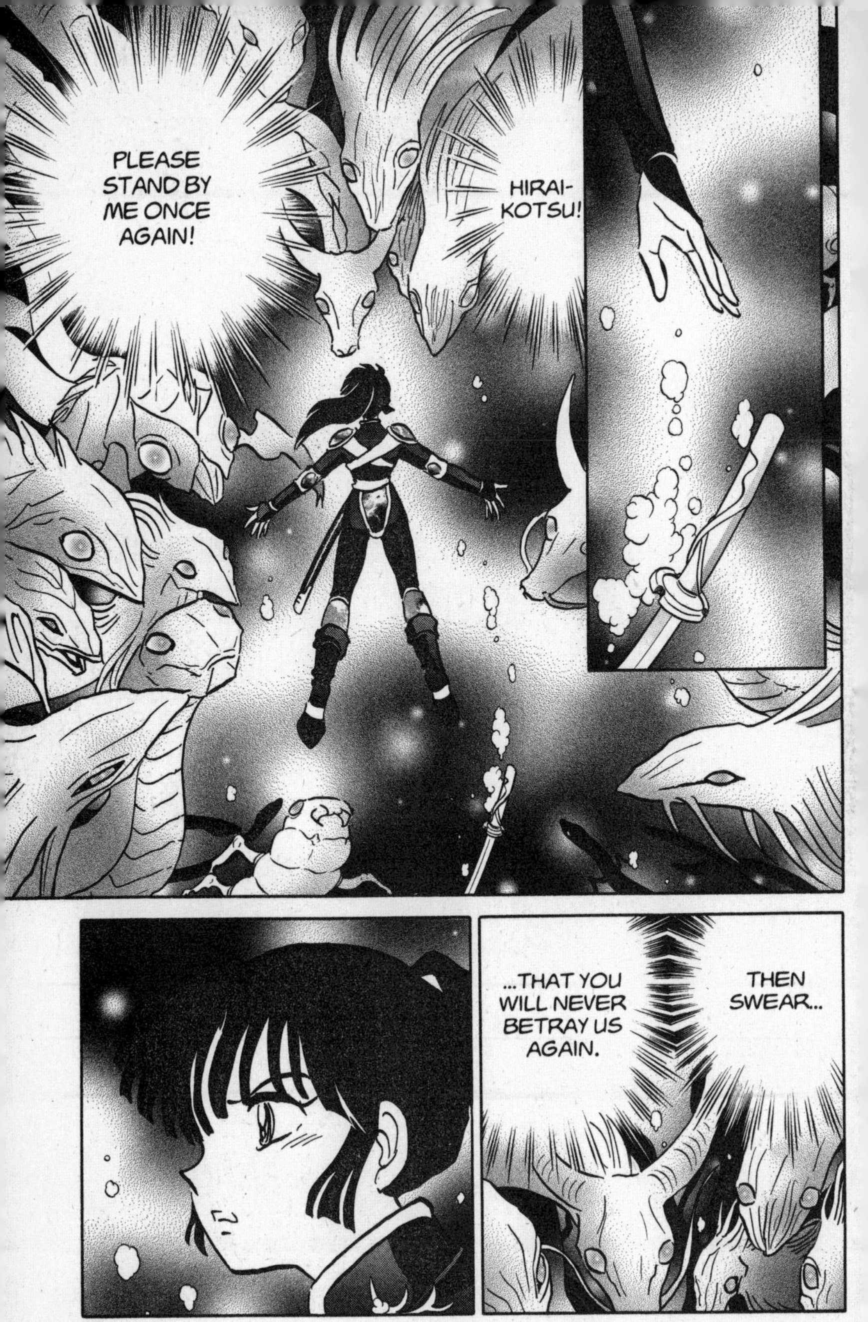
HIRAI-KOTSU!
PLEASE STAND BY ME ONCE AGAIN!
THEN SWEAR...
...THAT YOU WILL NEVER BETRAY US AGAIN.

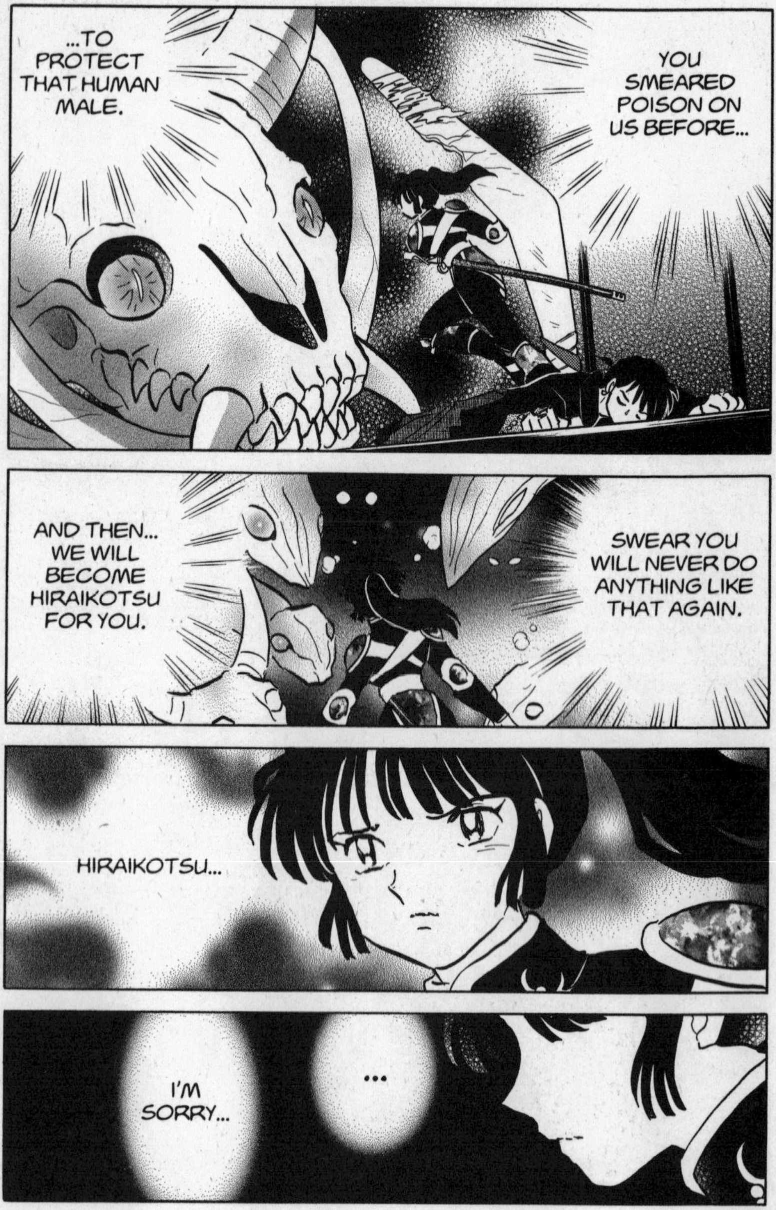
YOU SMEARED POISON ON US BEFORE...
...TO PROTECT THAT HUMAN MALE.
SWEAR YOU WILL NEVER DO ANYTHING LIKE THAT AGAIN.
AND THEN... WE WILL BECOME HIRAIKOTSU FOR YOU.
HIRAIKOTSU...
...
I'M SORRY...

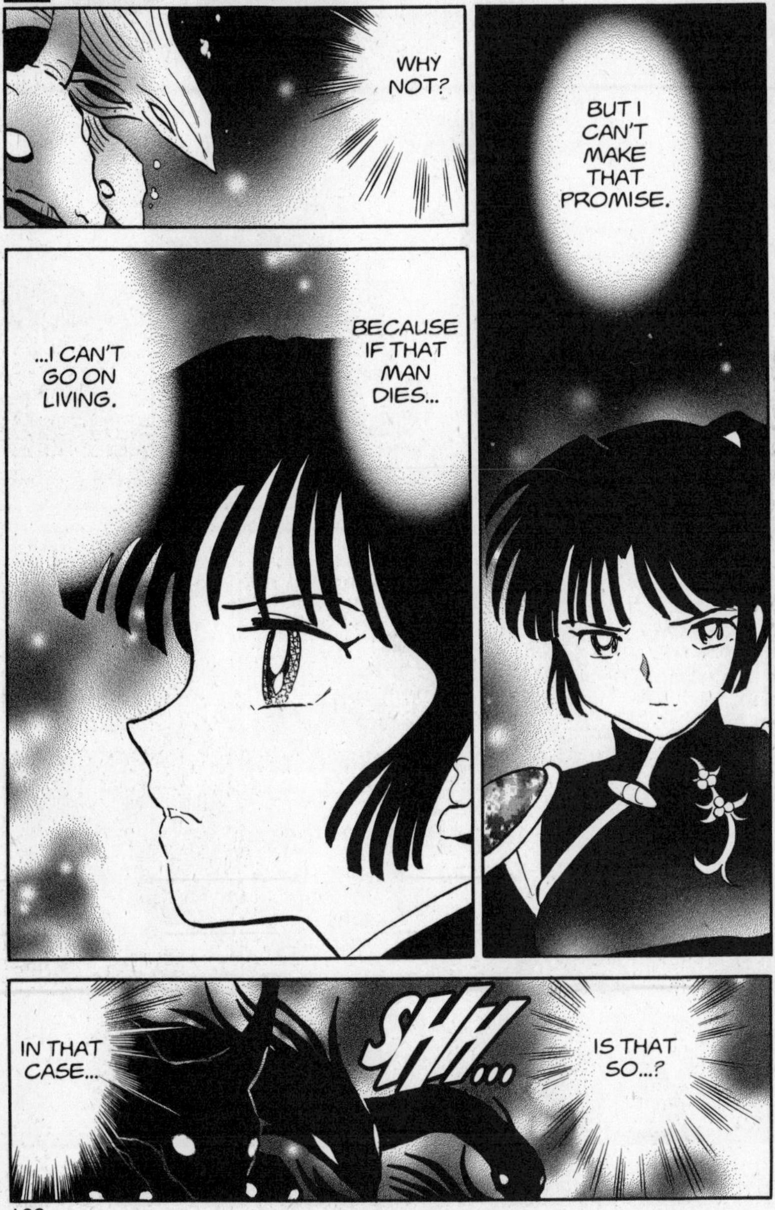
BUT I CAN'T MAKE THAT PROMISE.
WHY NOT?
BECAUSE IF THAT MAN DIES...
...I CAN'T GO ON LIVING.
IS THAT SO...?
SHH...
IN THAT CASE...

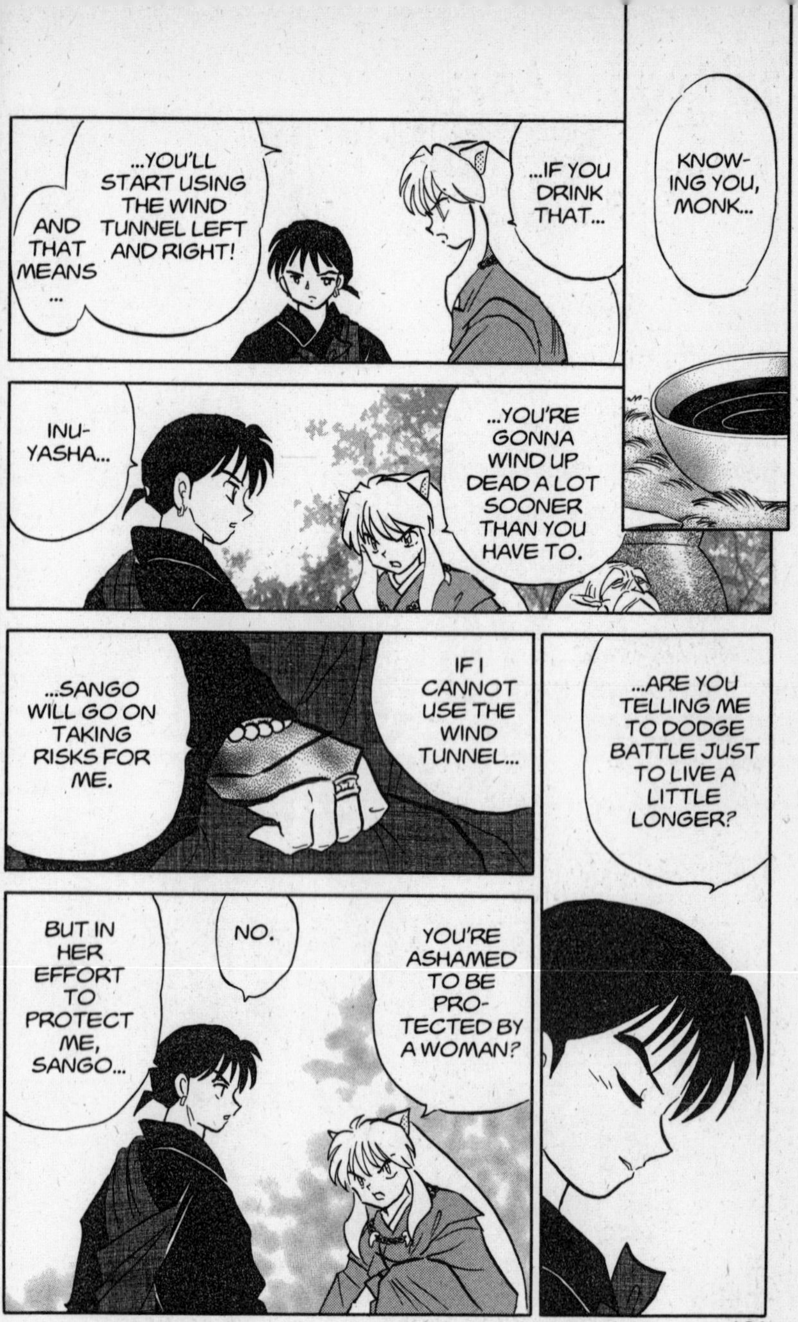
KNOWING YOU, MONK...
...IF YOU DRINK THAT...
...YOU'LL START USING THE WIND TUNNEL LEFT AND RIGHT!
AND THAT MEANS ...
...YOU'RE GONNA WIND UP DEAD A LOT SOONER THAN YOU HAVE TO.
INU-YASHA...
...ARE YOU TELLING ME TO DODGE BATTLE JUST TO LIVE A LITTLE LONGER?
IF I CANNOT USE THE WIND TUNNEL...
...SANGO WILL GO ON TAKING RISKS FOR ME.
YOU'RE ASHAMED TO BE PROTECTED BY A WOMAN?
NO.
BUT IN HER EFFORT TO PROTECT ME, SANGO...

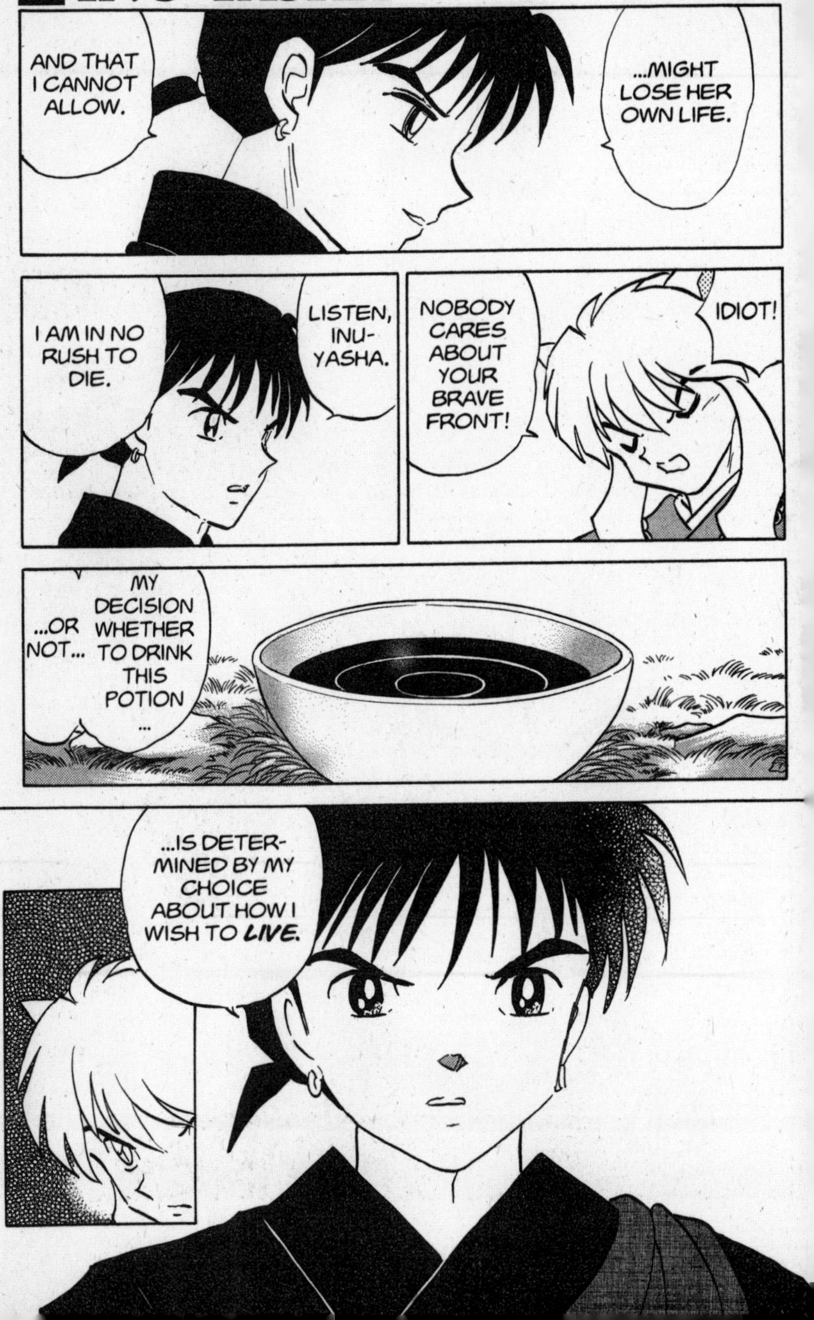
...MIGHT LOSE HER OWN LIFE.
AND THAT I CANNOT ALLOW.
IDIOT!
NOBODY CARES ABOUT YOUR BRAVE FRONT!
LISTEN, INU-YASHA.
I AM IN NO RUSH TO DIE.
MY DECISION WHETHER TO DRINK THIS POTION...
...OR NOT...
...IS DETERMINED BY MY CHOICE ABOUT HOW I WISH TO ***LIVE***.

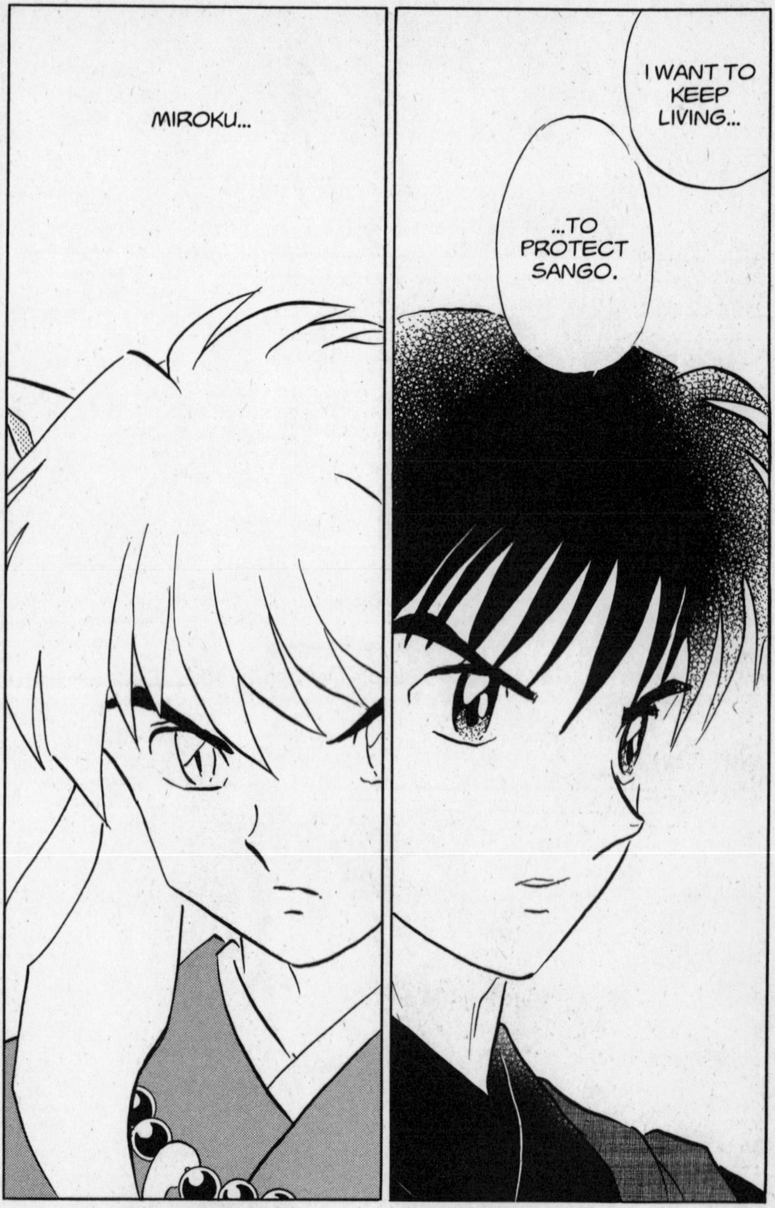
I WANT TO KEEP LIVING...
...TO PROTECT SANGO.
MIROKU...

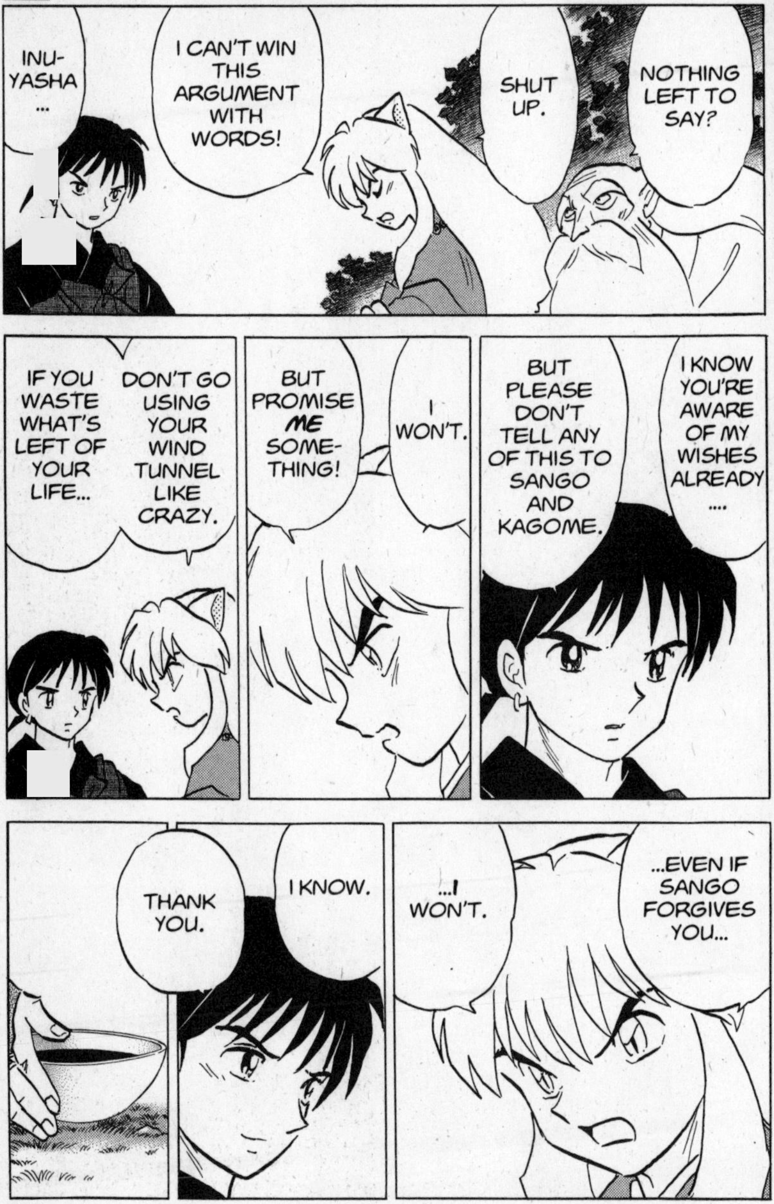
NOTHING LEFT TO SAY?
SHUT UP.
I CAN'T WIN THIS ARGUMENT WITH WORDS!
INU-YASHA ...
I KNOW YOU'RE AWARE OF MY WISHES ALREADY ....
BUT PLEASE DON'T TELL ANY OF THIS TO SANGO AND KAGOME.
I WON'T.
BUT PROMISE *ME* SOMETHING!
DON'T GO USING YOUR WIND TUNNEL LIKE CRAZY.
IF YOU WASTE WHAT'S LEFT OF YOUR LIFE...
...EVEN IF SANGO FORGIVES YOU...
...I WON'T.
I KNOW.
THANK YOU.

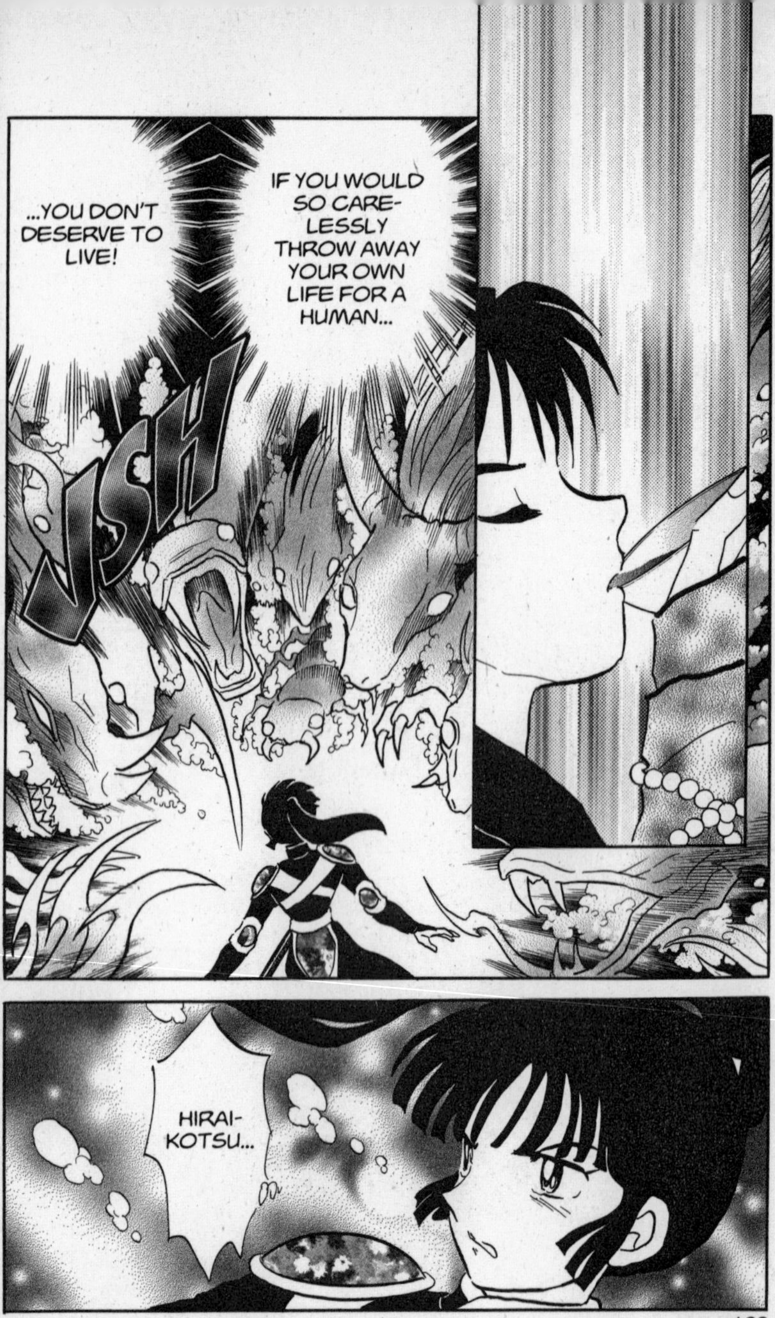
IF YOU WOULD SO CARELESSLY THROW AWAY YOUR OWN LIFE FOR A HUMAN...
...YOU DON'T DESERVE TO LIVE!
VSH
HIRAI-KOTSU...

SCROLL 10

THE RESPONSE

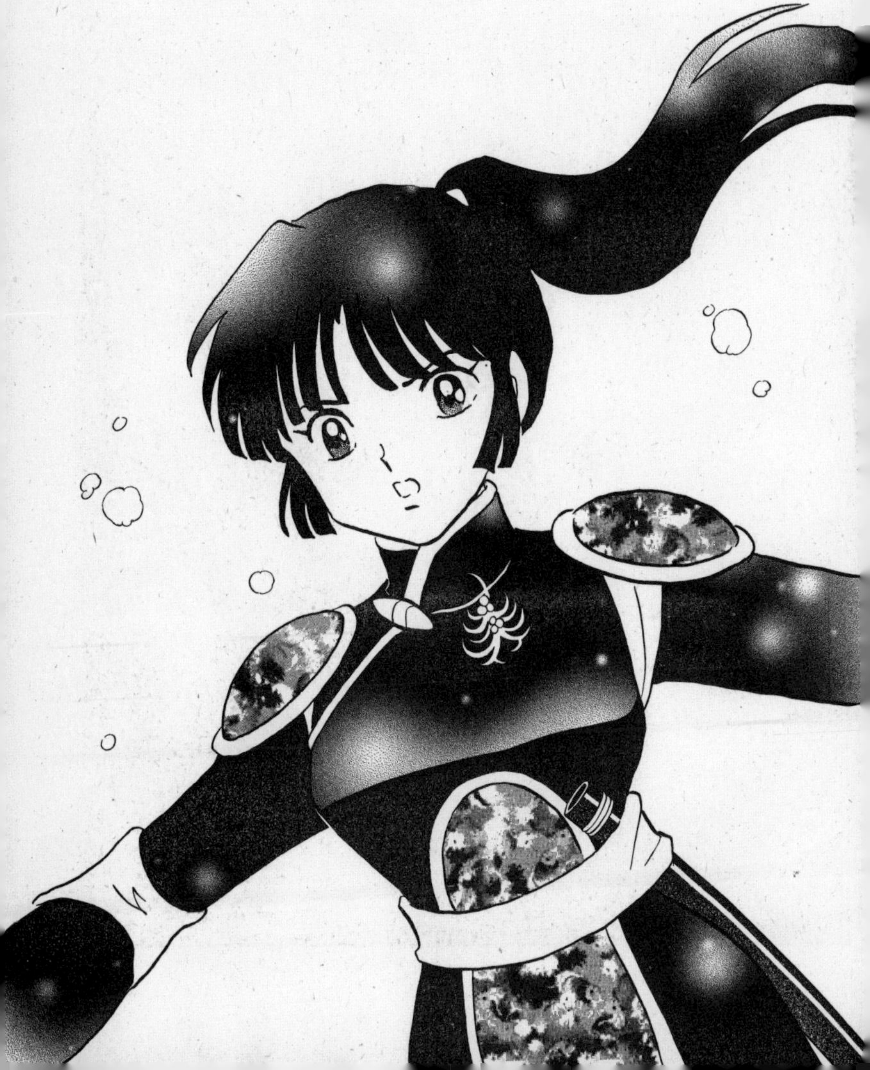

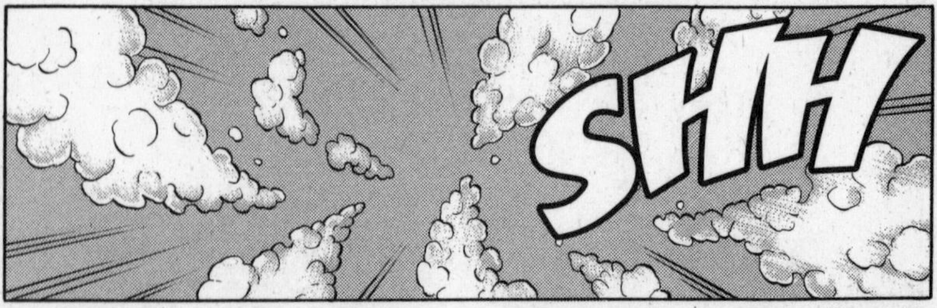
SHH
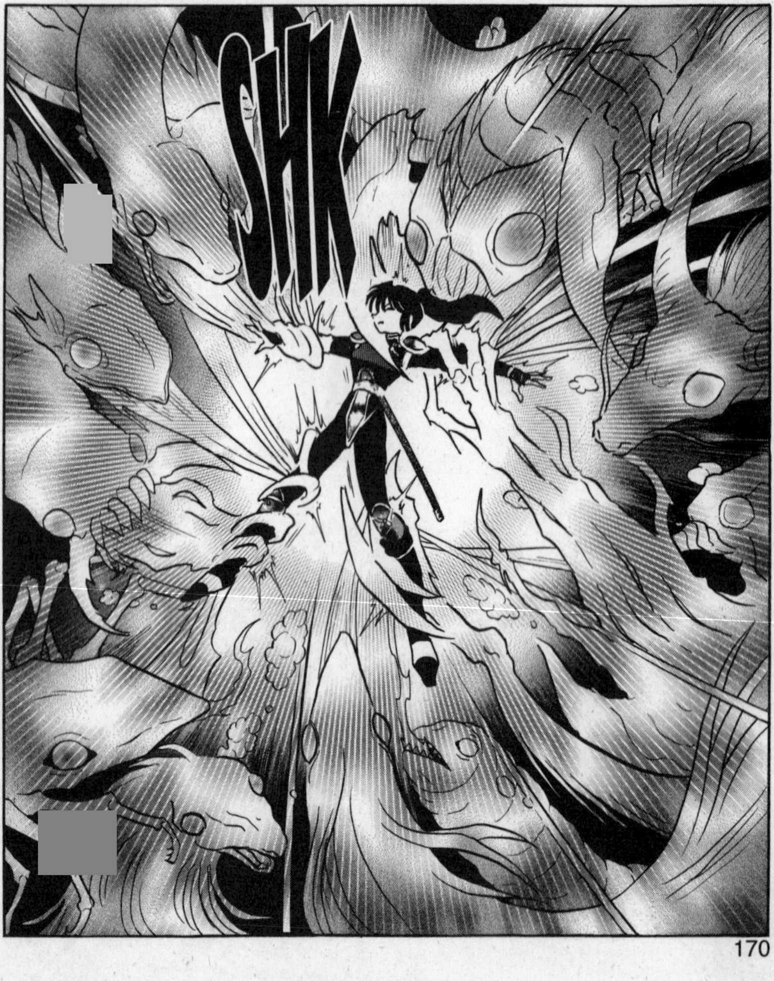
SHK

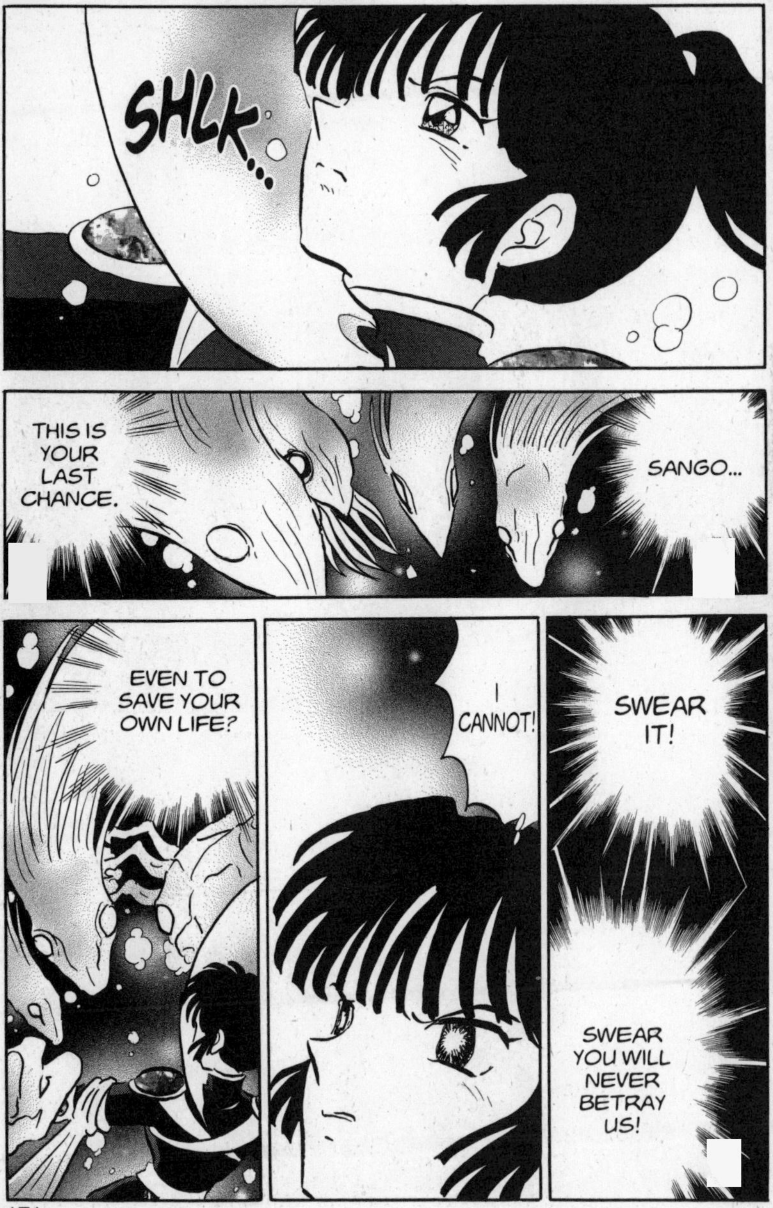
SHLK...
SANGO...
THIS IS YOUR LAST CHANCE.
SWEAR IT!
SWEAR YOU WILL NEVER BETRAY US!
I CANNOT!
EVEN TO SAVE YOUR OWN LIFE?

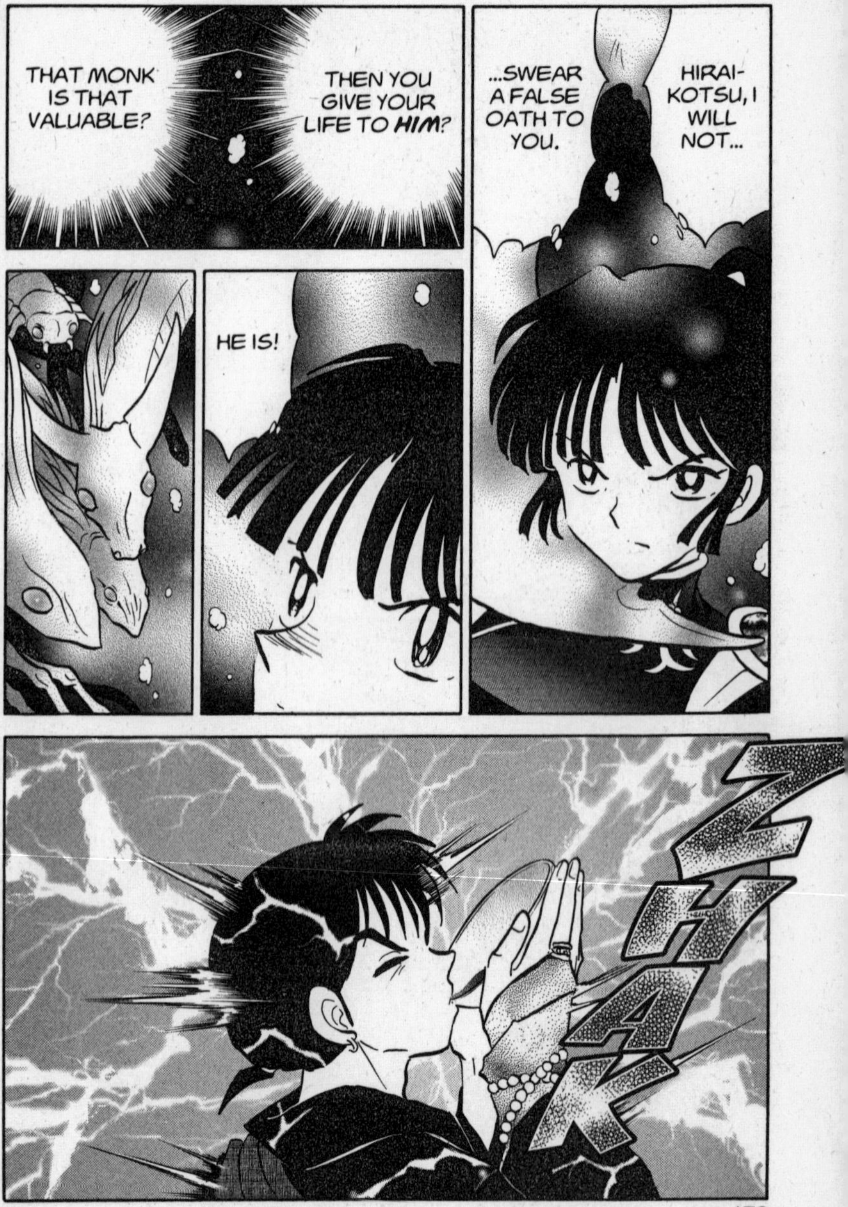
HIRAI-KOTSU, I WILL NOT...
...SWEAR A FALSE OATH TO YOU.
THEN YOU GIVE YOUR LIFE TO *HIM*?
THAT MONK IS THAT VALUABLE?
HE IS!
ZHAAK

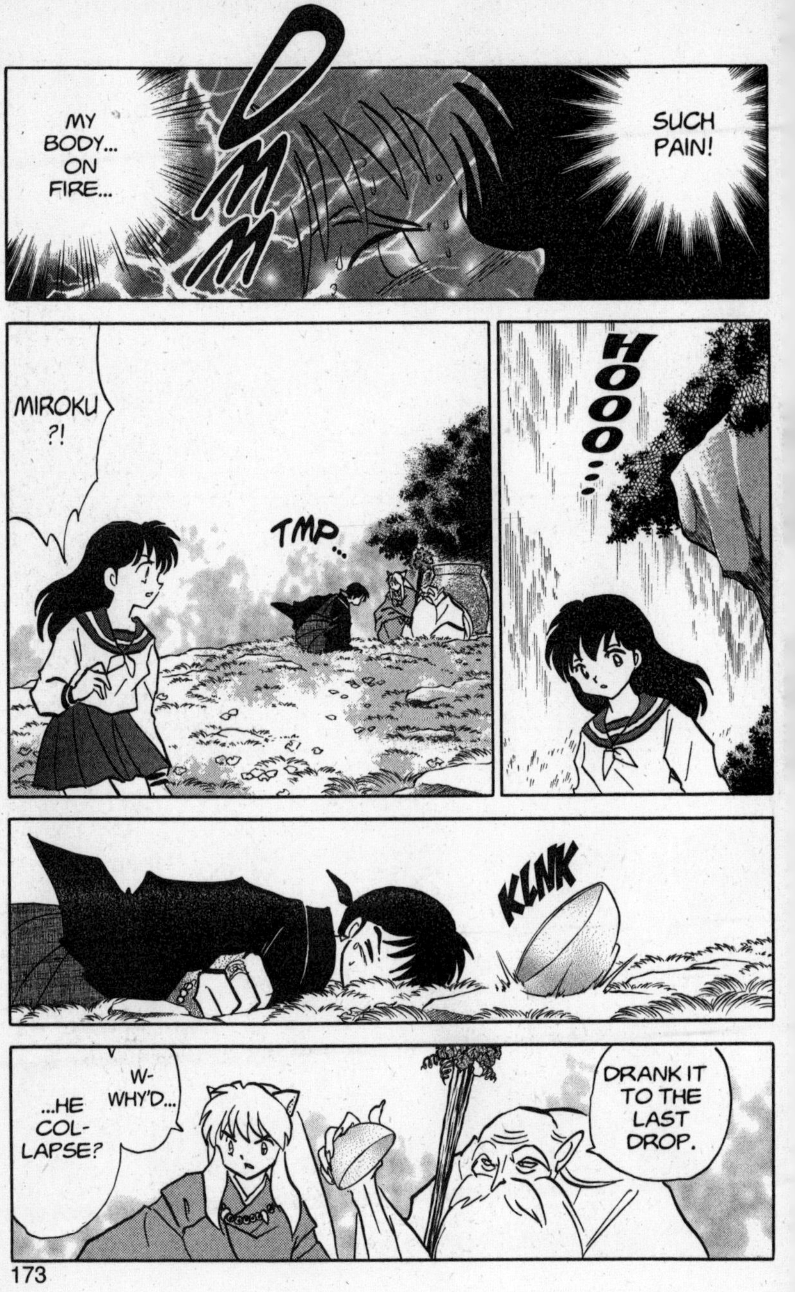
SUCH PAIN!
MY BODY... ON FIRE...
OMMM
HOOOO...
MIROKU ?!
TMP...
KLNK
DRANK IT TO THE LAST DROP.
W- WHY'D...
...HE COL-LAPSE?

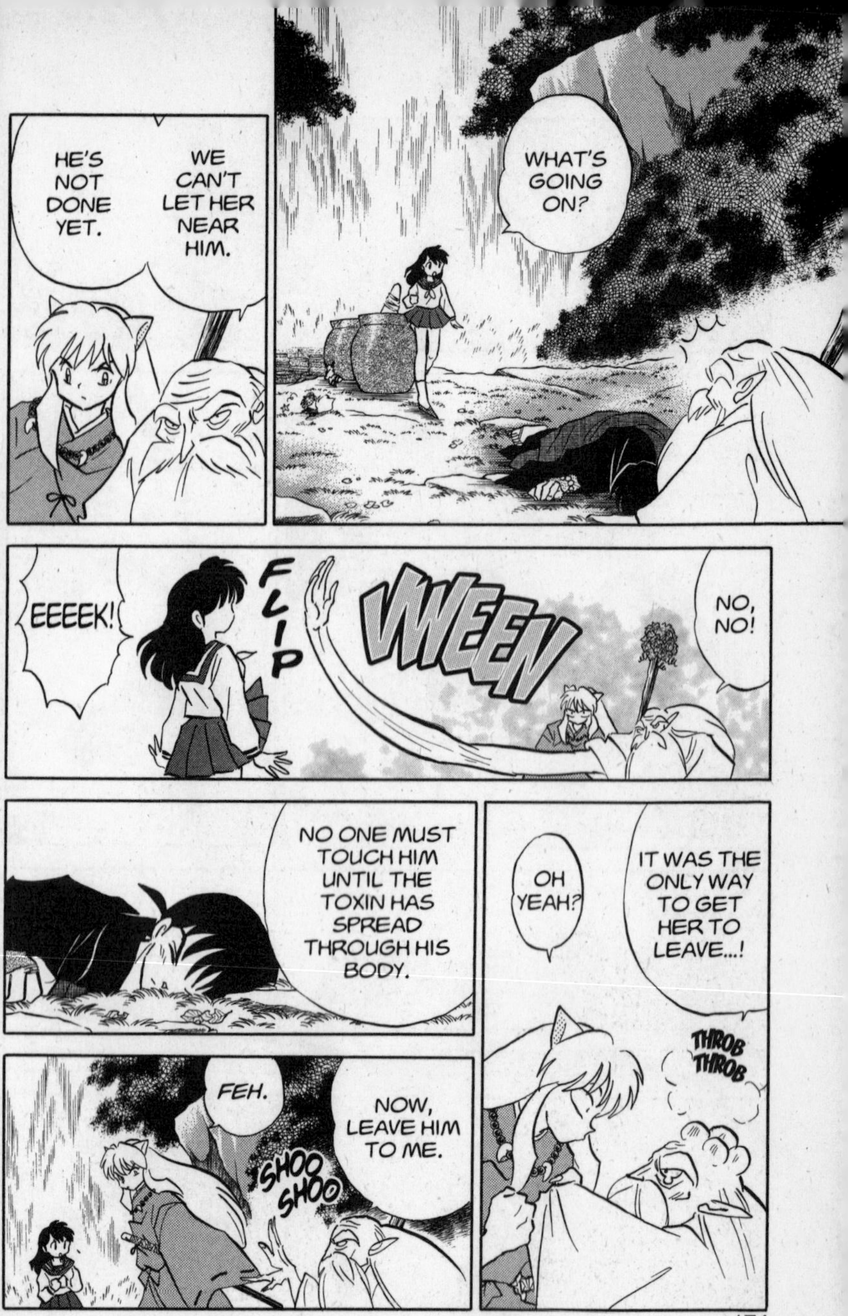
WHAT'S GOING ON?
WE CAN'T LET HER NEAR HIM.
HE'S NOT DONE YET.
NO, NO!
VWEEN
FLIP
EEEEK!
IT WAS THE ONLY WAY TO GET HER TO LEAVE...!
OH YEAH?
THROB THROB
NO ONE MUST TOUCH HIM UNTIL THE TOXIN HAS SPREAD THROUGH HIS BODY.
NOW, LEAVE HIM TO ME.
FEH.
SHOO SHOO

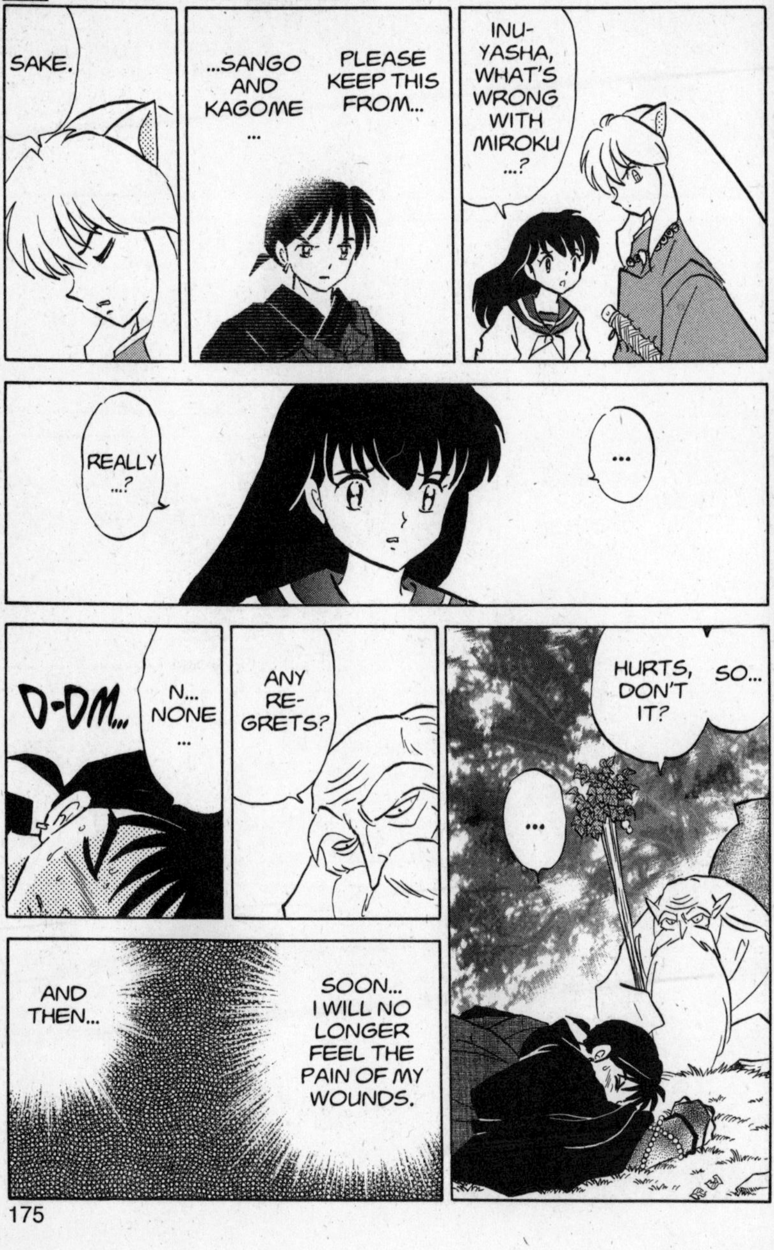
INU-YASHA, WHAT'S WRONG WITH MIROKU...?
PLEASE KEEP THIS FROM...
...SANGO AND KAGOME...
SAKE.
...
REALLY...?
SO...
HURTS, DON'T IT?
...
ANY RE-GRETS?
N... NONE...
D-DM...
SOON... I WILL NO LONGER FEEL THE PAIN OF MY WOUNDS.
AND THEN...

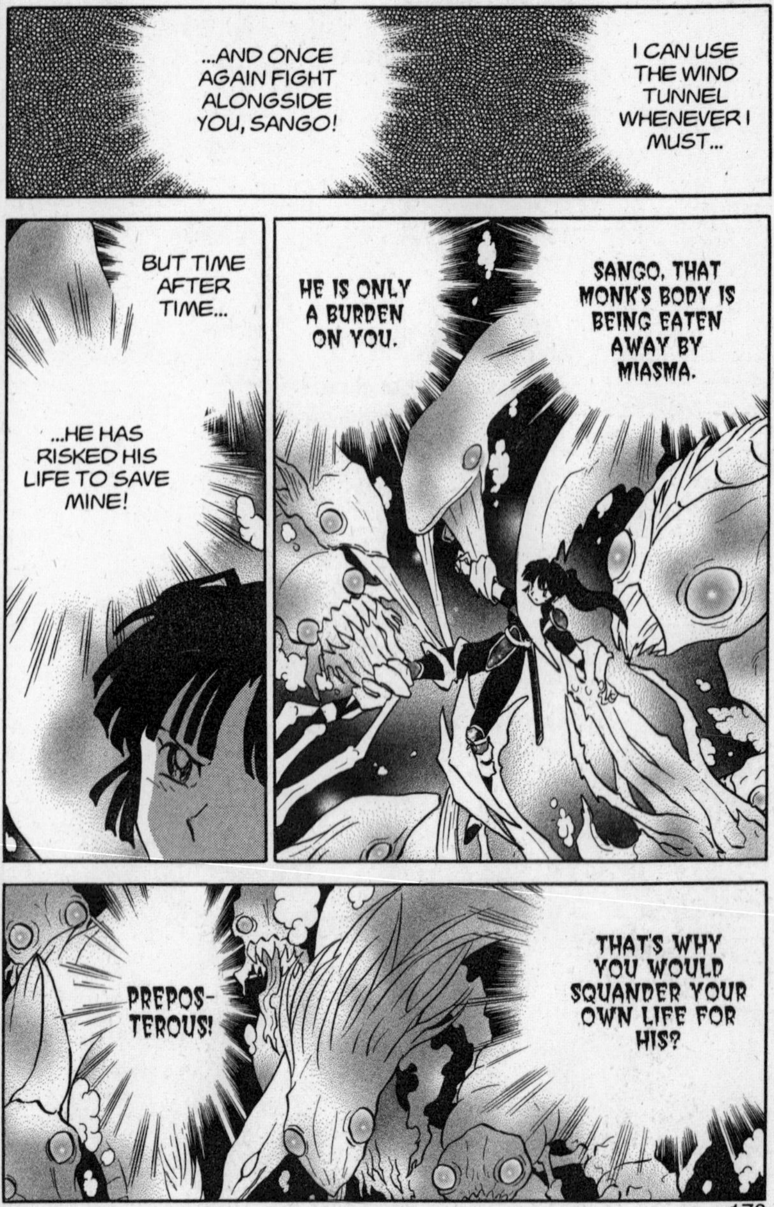
I CAN USE THE WIND TUNNEL WHENEVER I MUST...
...AND ONCE AGAIN FIGHT ALONGSIDE YOU, SANGO!
SANGO, THAT MONK'S BODY IS BEING EATEN AWAY BY MIASMA.
HE IS ONLY A BURDEN ON YOU.
BUT TIME AFTER TIME...
...HE HAS RISKED HIS LIFE TO SAVE MINE!
THAT'S WHY YOU WOULD SQUANDER YOUR OWN LIFE FOR HIS?
PREPOS-TEROUS!

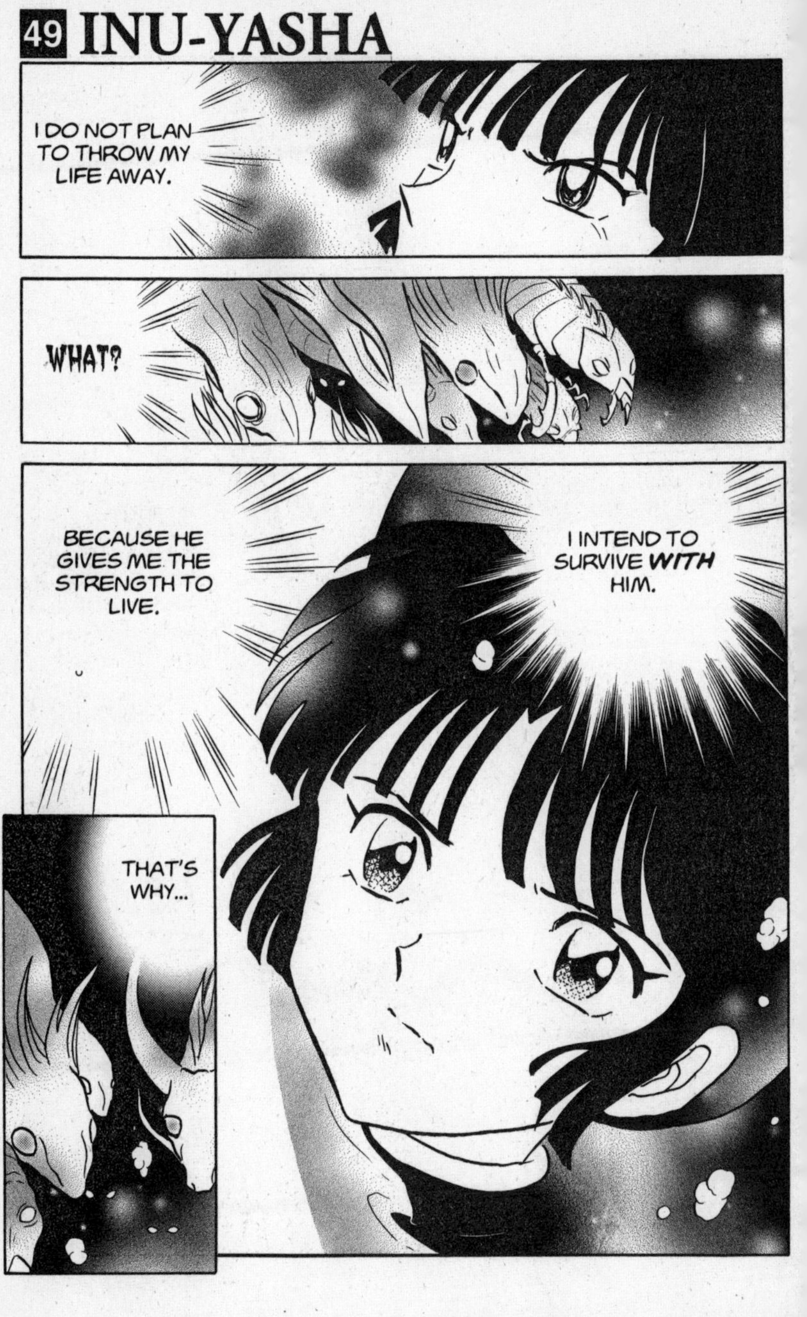
I DO NOT PLAN TO THROW MY LIFE AWAY.
WHAT?
I INTEND TO SURVIVE WITH HIM.
BECAUSE HE GIVES ME THE STRENGTH TO LIVE.
THAT'S WHY...

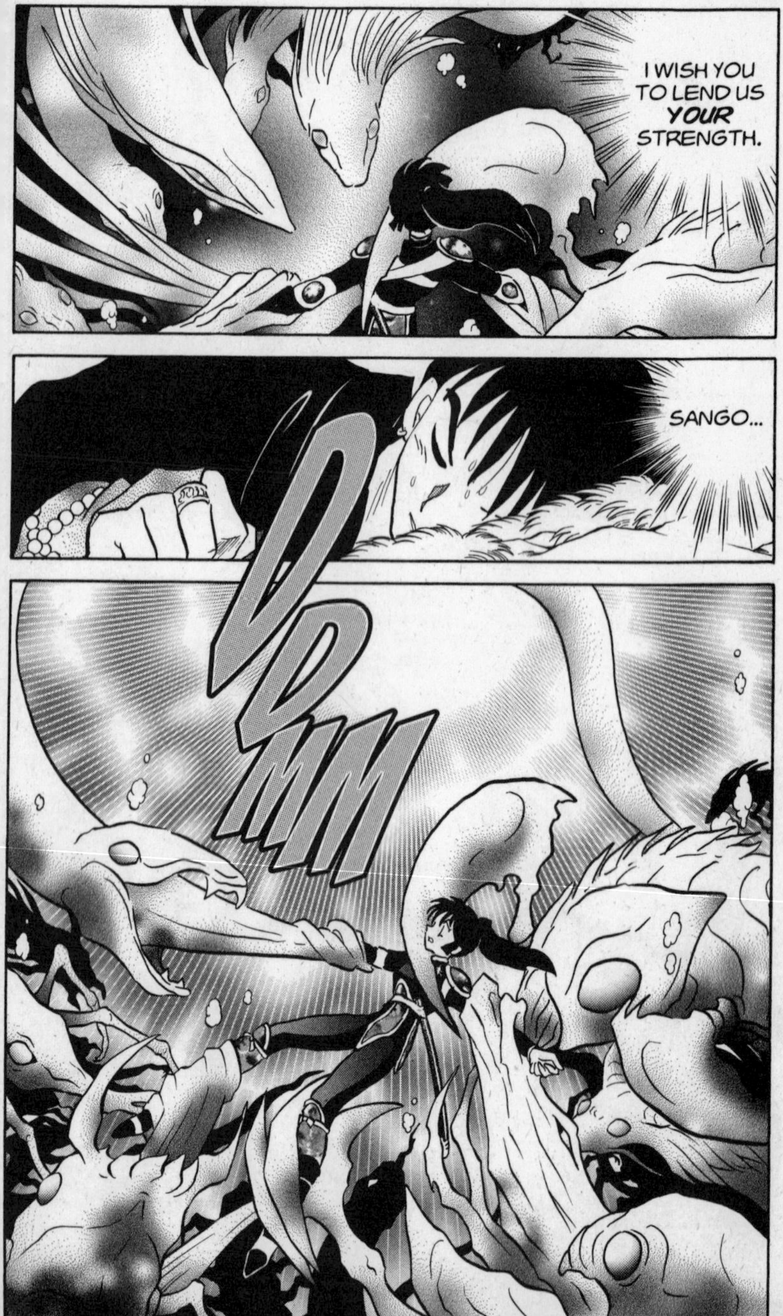
I WISH YOU TO LEND US **YOUR** STRENGTH.
SANGO...
DOMM

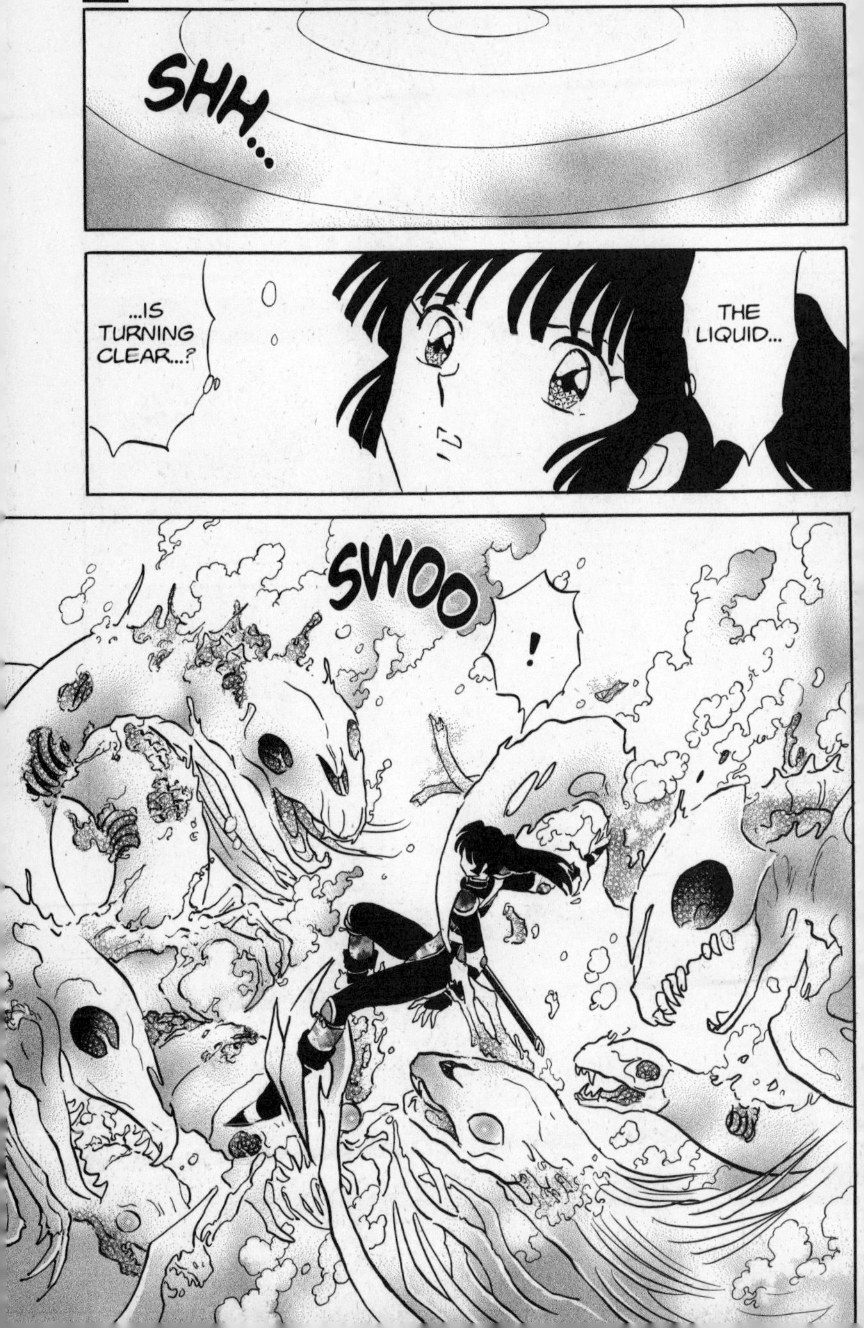
SHH...
THE LIQUID...
...IS TURNING CLEAR...?
SWOO
!

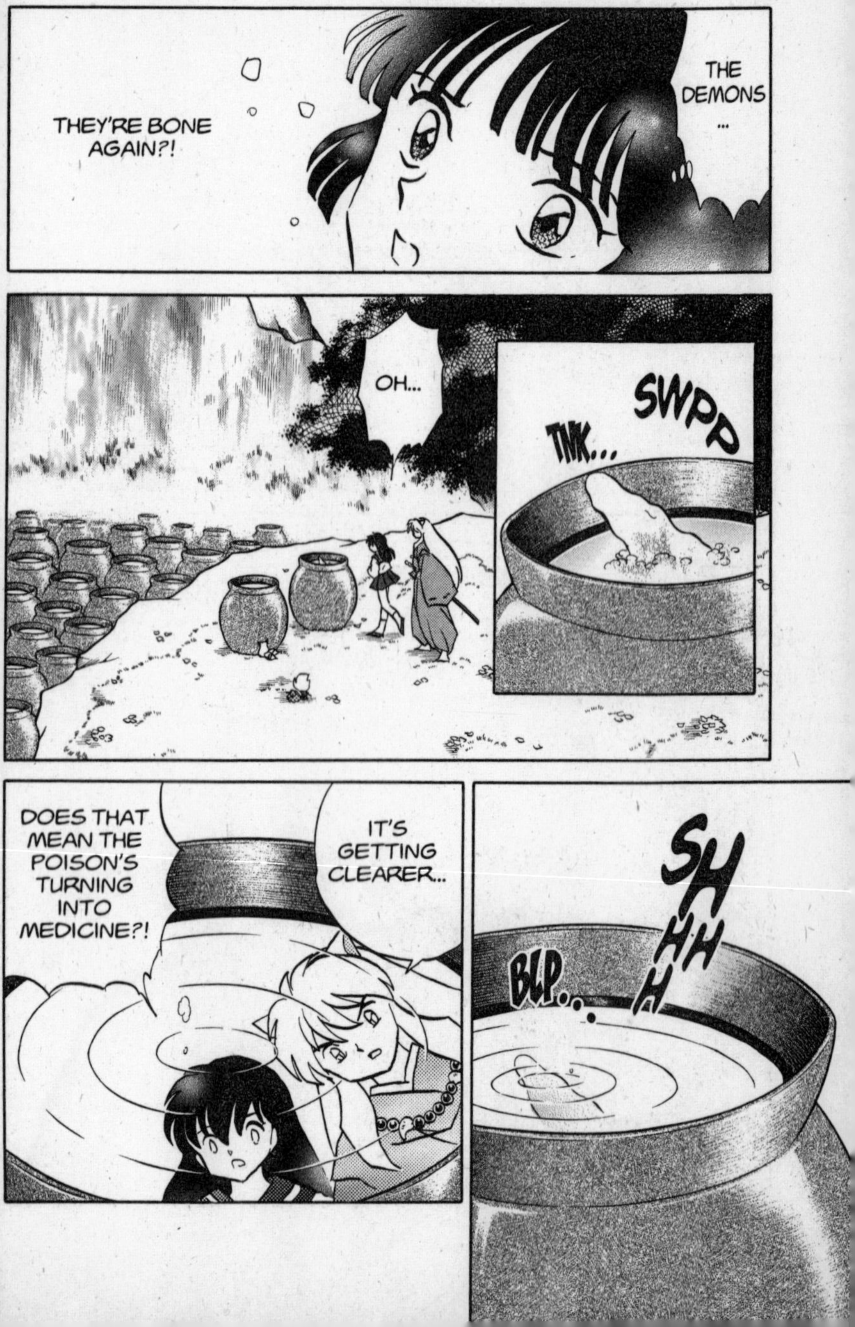

THE DEMONS ...
THEY'RE BONE AGAIN?!
SWPP
TNK...
OH...
SHHHH
BLP...
IT'S GETTING CLEARER...
DOES THAT MEAN THE POISON'S TURNING INTO MEDICINE?!

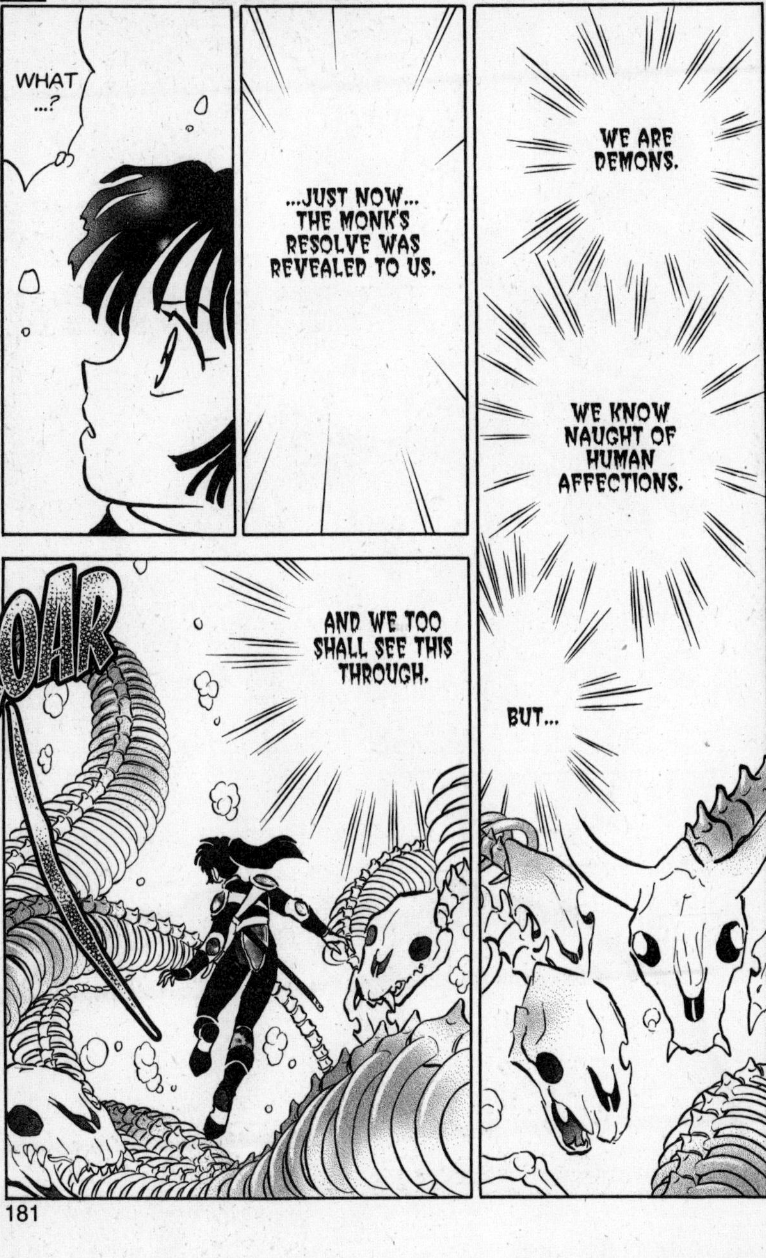
WE ARE DEMONS.
WE KNOW NAUGHT OF HUMAN AFFECTIONS.
BUT...
...JUST NOW... THE MONK'S RESOLVE WAS REVEALED TO US.
WHAT ...?
AND WE TOO SHALL SEE THIS THROUGH.
ROAR

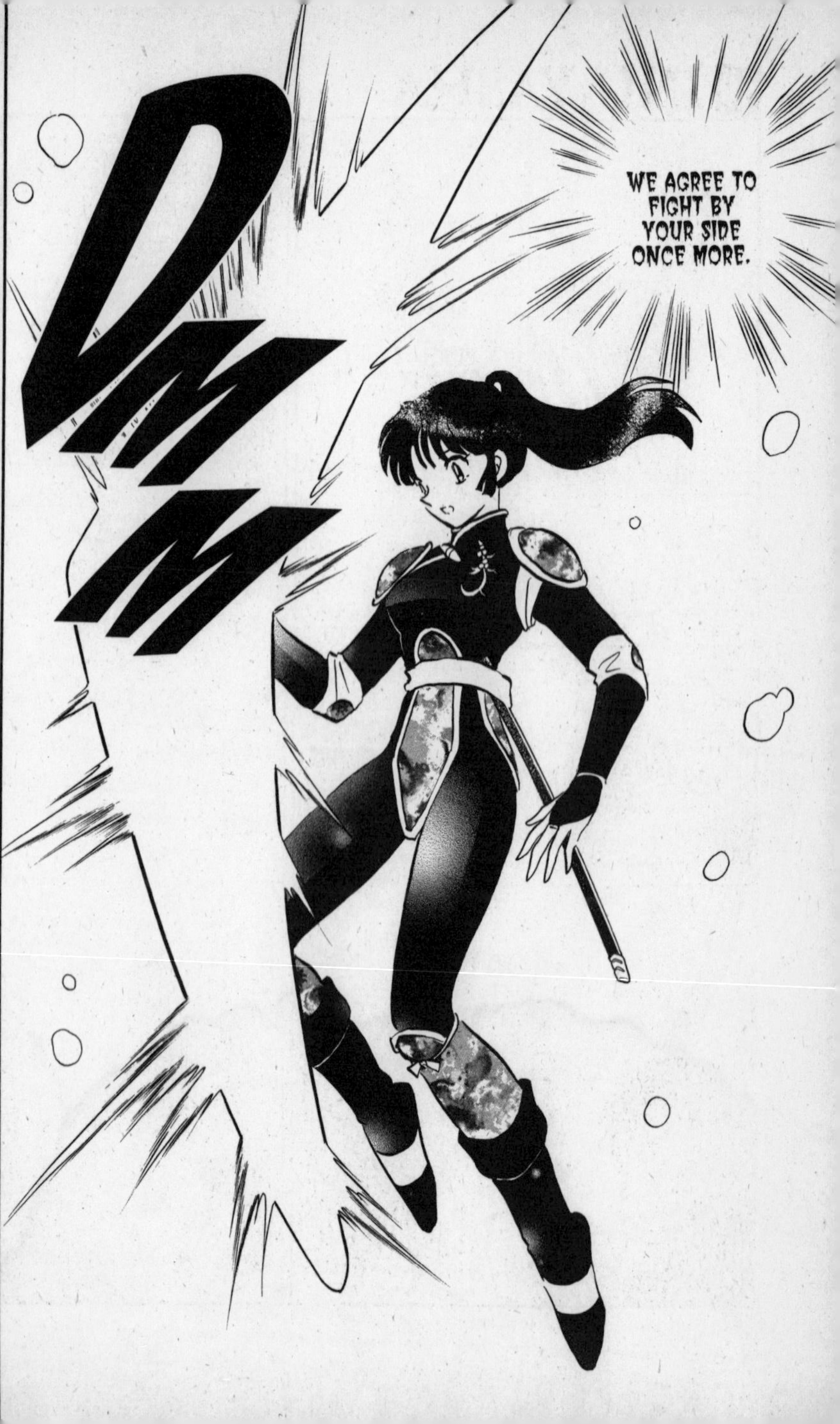
WE AGREE TO FIGHT BY YOUR SIDE ONCE MORE.
DMM

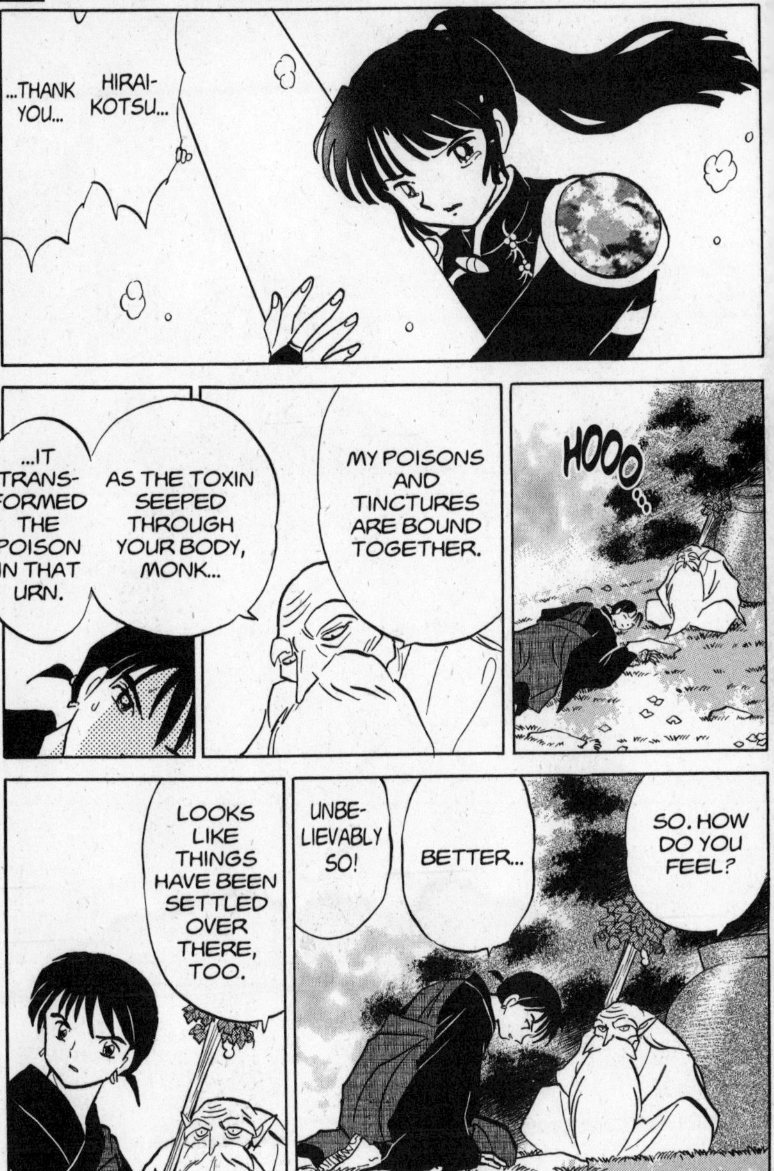
HIRAI-KOTSU...
...THANK YOU...
HOOO
MY POISONS AND TINCTURES ARE BOUND TOGETHER.
AS THE TOXIN SEEPED THROUGH YOUR BODY, MONK...
...IT TRANSFORMED THE POISON IN THAT URN.
SO. HOW DO YOU FEEL?
BETTER...
UNBELIEVABLY SO!
LOOKS LIKE THINGS HAVE BEEN SETTLED OVER THERE, TOO.

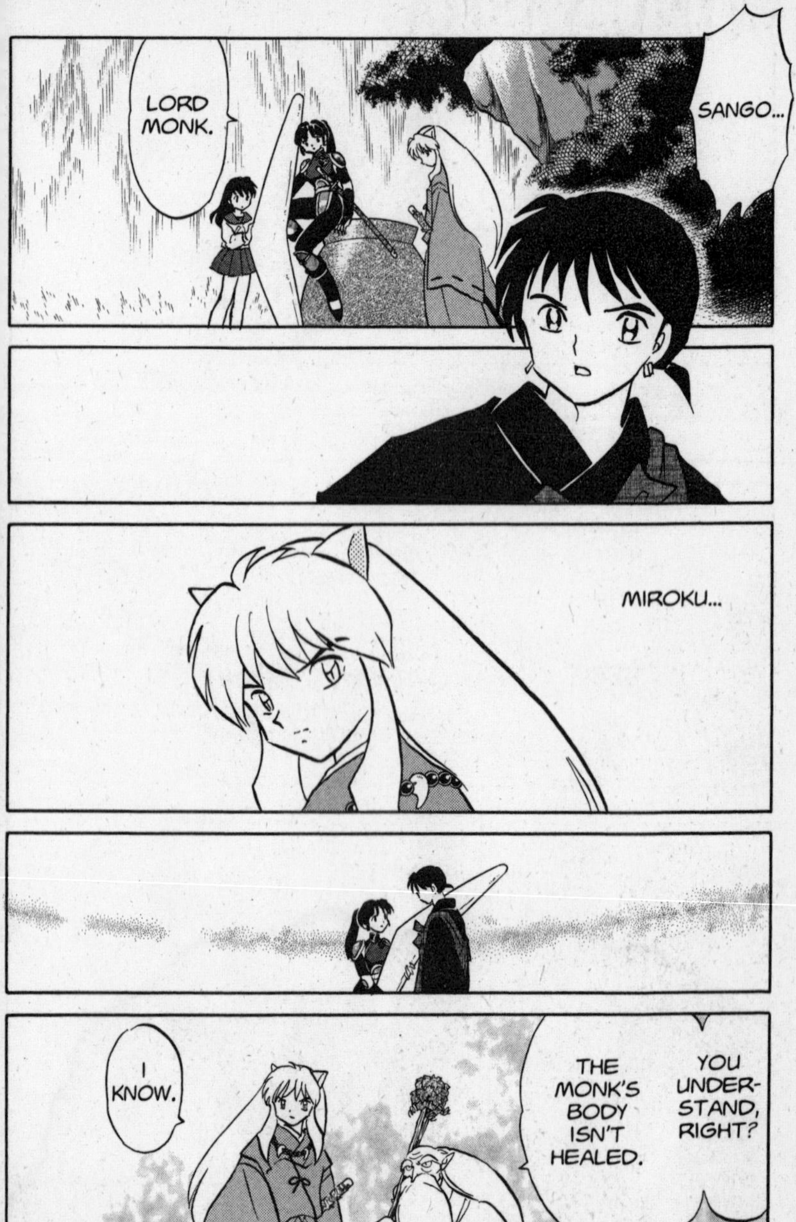
SANGO...
LORD MONK.
MIROKU...
YOU UNDERSTAND, RIGHT?
THE MONK'S BODY ISN'T HEALED.
I KNOW.

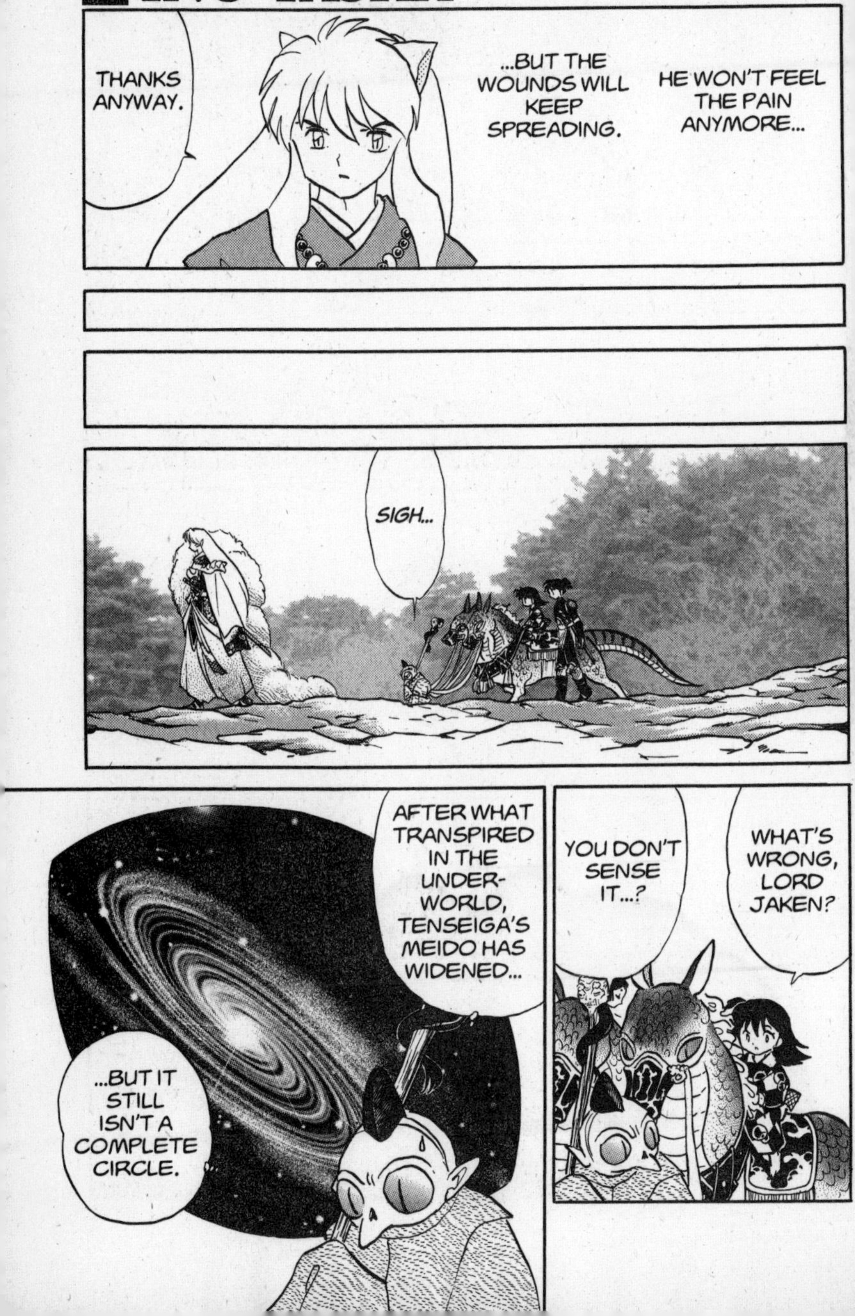
HE WON'T FEEL THE PAIN ANYMORE...
...BUT THE WOUNDS WILL KEEP SPREADING.
THANKS ANYWAY.
SIGH...
WHAT'S WRONG, LORD JAKEN?
YOU DON'T SENSE IT...?
AFTER WHAT TRANSPIRED IN THE UNDER-WORLD, TENSEIGA'S MEIDO HAS WIDENED...
...BUT IT STILL ISN'T A COMPLETE CIRCLE.

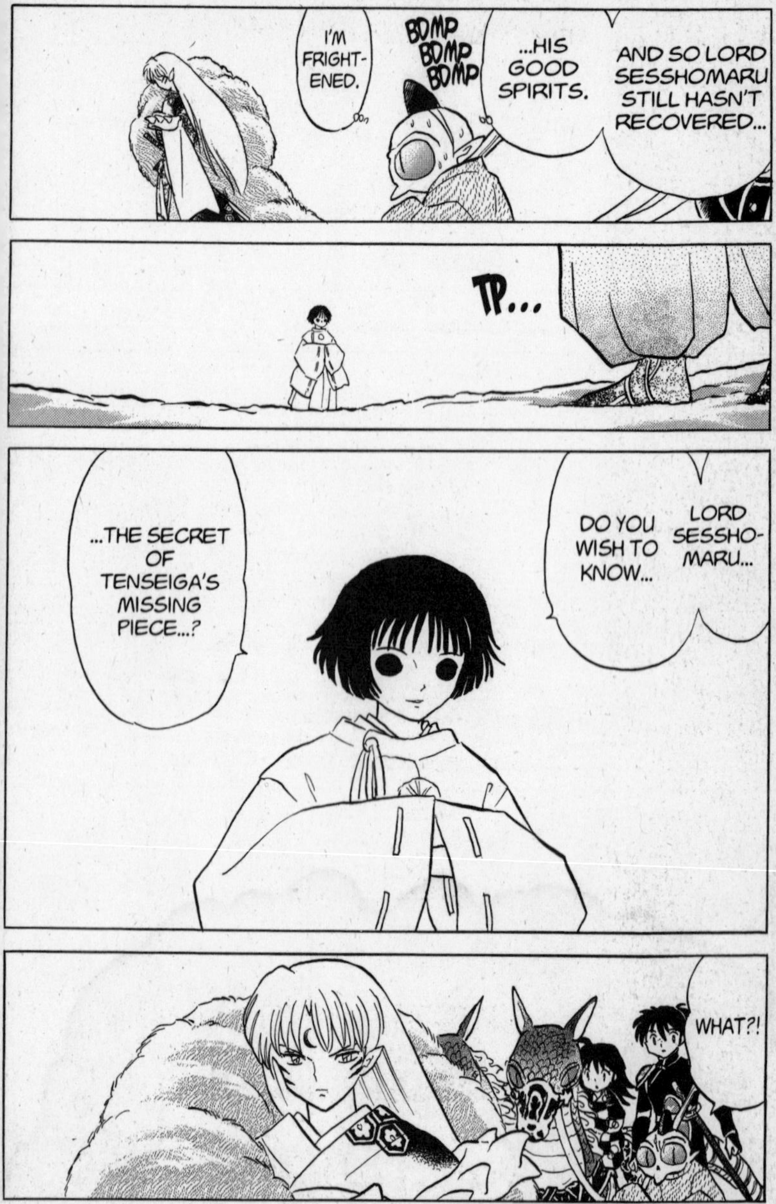
AND SO LORD SESSHOMARU STILL HASN'T RECOVERED...
...HIS GOOD SPIRITS.
BDMP BDMP BDMP
I'M FRIGHT-ENED.
TP...
LORD SESSHO-MARU...
DO YOU WISH TO KNOW...
...THE SECRET OF TENSEIGA'S MISSING PIECE...?
WHAT?!

TO BE CONTINUED...

INUYASHA

VOL. 49
Shonen Sunday Edition

Story and Art by
RUMIKO TAKAHASHI

© 1997 Rumiko TAKAHASHI/Shogakukan
All rights reserved.
Original Japanese edition "INUYASHA"
published by SHOGAKUKAN Inc.

English Adaptation by Gerard Jones

Translation/Mari Morimoto
Touch-up Art & Lettering/Bill Schuch
Cover & Interior Graphic Design/Yuki Ameda
Editor/Annette Roman

VP, Production/Alvin Lu
VP, Sales & Product Marketing/Gonzalo Ferreyra
VP, Creative/Linda Espinosa
Publisher/Hyoe Narita

The stories, characters and incidents mentioned
in this publication are entirely fictional.

No portion of this book may be reproduced or
transmitted in any form or by any means without
written permission from the copyright holders.

Printed in the U.S.A.

Published by VIZ Media, LLC
P.O. Box 77010
San Francisco, CA 94107

10 9 8 7 6 5 4 3 2 1
First printing, June 2010

PARENTAL ADVISORY
INUYASHA is rated T+ for Older
Teen and is recommended for
ages 16 and up. This volume
contains violence.
ratings.viz.com

www.viz.com   WWW.SHONENSUNDAY.COM

MANGA, ANI-MANGA™ & ART BOOKS!

RATED
T+
FOR OLDER
TEEN
ratings.viz.com

VIZ
MEDIA

www.viz.com
inuyasha.viz.com

INUYASHA

Read the action from the start with the original manga series

Full color adaptation of the popular TV series

Art book with cel art, paintings, character profiles and more

© 1997 Rumiko TAKAHASHI/Shogakukan Inc.
© 2001 Rumiko TAKAHASHI/Shogakukan Inc. © Rumiko TAKAHASHI/Shogakukan, Yomiuri TV, Sunrise 2000. Ani-Manga is a trademark of VIZ Media, LLC.
© 2001 Rumiko TAKAHASHI/Shogakukan Inc.

InuYasha

The Ultimate Source for Fans!

Based on the best-selling manga series

- Stunning, full color series artwork
- Historical feudal fairy tale facts
- Comments from Rumiko Takahashi on every aspect of her creative process
- Eight-page *Inuyasha* interview with Takahashi

Complete your Inuyasha collection—buy yours today at **store.viz.com**!

© 2003 Rumiko TAKAHASHI/Shogakukan Inc.
Cover art subject to change.

inuyasha.viz.com

www.viz.com

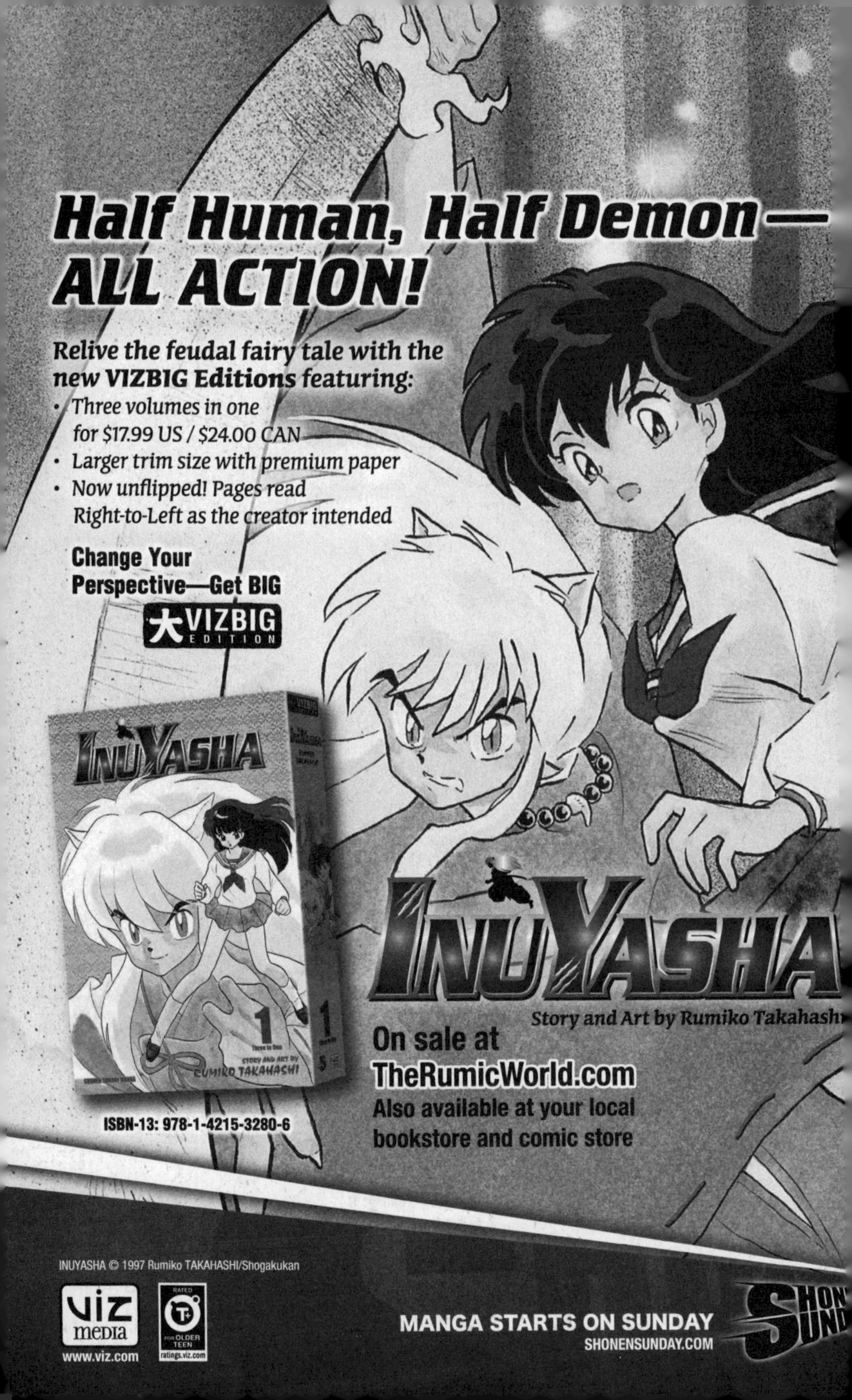
Half Human, Half Demon—
ALL ACTION!
Relive the feudal fairy tale with the new VIZBIG Editions featuring:
• Three volumes in one for $17.99 US / $24.00 CAN
• Larger trim size with premium paper
• Now unflipped! Pages read Right-to-Left as the creator intended
Change Your Perspective—Get BIG
大 VIZBIG EDITION
INUYASHA
1
Three in One
STORY AND ART BY RUMIKO TAKAHASHI
ISBN-13: 978-1-4215-3280-6
INUYASHA
Story and Art by Rumiko Takahashi
On sale at
TheRumicWorld.com
Also available at your local bookstore and comic store
INUYASHA © 1997 Rumiko TAKAHASHI/Shogakukan
viz media
www.viz.com
RATED T+ FOR OLDER TEEN
ratings.viz.com
MANGA STARTS ON SUNDAY
SHONENSUNDAY.COM

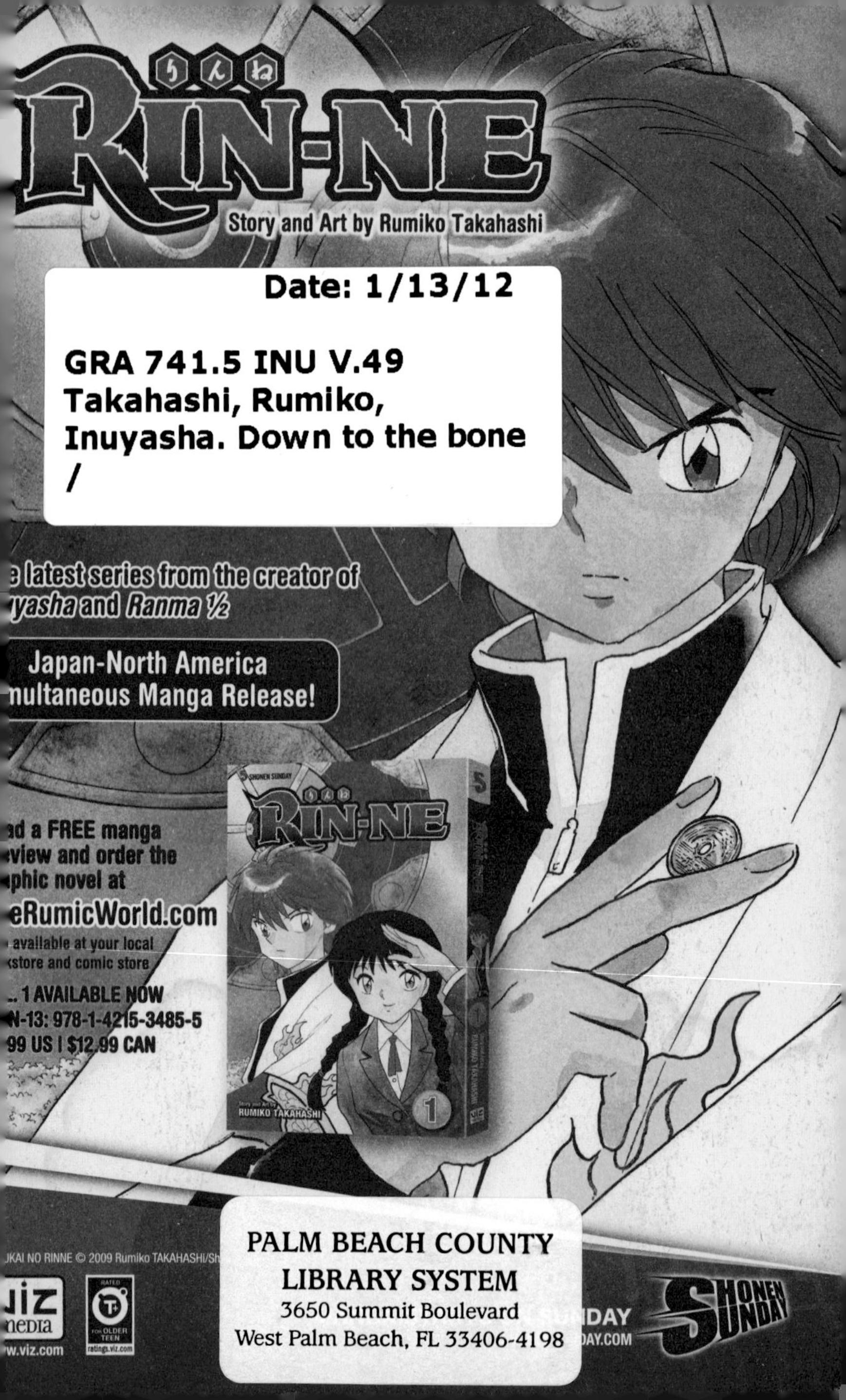
らんね
RIN-NE
Story and Art by Rumiko Takahashi
e latest series from the creator of
uyasha and Ranma ½
Japan-North America
multaneous Manga Release!
ad a FREE manga
eview and order the
aphic novel at
eRumicWorld.com
available at your local
kstore and comic store
. 1 AVAILABLE NOW
N-13: 978-1-4215-3485-5
99 US | $12.99 CAN
SHONEN SUNDAY
RIN-NE
Story and Art by
RUMIKO TAKAHASHI
1
KAI NO RINNE © 2009 Rumiko TAKAHASHI/Sh
viz media
w.viz.com
RATED T+ FOR OLDER TEEN
ratings.viz.com
SUNDAY
DAY.COM
SHONEN SUNDAY